China's Spatial (Dis)integration

Elsevier
Asian Studies Series

Series Editor: Professor Chris Rowley,
Cass Business School, City University, London, UK;
Institute of Hallyu Convergence Research, Korea University, Korea
Griffith Business School, Griffith University, Australia
(email: c.rowley@city.ac.uk)

Elsevier is pleased to publish this major Series of books entitled Asian Studies: Contemporary Issues and Trends. The Series Editor is Professor Chris Rowley of Cass Business School, City University, London, UK and Department of International Business and Asian Studies, Griffith University, Australia.

Asia has clearly undergone some major transformations in recent years and books in the Series examine this transformation from a number of perspectives: economic, management, social, political and cultural. We seek authors from a broad range of areas and disciplinary interests covering, for example, business/management, political science, social science, history, sociology, gender studies, ethnography, economics and international relations, etc.

Importantly, the Series examines both current developments and possible future trends. The Series is aimed at an international market of academics and professionals working in the area. The books have been specially commissioned from leading authors. The objective is to provide the reader with an authoritative view of current thinking.

New authors: we would be delighted to hear from you if you have an idea for a book. We are interested in both shorter, practically orientated publications (45,000+ words) and longer, theoretical monographs (75,000–100,000 words). Our books can be single, joint or multi-author volumes. If you have an idea for a book, please contact the publishers or Professor Chris Rowley, the Series Editor.

Dr Glyn Jones
Email: g.jones.2@elsevier.com

Professor Chris Rowley
Email: c.rowley@city.ac.uk

China's Spatial (Dis)integration

Political Economy of the Interethnic Unrest in Xinjiang

Rongxing Guo

ELSEVIER

AMSTERDAM • BOSTON • HEIDELBERG • LONDON
NEW YORK • OXFORD • PARIS • SAN DIEGO
SAN FRANCISCO • SINGAPORE • SYDNEY • TOKYO

Chandos Publishing is an imprint of Elsevier

CP CHANDOS PUBLISHING

Chandos Publishing is an imprint of Elsevier
225 Wyman Street, Waltham, MA 02451, USA
Langford Lane, Kidlington, OX5 1GB, UK

ISBN: 978-0-08-100387-9

British Library Cataloguing-in-Publication Data
A catalogue record for this book is available from the British Library

Library of Congress Cataloging-in-Publication Data
Library of Congress Control Number: 2015938349

For information on all Chandos publications
visit our website at http://store.elsevier.com/

Dedication

To the 90th birthday of my father.

Contents

List of abbreviations

BBC	British Broadcasting Corporation
CCP	Chinese Communist Party
CCPCC	Chinese Communist Party Central Committee
CCTV	China Central Television
CNN	Cable News Net
CRI	China Radio International
ETIM	East Turkestan Islamic Movement
ETR	East Turkistan Republic
FDI	foreign direct investment
GDP	gross domestic product
GNP	gross national product
GRP	gross regional product
IKAP	Ili Kazakh autonomous prefecture
KMT	Kuomintang
LAC	line of actual control
MOF	Ministry of Finance
NDRC	National Development and Reform Commission
NPC	National People's Congress
PLA	People's Liberation Army
PRC	People's Republic of China
ROC	Republic of China
SAR	special administrative region
SEAC	State Ethnic Affairs Commission
SITE	Search for International Terrorist Entities
TBS	Tibet Bureau of Statistics
TIP	Turkestan Islamic Party
UAA	Uyghur American Association
UN	United Nations
UNDP	United Nations Development Program
UNHCR	United Nations High Commissioner for Refugees
USSR	Union of Soviet Socialist Republics
WHO	World Health Organization
WTO	World Trade Organization
WUC	World Uyghur Congress
XASS	Xinjiang Academy of Social Sciences
XBS	Xinjiang Bureau of Statistics
XPCC	Xinjiang Production and Construction Corps

List of figures

List of tables

Preface

The first decade of the 21st century was unusual to China. Promoted by its entry into the World Trade Organization (WTO) on December 11, 2001, China's economic growth has been significantly driven by its remarkable performance in foreign trade. WTO data show that China's exports and imports enjoyed an average annual growth rate of 18 percent and 16 percent from 2000 to 2010, respectively, much higher than the average annual growth rate of the global trade volume in the same period, which was only 3 percent.[1]

When looking inside China, however, one can only find less encouraging news. For example, compared with its surging foreign trade, which has increased by more than four (for exports) or three (for imports) times from 2000 to 2010, China's domestic trade has only achieved a growth of 86.26 percent during the same period (see Table 4.1). This means that China's , China was the 7th leading exporter and 8th largest importer of merchandise trade. Since 2001, China has steadily increased its share of global manufactured exports. Notwithstanding the global reductions in trade, which resulted from the U.S. financial crisis in 2008, China replaced Germany as the world's largest exporting nation in 2009. In 2010, China continued to be the leading merchandise exporter (US$1.58 trillion, or 10.4 percent of world exports) followed by the United States (8.4 percent of world exports), Germany (8.3 percent of world exports), and Japan (5.1 percent of world exports).[2] Domestic trade—both intra- and interprovincial—has only had an average annual growth rate of about 6 percent from 2000 to 2010. Frankly speaking, this may not have been treated as a low figure in many other countries during that period of time. However, compared with its 16 to 18 percent of annual foreign trade growth rate and 10 percent of annual gross domestic product growth rate from 2000 to 2010, China's domestic trade performance can only but be labeled as "poor."

Even worse news comes from China's interprovincial trade performance. China's official statistics on interprovincial trade (in terms of freight exchange via national railways) are puzzling. For example, except for China's two peripheral territories (i.e., Hainan and Tibet) whose data are not available for 2000, the proportions of interprovincial trade to total domestic trade have risen in only 17 provincial economies (i.e., Beijing, Jiangsu, Guizhou, Ningxia, Shandong, Gansu, Chongqing, Jilin, Guangxi, Yunnan, Inner Mongolia, Fujian, Guangdong, Sichuan, Shanghai, Hubei, and Shaanxi) from 2000 to 2010. By way of contrast, the proportions for the remaining provincial economies have either decreased (i.e., in Tianjin, Zhejiang,

[1] Calculated by author based on the data released by the World Trade Organization (WTO) (http://www.wto.org/english/thewto_e/countries_e/china_e.htm).

[2] Data sources: Rumbaugh and Blancher (2004) and WTO (2011).

Qinghai, Anhui, Henan, Jiangxi, Heilongjiang, Hebei, Hunan, and Liaoning) or were almost unchanged (i.e., in Shanxi and Xinjiang) during the same period (see Table 4.1 in Chapter 4 for more details).[3]

Indeed, the above phenomenon is unusual, especially after the following facts are taken into account:

(i) Since the 1990s, there has been a significant improvement of transport infrastructures (including inter alia, the completion of various expressways and high-speed railways across the nation) in China.

(ii) Since 1999, the "Western Regional Development Policy" has been implemented by the Chinese central government speed up the development of the western and central provinces by encouraging the economic cooperation between the East and West provinces.

(iii) Since 2008, and as a result of the global reductions in trade, which resulted from the U.S. financial crisis, the Chinese government has made various efforts to stimulate China's domestic consumption.

Throughout history, race, ethnicity, language, and religion have divided states into separate political entities as much as physical terrain, political fiat, or conquest. In China, most provinces (or autonomous regions and municipalities directly under the central government) are on a size and scale equivalent to a European country in population and land area. They are considerable political and economic systems in their own right. The differences among these provinces have long been a defining characteristic of China's politics. In China, culture is not homogeneous across provinces, and many ethnic groups also have their own languages and religions. All of these imply that it is unlikely to enhance the chances of the adoption of a common standard among different groups of peoples.

In February 2013, when I conducted a quantitative research on the driving forces behind China's interprovincial (dis)integration, I found two strange results. The first one relates to the negative effect of distance-related transactions costs on interprovincial trade, which tended to rise over time from 2000 to 2010, and the second one concerns the different roles that some non-Han ethnic groups have played in China's interprovincial relations. As for the latter, the Uyghur ethnic group, unlike the 13 ethnic groups (each of which tends to contribute to China's interprovincial trade), is not found to contribute to China's spatial economic integration (Guo, forthcoming). The first finding is unusual because it does not reflect China's considerable improvement in transport infrastructures during the past decades, and it does not conform to the general dynamic pattern of international trade. More unusual is the second finding. Why have China's ethnic groups played different roles in its interprovincial trade?

This book is intended to provide the narratives and analytics of China's spatial (dis)integration. Indeed, the Chinese nation is far too huge and spatially complicated and diversified to be misinterpreted. The only feasible approach to analyzing it is therefore to divide it into smaller geographical elements through which one can have a better insight into the spatial mechanisms and regional characteristics.

[3] Note that Beijing and Shanghai's reductions of domestic trade from 2000 to 2010 are mainly attributable to their removals of large industrial, pollution-making plants during the period.

To this end, I chose Xinjiang—China's far western autonomous region—as an in-depth case study, focusing on its special geopolitical and socioeconomic features and external and boundary conditions. The rationale for this kind of case selection is threefold:

- Xinjiang, in terms of land area, is much larger than any other Chinese provincial administrations.
- The Uyghurs—which are the ethnic majorities of Xinjiang—have much more cultural differences from the Han Chinese (the ethnic majority of China as a whole) than another other non-Han ethnic groups in China.
- Xinjiang, which had been an independent state in history, has been treated by the Chinese central government as the most "sensitive" and, to some extent, "problematic" region in China.

China's great diversity in physical geography, resource endowment, and political economy as well as ethnicity and religion has posed challenges to the studies of spatial and interprovincial issues. Historical record provides an ample source of narrative. And narrative matters because it is inherently concerned with causality recognizing that from the historical perspective, specific events can yield a multiplicity of equilibria. But narrative alone is insufficient because many questions relate to events that did not take place (or have not yet taken place) or are concerned with the motivations behind why certain behavior or events have not occurred. This is arguably especially true when the accuracy or adequacy of the data and information on which the narrative are based is in question. Addressing these issues requires an appropriate model for linking what is observed (or observable) with what is not observed.

In this book, to produce more rigorous, convincing research results, I use both analytic and narrative approaches. More often than not, analytics (focusing on theory and analytical models) and narrative (focusing on data and historical events) each have both advantages and disadvantages in presenting a research project. However, the combination of analytics and narrative can capture the conviction that data linked to theory is more powerful than either data or theory alone. A priori, the most relevant advantage of the analytic narrative method is that it allows us to model historical "one-off" processes and events that have unique characteristics. Likewise, the method renders some problems of empirical testing of hypotheses manageable. Some political and cultural events pose insurmountable difficulties to traditional panel data or time series methods.

Tips for readers

- The Prologue and Chapters 1, 2, 3, 5, and 6 are either narratives or analytical narratives. They may be the most interesting to general readers.
- Chapters 4, 5, and 6 are either qualitative (narrative) or quantitative analyses. They may (also) be interesting to professional readers.
- The Annexes of Chapters 2, 4, and 5 include provincial and interprovincial panel data and information that are collected and complied by the author. They may be useful for those who want to conduct their own research on China's interprovincial relations.
- Chapter 4 and the Annexes of Chapter 6 include some specialized mathematics and statistical techniques. They may not fit in with general audience.

Acknowledgments

First of all, my sincere thanks go to two anonymous residents of Xinjiang (I use their names as Hamier and Korlar because their residential places are in Hami [or Kumul in Uyghur] and Korla, respectively). Their accompanying of me during the trip to Urumqi and their interesting stories about Xinjiang enabled me to believe that writing a book on Xinjiang is not a difficult job. (Their stories have been included in the Prologue.) I must also thank Mr. Yang Liming (my former colleague and now a resident of New York City) who accompanied me in my first visit to Xinjiang in the late 1980s.

I would highly appreciate the active cooperation by Miss Xiaoxuan Lu (Ph.D. candidates of Harvard University and of Peking University). That she let me share the story about her experiences in Urumqi in the summer of 2009 helped me to delve into an in-depth understanding of the most serious Han–Uyghur violence that has occurred there. (This has been included in a quotation in Chapter 3.)

This book also adopts the published materials of mine as well as of other colleagues. Specifically, the first three sections of Chapter 4 draw heavily on my paper titled "Spatial (Dis)integration and Multiethnic Economics: Evidence from China's Interprovincial Data" (forthcoming). The quotation included in Chapter 3 is based on an internal report written in Chinese; its author is anonymous. I would also thank Mr. Kelly Olsen (correspondent of the French Press Agency) for his article cited in Chapter 2, Mr. William Smith (correspondent of *The Diplomat*) for his article quoted in Chapter 3, and Ms. Didi Tang and Louise Watt (correspondents of the Associated Press) for their article quoted in Chapter 3.

Last but not least, I have benefited from Mr. George Knott (Editor of the Chandos Publishing, Elsevier) and other editors and readers of the Chandos Asian Studies series and five anonymous reviewers who were either arranged by Elsevier or elsewhere. All of their comments and suggestions have helped me refine many parts of the manuscript. However, all views and errors in this book certainly are mine.

Rongxing Guo
Huairou, Beijing, China
September 2014

Prologue: A long journey

Day 1: Making friends

The following story happened before the Tiananmen protests in 1989. In reward for my contribution to his academic work, my boss decided to let me participate and, on behalf of him, give a presentation at a conference held in Urumqi, capital of Xinjiang Uyghur autonomous region. I was quite anxious about how I could fulfill this task; obviously, I was not qualified as a keynote speaker because I had only been a junior university staff at that time. But my boss had other, more pressing business to do, and more important, he was not familiar with *his* paper.

My colleagues had reminded me of trying to keep away from Uyghur Muslims. Just before my departure, a series of Han–Uyghur tensions had just occurred in Xinjiang. Through the Voice of America,[1] I learned that the Uyghurs in Xinjiang marched through the streets of Urumqi protesting against a wide range of issues, including nuclear testing in the Taklimakan, increased Han immigration to Xinjiang, and ethnic insults at Xinjiang University. In the meantime, there were also reports that Muslims throughout China protested against a children's book that portrayed Muslims, particularly their restriction against pork, in a derogatory fashion. At last, tensions began to ease after the Chinese government promised to meet most of the Muslims' demands by condemning the publications, arresting the authors, and closing down the printing houses.

Nevertheless, I felt quite lucky that there was no Uyghurs in my railway car. Beside myself, the two other passengers were Han Chinese—one from Hami (or Kumul in Uyghur) and the other from Korla, both in Xinjiang. Throughout the whole journey, I simply referred to them as "Hamier" and "Korlar," respectively, and they called me "Beijinger" (although I am not a native of Beijing).

Even luckier was that both Hamier and Korlar were very hospitable. They told me many interesting stories about Xinjiang as well as their daily lives there. But it seemed that my stomach was not good because of the long trip on the train. I had never had such a long trip via train before. I could not even eat anything on the last day's journey to Urumqi. Most passengers were complaining that the style and taste of the food provided by the train had never been changed all the days.

> *"Having nothing to eat is not good for you, young man! Not like us, you are going to be away from your home. Try to eat something so that you will be able to do your business well," Hamier kindly advised me.*

[1] It was one of the most important sources that I used to learn English and to get access to politically sensitive news in China during the 1980s.

He picked up a bottle of wine, saying:

> *"Come on! Try to drink it as much as you can. And you will then be able to finish your food. Every time when I travelled from Kumul [he used a Uyghur name to the city of Hami] to inland cities, I would have brought a box [ten bottles] of wine with me—that is life. You know, my company produces the best wine as Xinjiang produces the best grapes."*

Hamier looked older than I, so he always spoke and acted like an elder brother. And I accepted this—according to Chinese tradition, elders should be respected.

Hamier introduced him as a salesman of a wine production company in Hami. As a Han-Chinese migrant in Xinjiang, his great grandfather came from somewhere in central China. Hamier did not give more details about why and how his ancestor had moved from central China to Xinjiang. And neither did I make further inquiries; I learned that before the 20th century, many of the Han immigrants in Xinjiang were either criminals or officials who had been exiled from inland China.

I still remember I was half drunk with the wine Hamier offered. But I felt better now, and I was able to finish the food.

> *"Dear passengers: Attention, please! We are going to arrive at the Yumen Station," the broadcaster announced.*

"I am now in Yumen (Jade Pass)!" I shouted. I recalled that I had learned many Tang-style poems about the Jade Pass when I was in school. According to the traditional Chinese culture, a more intelligent man is usually judged to know more ancient Chinese poems. As a smart young scholar (at least I believed so at that time), I decided to recite an ancient poem written by Wang Zhihuan (AD 688–742):[2]

> *Where the Yellow river climbs to as far as the clouds,*
> *There is a city among ten-thousand-foot mountains.*
> *A mourning man is playing the willow song on a flute,*
> *As spring breezes never blow through the Jade Pass.*

This is a folk song–styled verse titled "Beyond the Border" (or *chusai* in Chinese). Even though most Chinese know some ancient Chinese poems, perhaps many of them could not understand what each word exactly means. For example, in this poem, the term "willow song" (i.e., *yangliu qu* in Chinese) refers to a popular Han-Chinese music in the Tang dynasty; it was usually played for those who had been drafted into the army. And the "flute" is a music instrument made in bamboo. It was invented and used by the Tartar people living in modern-day Gansu and Xinjiang, although it has also been very popular throughout China.

[2] Even though Wang is less famous than other Tang (AD 619–907) poets such as Li Bai, Du Fu, and Bai Juyi, his poem "yu qiong qianli mu, geng shang yicheng lou" ("Enjoy a Grander Sight by Climbing to a Greater Height") has been a popular saying in Chinese circle.

Figure 0.1 The ruins of the Jade Pass.

I was quite confident that I had known more about Chinese history than both Hamier and Korlar, just as they had about Xinjiang than I. I thought my presentation should have received applause.

"The Yumen you mentioned is still quite far away from here; it is on the west of Dunhuang city. As an important border pass in ancient times, it has now become ruins," Korlar responded.

"Then, why here is also called the Jade Pass?" I asked. Korlar explained that probably it was because ancient Chinese rulers had a strong attachment to jade. He told me that he had watched a TV show in which it was reported that all of the jade items excavated from the Fuhao tomb of the Shang dynasty (3,000 years ago), including hundreds of pieces, were imported from Hotan in modern Xinjiang. He further quoted a textbook of Chinese history as saying that the Yuezhi were the earliest people engaging in the jade trade, of which the major consumers were the rulers of inland China. The Jade Pass I mentioned in Wang Zhihuan's poem was built by Emperor Wu of the Han dynasty (Figure 0.1).

Day 2: "We" versus "They"

Korlar was a native of Xinjiang. But his parents were from Shanghai and, together with other Chinese soldiers and young female graduates, were resettled in Korla in 1954. And all of them comprised the first batch of members for the No. 2 Agricultural Division of the Xinjiang Production and Construction Crops (Xinjiang Production and Construction Corps, or XPCC, is also known as *bingtuan* in Chinese for short). Korlar did not receive a good education (neither did I) during the 1970s. But because his mother, a graduate from a very prestigious middle school in Shanghai, had been a historian teacher, Korlar had a better knowledge of Chinese history than many others of his age.

Korlar was quite outspoken. He told me many interesting stories about his family, his childhood, and his colleagues and friends in Xinjiang. And after the train left the Hami Station, he decided to tell me his personal experiences with the Uyghurs; most of his childhood was spent in a Uyghur-dominated community.

When I was wondering why he had not told his stories earlier, Korlar noted Hamier who had just got off the train, reminding me:

> *"Maybe Hamier's wife is a Uyghur. So* we *must have been very cautious of him!"*
>
> *"Why is that?" I was rather confused.*
>
> *"I can tell you that Hamier's Uyghur is more fluent than his Chinese. You know, even though the Han–Uyghur marriage can hardly be found in many places, especially in Nanjiang [southern Xinjiang], it is not the case in the city of Hami, which is located in Beijiang [northern Xinjiang]. Nanjiang and Beijiang are quite different from each other. So Hamier may not be happy if we Han Chinese were talking about Uyghurs if he has a mixed Han–Uyghur family," he further explained.*

I began to recall that during our conversions, Hamier had frequently used the Uyghur name "Kumul" when we referred to the city of Hami. Obviously, Korlar's judgment was fairly reasonable. I was a little bit jealous of Korlar for his intelligence. I was even thinking of a hypothesis that a man, after a long period of living experiences in a culturally diverse community, can become more intelligent.

Day 3: "Beating their noses!"

Now, the train, after 3 days since my departure—was near its destination. Before the train arrived at the Urumqi station, Korlar moved closer toward me and wanted to let me share his special knowledge about how to deal with the Uyghurs. After looking around and finding that no Uyghur could hear us, he whispered that a counteraction must be done when some Uyghurs' actions were proved to be physically harmful to me. Obviously, the method had been invented by Korlar during his childhood:

> *"Beating their noses! I have found many Uyghurs are blood-sick. Upon seeing blood comes out of the nose of one Uyghur guy, the other Uyghurs would become frightened and immediately run away from you. And you will be safe then."*

After hearing his instructions, I immediately had a feeling that I was fully prepared to live in a foreign land. When we were going to leave the railway station, I tried to invite Korlar to have a dinner with me; the food we had for the past days on the train was so bad. I wished to taste the delicious Muslim-style food. But this time, he simply rejected my proposal:

> *"My Uyghur friends here in Urumqi are still waiting for me. They will host me with a big dinner. You see, I am also bringing so many gifts to them."*

Within a few minutes, Korlar disappeared from my sight. And I suddenly found that I became a foreigner. During my stay at Urumqi, I never used Korlar's "beating-nose" method. And I never I confirmed if the Uyghurs would be liable to blood-sickness. I spent a very pleasant time in Urumqi.

. . .

On my way back to Beijing, I became rather lonely. There were occasionally Han or Uyghur passengers sitting in my coach for a few of stops, but none of them left me with a deep impression as Hamier and Korlar did. When the train passed through the Yumen station, I was feeling that I missed the two of them.

But at that movement, one question suddenly emerged from my mind: "Which side would Korlar take if there were a zero-sum game between his Uyghur friends and me?"

A brief history of Xinjiang

1

Xinjiang: New frontier

> *I now refer to the records of the far west—a vast area covering both the southwest and the northwest.... Mt. Qiong lies north of the territory of Xuanyuan [name of Emperor Huang]. On the mountain, nobody dared to shoot the west where Emperor Huang's residence was located at the top of a hillock. The hillock is surrounded and protected by four snakes.... And at the north is a place where fish dragons lived.... Beyond its far northern edge there is a place in which there were white people with lightish hair....*
>
> —Shanhaijing *(2001, 2: 2)*[1]

Located in the northwestern part of China, Xinjiang Uyghur autonomous region is a large, sparsely populated area (comparable in size to Iran) that takes up about one sixth of the country's territory. Domestically, it borders Tibet autonomous region to the south and Qinghai and Gansu provinces to the southeast. Internationally, Xinjiang shares a 5,000-km land border with eight countries (including Mongolia to the northeast, Russia to the north; and Kazakhstan, Kyrgyzstan, Tajikistan, Afghanistan, Pakistan, and India to the west). The Tian Shan mountain range marks the Xinjiang–Kyrgyzstan border at the Torugart Pass. The Karakorum Highway links Islamabad in Pakistan with Kashgar over the Khunjerab Pass. The name "Xinjiang," which was first given to it during the Qing dynasty (AD 1644–1911), literally means "a new frontier/territory."

At present, Xinjiang is home to a number of ethnic groups, including the Uyghur, Han, Kazakh, Hui, Kyrgyz, and Mongol. These groups follow various religious traditions, with the majority of the population adhering to Islam. Afaq Khoja Mausoleum and Id Kah Mosque in Kashgar are among the most important Islamic sites in Xinjiang. Emin Minaret is another key Islamic site, in Turfan. In addition to Islam, Lamaism (Tibetan Buddhism), Buddhism, Taoism, Christianity, Catholicism, Eastern Orthodoxy, and Shamanism all thrive side by side in the country's foremost multicultural melting pot.

Early encounters

Ancient Xinjiang was described in the *Shanhaijing* (*The Classic of Mountains and Seas*), an ancient Chinese book written during the Eastern Zhou dynasty (771–221 BC) and compiled by Liu Xin (c. 53–23 BC), as a place where there were "white people with lightish hair," or the Bai people, who lived beyond their northwestern border. Such a description could accord well with a Caucasoid population beyond the frontiers

[1] Translated by author based on the Chinese text.

China's Spatial (Dis)integration.

of ancient China, and some scholars have identified these whites as Yuezhi (Mallory & Mair, 2000, p. 55). The well-preserved Tarim mummies with a Caucasoid physical type, often with reddish or blond hair, today displayed at the Urumqi Museum and dated to the 3rd century BC, have been found in precisely the same area of the Tarim basin (Saiget, April 19, 2005). Various nomadic tribes, including the Yuezhi (officially called Rouzhi in China), were part of the large migration of Indo-European–speaking peoples who were settled in today's Xinjiang and the western part of Gansu.

The Yuezhi continued to be one of the strongest tribes in the northwest of China until the early Han dynasty. Because of conflicts with another, more aggressive nomadic tribe, the Xiongnu, the Yuezhi migrated to the west in the following century. The nomadic tribes of the Yuezhi are documented in detail in Chinese historical accounts, in particular *Shiji* (*Records of the Great Historian*) by Sima Qian (145–87 BC), which states that they "were flourishing" but regularly in conflict with the neighboring tribe of the Xiongnu to the northeast. According to *Shiji* (vol. 123, *Account of Dayuan*):

> *The Yuezhi originally lived in the area between the Qilian and Tian Mountains and Dunhuang, but after they were defeated by the Xiongnu they moved far away to the west, beyond Dayuan, where they attacked and conquered the people of Daxia and set up the court of their king on the northern bank of the Gui [Oxus] River. A small number of their people who were unable to make the journey west sought refuge among the Qiang barbarians in the Southern Mountains, where they are known as the Lesser Yuezhi.*[2]

Rise and fall of Xinjiang

Quest for a Uyghur khanate

In 138 BC, Emperor Wu (reign 140–87 BC) of the Han dynasty sent Zhang Qian as an envoy to the states in the present-day Xinjiang region. The following decades saw struggles between the Xiongnu and Han China over dominance of the region, which eventually ended in Chinese success. In 60 BC, the Han established the Protectorate of the Western Regions to oversee the entire region as far west as the Pamir. Tarim basin was under the influence and control of the Han dynasty. After the fall of the Han dynasty, the Western Regions continued to be maintained by various short-lived kingdoms (both Han and non-Han) that ruled northwestern China one after the other, with varying extents and degrees of success.

Established in AD 618, the Tang dynasty (AD 618–907) proved to be one of the most expansionist dynasties in Chinese history. During the early Tang period, China conducted a series of expeditions against the Tujue, eventually forcing the surrender of the western Tujue in AD 657. As a result, Xinjiang was placed under

[2] Cited from Watson (1993, p. 234).

the Anxi Protectorate ("Anxi" means "pacifying the West"). The protectorate did not outlast the decline of the Tang dynasty in the 8th century. In AD 763, Tibet invaded Tang China on a wide front from Xinjiang to Yunnan. As a result, the Tang lost its control of southern Xinjiang by the end of the century. At the same time, the Uyghur khanate took control of northern Xinjiang, as well as much of the rest of Central Asia, including the western part of Mongolia.

In the mid-9th century, the Uyghur khanate began to decline. As a result, the Kara-Khanid khanate, which arose from a confederation of Turkic tribes scattered, took control of western Xinjiang in the 10th and 11th centuries. Meanwhile, after the Uyghur khanate in modern-day Mongolia had been smashed by the Kirghiz in AD 840, branches of the Uyghurs established themselves a new Uyghur state in the area around today's Turpan and Urumqi. This state remained in eastern Xinjiang until the 13th century.

Decline of the khanate

After Genghis Khan unified China and began his advance west, the Uyghur state in the Turpan-Urumqi area offered its allegiance to the Mongols in AD 1209, contributing taxes and troops to the Mongol empire. After the break-up of the Chagatai khanate into smaller khanates in the mid-14th century, the region fractured and was ruled by various Mongol Khans simultaneously. These leaders engaged in numerous wars with each other and both the Timurids of Transoxania to the west and the Western Mongols to the east.

During the Ming dynasty (AD 1368–1644) and the following decades, Xinjiang was independent from China proper. In the 17th century, the Mongolian Zungars established an empire over much of the today's Xinjiang region. The Mongolian Zungar (also Dzungar, Jungar, or Zunghar) is the collective identity of several Oirat tribes that formed and maintained one of the last nomadic empires. The Zungar khanate covered the area called Zungaria and stretched from the west end of the Great Wall of China to present-day eastern Kazakhstan and from present-day northern Kyrgyzstan to southern Siberia (most of this area is renamed to Xinjiang after the fall of the Zungar Empire). It existed from the early 17th century to the mid-18th century.

After the Qing dynasty (AD 1644–1911) consolidated its rule of the Han-Chinese areas, it gained control over eastern Xinjiang. As a result of a long struggle with the Zungars, the Qing troops attacked Ghulja (Yining in Chinese) and captured the Zungar khan. After the defeat of the Zungars, the Qing court established state farms, especially in the vicinity of Urumqi, which had fertile, well-watered land and few people. From AD 1760 to 1830, as the result of a series of the successful Chinese Campaign against rebels in Xinjiang (Figure 1.1), more state farms were opened, and the Chinese population in Xinjiang grew rapidly. At the start of the 19th century, 40 years after the Qing reconquest, approximately 155,000 Han and Hui Chinese lived in northern Xinjiang, and about 320,000 Uyghurs lived in southern Xinjiang (Millward, 2007, p. 306).[3] The Han Chinese of Xinjiang arrived from

[3] A census of the time tabulated ethnic shares of the population as 60% Turkic and 30% Han (Toops, 2004).

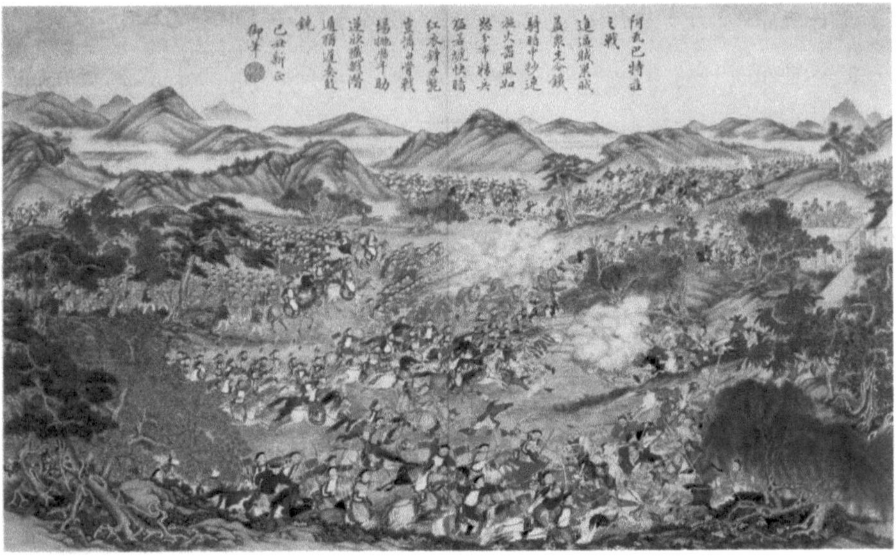

《平定回疆战图册·阿瓦巴特庄之战》
清宫廷画家绘，纸本，设色，14开，每开纵51．4厘米，横89．4厘米，故宫博物院藏。

Figure 1.1 A scene of the Chinese campaign against rebels in Xinjiang, AD 1828.
Source: Wikipedia Commons.

different directions and social backgrounds: they were descendants of criminals and officials who had been exiled from China proper during the second half of the 18th and first half of the 19th centuries; descendants of families of military and civil officers from Hunan, Yunnan, Gansu, and Manchuria; descendants of merchants from Shanxi, Tianjin, Hubei, and Hunan; and descendants of peasants who started immigrating into the region in 1776 (Bellér-Hann, 2008, pp. 51–52).

Before 1831, only a few hundred Chinese merchants lived in southern Xinjiang, and only a few number of Uyghurs lived in northern Xinjiang. Thereafter, the Qing court encouraged Han Chinese migration into the Tarim basin in southern Xinjiang and stationed permanent troops on the land there as well (Millward, 2007, pp. 104–105). Political killings and expulsions of non-Uyghur populations in the uprisings of the 1860s and 1930s saw a sharp decline of the Han Chinese as a percentage of the total population (Bellér-Hann, 2008, p. 52).

Xinjiang becomes a province

By the mid-19th century, Russia encroached upon China along its entire northern frontier. The Opium Wars and the Taiping and other rebellions during the mid-19th century in China proper had severely restricted the dynasty's ability to maintain its garrisons in distant Xinjiang. In 1864, both Chinese Muslims (called *Hui*) and Uyghurs rebelled in Xinjiang cities after an ongoing Chinese Muslim Rebellion in Gansu and Shaanxi provinces farther east. Because all of the non-Muslim populations in Xinjiang were regarded as infidels and enemies to be exterminated, the rebellion resulted in incredible cruelties whenever the towns held by the Qing force were taken (Kim, 2004, p. 71). In 1871, Russia took advantage of the chaotic situation and seized the rich Ili River Valley, including Gulja. In 1881, the Qing court recovered the Gulja region through diplomatic negotiations. Several years later, a Chinese provincial administration was established on the new frontier (called *xin jiang* in Chinese).

In 1912, the Qing dynasty was replaced by the Republic of China (ROC). However, Xinjiang was among China's most instable territories in the following decades. On November 12, 1933, the short-lived, self-proclaimed East Turkistan Republic (ETR) was declared in the Kashgar region, which in theory encompassed today's Kashgar, Hotan, and Aksu prefectures in southwestern Xinjiang (Millward, 2007, p. 24). The Chinese Muslim 36th Division (National Revolutionary Army) destroyed the army of the ETR at the Battle of Kashgar in 1934, bringing the latter to an end. A Second East Turkistan Republic (Second ETR) existed from 1944 to 1949 with Soviet support in what is now called Ili Kazakh autonomous prefecture (including Ili, Tarbagatay, and Altay Districts) in northern Xinjiang (Gladney, 2004a, pp. 161–168). The Second ETR came to an end when the People's Liberation Army (PLA) entered Xinjiang in 1949.

Xinjiang in the People's Republic of China Era

With a history of at least 2,500 years, a succession of peoples and empires has vied for control over all or parts of Xinjiang's territory. Before the People's Republic of China (PRC) was founded in 1949, all or part of the region has been ruled or influenced at times by the Tocharians, the Yuezhi, the Xiongnu empire, the Kushan empire, the Han empire, the Former Liang, the Former Qin, the Later Liang, the Western Liang, the Tang dynasty, the Uyghur khaganate, the Kara-Khanid khanate, the Yuan dynasty, the Zungar khanate, the Qing dynasty, and the ROC.

Territorial changes in Xinjiang

In 1950, China occupied the northeast portion of Kashmir, a region known as Aksai Chin. In 1962, there was a short border war between China and India. The war lasted from October 20 to November 22. It ended with a Chinese victory and the birth of the Line of Actual Control (LAC). In 1963, Pakistan ceded to China another portion of land claimed by India. Aksai Chin is currently under the administration of Xinjiang, with the majority of it being part of Hotan county (Figure 1.2). India claims the area as part of Ladakh district of the state of Jammu and Kashmir. Aksai Chin is of strategic importance to China because it contains National Highway No. 219, a major road connecting Tibet and Xinjiang.

China had dozens of disputable segments on the boundaries with the Central Asian republics of the former Union of Soviet Socialist Republics (USSR). This

Figure 1.2 The administrative divisions of Xinjiang Uyghur autonomous region.

included Kazakhstan, Kyrgyzstan, and Tajikistan, all sharing land boundaries with Xinjiang. Despite numerous negotiations, the problem of disputable borderlines had still not been resolved until the break-up of the USSR. The common boundary between China and the Central Asian republics of the former USSR included 19 disputed areas.

Since 1992, Kazakhstan as an independent state has had talks with China on their joint boundary. The most complicated issue was the demarcation of a 120-km-long boundary. According to a treaty signed by the two countries on July 3, 1998, disputable lands were divided into equal parts (50/50) by China and Kazakhstan. A treaty on delimitation of tripoint between China, Kyrgyzstan, and Tajikistan was signed by the three countries in July 2000. According to the treaty, China obtained 2,000 sq km of land area beyond its LAC. The total length of the China–Kazakhstan boundary is 1,782.75 km, all bordered with China's Xinjiang Uygur autonomous region (Guo, 2007a, p. 202).

Xinjiang Uyghur autonomous region

On October 1, 1955, Xinjiang Uyghur autonomous region of the PRC was established, replacing the province.

At present, in terms of territorial size, Xinjiang is the largest political subdivision of China (Table 1.1). It is divided into 2 prefecture-level cities, 7 prefectures, and 5 autonomous prefectures for the Mongol, Kirgiz, Kazakh, and Hui minorities. These are then divided into 11 districts, 20 county-level cities, 62 counties, and 6 autonomous counties, and then 5 subprefectural level cities (Aral, Beitun, Shihezi, Tumxuk, and Wujiaq), which do not belong to any prefecture, are administered by the Xinjiang Production and Construction Corps, a de facto subprovincial unit directly under Chinese central government. The Tian Shan mountain range marks the Xinjiang–Kyrgyzstan border at the Torugart Pass. The Karakorum Highway links Islamabad in Pakistan with Kashgar over the Khunjerab Pass.

Annex: Chronology of key events related to Xinjiang

138 BC: Emperor Wudi of the Han dynasty sends Zhang Qian as an envoy to the states in the Xinjiang region, beginning several decades of struggle between the Xiongnu and the Han dynasty over dominance of the region, eventually ending in Chinese success.

60 BC: The Han dynasty establishes the Protectorate of the Western Regions (xiyu duwei fu) at Wulei (near modern Luntai) to oversee the entire region as far west as the Pamir. Tarim Basin is under the influence and control of the Han dynasty.

AD 13: During the usurpation of Wang Mang in China, the dependent states of the protectorate rebel and become independent from China. Han China conducts several expeditions into the region, reestablishing the protectorate from AD 74 to 76, AD 91 to 107, and AD 123 onward. These campaigns expand Han sovereignty into the Tarim Basin and Central Asia.

AD 640: Campaigns against the oasis states begin under Emperor Taizong of the Tang dynasty with the annexation of Gaochang.

Table 1.1 **The administrative divisions of Xinjiang***

Name	Administrative seat	Population
Aksu P	Aksu	2,370,887
Altay P	Altay	526,980
Aral SPM	Aral	166,205
Bayingolin Mongol AP	Korla	1,278,492
Beitun SPM	Beitun	76,300
Bortala Mongol AP	Bole	443,680
Changji Hui AP	Changji	1,428,592
Hotan P	Hotan	2,014,365
Ili Kazakh AP	Yining	2,482,627
Karamay PM	Karamay District	391,008
Kashgar P	Kashgar	3,979,362
Kizilsu Kirgiz AP	Artux	525,599
Kumul P	Kumul	572,400
Shihezi SPM	Shihezi	635,582
Tacheng P	Tacheng	1,219,212
Tumxuk SPM	Tumxuk	147,465
Turpan P	Turpan	622,679
Urumqi PM	Tianshan District	3,110,280
Wujiaqu SPM	Wujiaqu	72,613

AP, Autonomous prefecture; *P*, prefecture; *PM*, prefectural-level municipality; *SPM*, subprefectural level municipality (administered by the Xinjiang Production and Construction Corps).
*All data are as of 2010.

AD 644: The kingdom of Karasahr is captured by the Tang dynasty.
AD 649: The kingdom of Kucha is conquered by the Tang dynasty.
AD 657: The expansion into Central Asia continues under Taizong's successor, Emperor Gaozong, who dispatches an army led by Su Dingfang against the Western Turk qaghan Ashina Helu.
AD 670: Xinjiang is invaded by the Tibetan Empire to the south. Xinjiang alternates between Tang and Tibetan rule as they compete for control of Central Asia.
AD 763: The Uyghur Khaganate takes control of northern Xinjiang and much of the rest of Central Asia, including Mongolia.
AD 840: After the Uyghur khanate in Mongolia has been smashed by the Kirghiz, branches of the Uyghurs establish themselves in Qocha (Karakhoja) and Beshbalik near the modern cities of Turfan and Urumchi. This Uyghur state remains in eastern Xinjiang until the 13th century, although it is subject to foreign overlords during that time. The Kara-Khanids convert to Islam. The Uyghur state in eastern Xinjiang remained Manichaean but later converts to Buddhism.
1132: Remnants of the Khitan Empire from Manchuria enter Xinjiang, fleeing the rebellion of their neighbors, the Jurchens. They establish an exile Chinese empire, the Western Liao, which rules over both the Kara-Khanid–held and Uyghur-held parts of the Tarim Basin for the next century.
1209: After Genghis Khan unifies Mongolia and begins his advance west, the Uyghur state in the Turpan-Urumchi area offers its allegiance to the Mongols, contributing taxes

and troops to the Mongol imperial effort. In return, the Uyghur rulers retain control of their kingdom.
1218: Genghis Khan's Mongol Empire conquers the Western Liao.
1755: With the help of the Oirat nobel Amursana, the Qing attacks Ghulja and captures the Dzunghar khan. After Amursana's request to be declared Zunghar khan goes unanswered, he leads a revolt against the Qing. Over the next 2 years, Qing armies destroy the remnants of the Dzunghar khanate, and many Chinese Muslims (Hui) move into the pacified areas.
1758–1759: After the defeat of the Dzungars, the Qing make members of a clan of Sufi shaykhs known as the Khojas, rulers in the western Tarim Basin, south of the Tianshan Mountains. Rebellions against this arrangement broke out both north and south of the Tian Shan mountains.
1759: State farms are established in the region of Xinjaingh, especially in the vicinity of Urumqi, which has fertile, well-watered land and few people.
1760–1830: More state farms are opened, and the Chinese population in Xinjiang grows rapidly to about 155,000.
1776: The Qing resorts to incentives such as issuing a subsidy that is paid to Han who are willing to migrate to northwest to Xinjiang.
1803: Around 155,000 Han and Hui peoples live in Xinjiang, mostly in Dzungaria, and around 320,000 Uyghurs, living mostly in Southern Xinjiang (the Tarim Basin), as Han and Hui are allowed to settle in Dzungaria but forbidden to settle in the Tarim; the small amount of Uyghurs living in Dzungaria and Urumqi is insignificant.
1800: The Han population is around one third of Xinjiang's population, during the time of the Qing dynasty.
1830: The Qing rewards the Han and Hui merchants for fighting off Khoja by allowing them to settle down.
1864: Both Chinese Muslims (Hui) and Uyghurs rebel in Xinjiang cities after ongoing Chinese Muslim Rebellions in Gansu and Shaanxi provinces farther east.
1865: Yaqub Beg, a warlord from the neighboring khanate of Kokand, enters Xinjiang via Kashgar and conquers nearly all of Xinjiang over the next 6 years.
1871: Russia takes advantage of the chaotic situation and seizes the rich Ili River Valley, including Gulja. At the end of this period, forces loyal to the Qing hold onto only a few strongholds, including Tacheng.
1875–1877: The Qing general Zuo Zongtang reconquers the region.
1881: The Qing recovers the Gulja region through diplomatic negotiations via the Treaty of Saint Petersburg (1881).
1884: The Qing dynasty establishes Xinjiang ("new frontier") as a province, formally applying to it the political systems of the rest of China and dropping the old name of Huijiang, or "Muslimland."
1912: The Qing dynasty is replaced by the ROC. Yuan Dahua, the last Qing governor of Xinjiang, flees. One of his subordinates, Yang Zengxin, takes control of the province and accedes in name to the ROC in March of the same year.
1928: Yang's control over Xinjiang ends with his assassination.
1933: In the Kashgar region, the ETR is declared on November 12, after some debate over whether the proposed independent state should be called "East Turkestan" or "Uyghuristan."
1934: The Chinese Muslim 36th Division (National Revolutionary Army) destroys the army of the ETR at the Battle of Kashgar, bringing the latter to an end.

1944: With Soviet support, the Second ETR is established in what is now called Ili Kazakh autonomous prefecture (Ili, Tarbagatay, and Altay Districts) in northern Xinjiang.
1949: The Second ETR comes to an end when the PLA enters Xinjiang.
1950: In the 14th meeting of the Central People's Government Administration Council, held on January 6, the "current policy objectives of the Xinjiang People's Government Committee" are ratified.
1952: In the 125th meeting of the Central People's Government Administration Council, held on February 22, the "Regional Ethnic Autonomy Programs of People's Republic of China" are approved.
1954: The Xinjiang Production and Construction Corps (XPCC) is formed in Xinjiang.
1955: The Chinese Communist Party Central Committee (CCPCC) issues "some comments on the organization of youth to participate in the construction of the frontier issues" in July, requesting junior and senior graduates, and other unemployed youth to participate in reclamation work of Xinjiang. Xinjiang autonomous region is established on October 1.
1958: The CCPCC implements the "Decision on the mobilization of young people to participate in border areas and ethnic minority areas of socialist construction" on August 29.
1962: After the Sino–Soviet split, rioting occurs in Yining, and 60,000 ethnic minorities living across the border flee to the Soviet Union.
1964: The CCPCC and the State Council issue the "decision (draft) on the mobilization and organization of urban educated youth in rural socialist construction."
1970: The Office of the State Council issues "telegram on cadres drawn from various departments of the State Council to strengthen the leadership of key enterprises in Xinjiang" on October 28.
1975: The XPCC is abolished, with all of its powers transferred to the government of Xinjiang Uyghur autonomous region and the local authorities thereof.
1981: The CCPCC and the State Council issue the "Decision on the restoration of the Xinjiang Production and Construction Corps" on December 3. In December, the Chinese government reopened the XPCC.
1984: The second meeting of the Sixth National People's Congress through the "Law of People's Republic of China concerning Regional Ethnic Autonomy" on May 31.
1985: The construction of the 500-km-long Northern Xinjiang Railway is announced. This Railway connects the West Urumqi Station with the Alashankou (i.e., the Ala Pass) Station on the China–Kazakhstan boundary.
1986: Uyghurs in Xinjiang march through the streets of Urumqi protesting against a wide range of issues, including the environmental degradation of the Zungharian plain, nuclear testing in the Taklimakan, increased Han immigration to Xinjiang and ethnic insults at Xinjiang University.
1987: A book titled *Sexual Customs* is published, which purports to describe the sexual lives of Muslims and provokes Hui people from Gansu, Ningxia, and Xinjiang. The General Administration of Customs releases the "Notification concerning preferential treatment on foreign-invested enterprises in four cities including Urumqi" on September 17.
1988: The Special Economic Zone Office of the State Council issues "Notification concerning the opening up policy granted to Xinjiang" on January 5.
1989: On May 19, Muslim protesters march and finally escalate into violent attack against the CCP Xinjiang Committee tower at People's Square in Urumqi. During this turmoil, more than 40 saloon cars are destroyed, and more than 150 members of the armed police forces, public security policemen, and governmental functionaries are injured. In October, Muslims throughout China protest against a children's book that portray Muslims, particularly their restriction against pork, in a derogatory fashion. In each case, the Chinese government

responds quickly with a promise to meet most of the Muslims' demands by condemning the publications and arresting the authors and closing down the printing houses. The State Council approved the "proposal submitted by the State Ethnic Affairs Commission (SEAC) and the State Council Leading Group for Economic Development in Poor Areas concerning policy issues related to poverty alleviation in minority areas on" on August 28.

1990: On April 4, Zeydun Yusup, head of the East Turkistan Islamic Party, leads 200 or more men to protest against the 250 forced abortions enforced by the government on the local Uyghur women. The State Council issues "Notification concerning the adjustment of program management system and issues in the Xinjiang Production and Construction Corps" on March 13. On April 10, the conflict ends with the eventual capture of hundreds of Uyghur fighters.

1992: The General Department of the State Council issues "Notes on the training of technological personnel of Xinjiang minorities" on August 13.

1994: The State Council approves "Issues concerning the establishment of the Urumqi Economic and Technological Development Zone" on August 25.

1997: On February 5, protesters in the city of Yining (Ghulja) of Ili Kazakh autonomous prefecture are dispersed using clubs, water cannons, and tear gas, and the demonstrations are crushed by the PLA using gunfire. Official reports put the death toll at nine. The CCPCC and the State Council issue the "Notification on further strengthening the work of the Xinjiang Production and Construction Corps" on October 10. The first batch of paring-aid cadres arrives in Xinjiang, opening the curtain the paring-aid work.

1998: The second batch of paring-aid cadres arrives in Xinjiang in March.

1999: The third batch of paring-aid cadres arrives in Xinjiang in June.

2000: On April 24, the State Council approves the Shihezi Economic and Technological Development Zone of the XPCC to upgrade to national level. On October 26, the State Council approves the "Notification of the State Council concerning the implementation of policy measures in the western development." The Ministry of Science and Technology establishes a Joint Conference System among 10 Eastern provinces and Xinjiang. The CCP Central Organization Department, the Central United Front Work Department and the SEAC issue the "Plan of selecting cadres from the western region and other ethnic minority areas to work in the central and state organs (2000–2009)."

2001: The State Council approves the "Plan of the Tarim River comprehensive management" on June 27.

2002: In July, China begins to construct the West-East Gas Pipeline. The project, which starts in the Tarim Basin of the Xinjiang Uyghur autonomous region in northwest China and ends in the east China coastal city of Shanghai, is part of the efforts of the country to make full utilization of the rich resources in the western part of the country and ease energy hunger in the economically developed eastern part. The State Taxation Administration issues "Opinions concerning the implementation of the preferential tax rates in western development" in March. The fourth batch of paring-aid cadres is chosen by the central state organs in August.

2003: On April 2, the CCPCC Xinjiang Coordination Group holds its first meeting, focusing on further strengthening and improving education in Xinjiang.

2004: In May, the CCPCC Xinjiang Coordination Group publishes a Strategic Research Report on the Development and Stability in Xinjiang. In July, the State Council approves the "Catalogue of Advantageous Industrial Sectors for Foreign Investment in Central and West Regions." On September 7, the Dunhuang Railway is announced.

2005: On April 18, the CCPCC and the State Council issue "Establishment of paring-aid relations between relevant provinces, municipalities, business enterprises and the four prefectures in southern Xinjiang Uygur autonomous region and the Xinjiang Production and Construction Corps." The fifth batch of paring-aid cadres from 14 provinces and 15 key state-owned enterprises arrives in Xinjiang.

2006: On August 5, the Dunhuang Railway goes into operation. This 170-km-long railway starts at the Liugou Station of the Lanzhou-Xinjiang Railway and ends at the city of Dunhuang, Gansu province. In September, President Hu Jintao visits Xinjiang to promote economic and social development in Xinjiang and to achieve long-term stability in Xinjiang.

2007: On January 5, Chinese police in Xinjiang carry out a raid against a suspected East Turkestan Islamic Movement training camp in Akto county in the Pamir plateau near the border with Afghanistan and Pakistan, with 18 terror suspects killed and 17 captured. The raid also results in the death of one Chinese paramilitary officer and the injury of another. On September 28, the State Council issues the "Opinions on further promoting economic and social development in Xinjiang."

2008: In July, the Ministry of Land Resources and the Xinjiang government sign an "agreement concerning the cooperation on the geological survey and mineral exploration of key minerals." The sixth batch of paring-aid cadres, coming from more than 90 ministries and central state organs, arrives in Xinjiang. On August 4, a Uyghur separatist group of approximately 70, attacks police officers in the city of Kashgar. This attack results in the deaths of 16 policemen and another 16 being hurt.

2009: In March, National Development and Reform Commission approved "Special plan for the construction projects in the three southern prefectures (2009–2013)." In November, a delegation of about 400 people from various ministries comes to Xinjiang to conduct a comprehensive study. On June 25, two Uyghur factory workers are killed and 118 people (including 79 Uyghurs) injured in an ethnic brawl between Uyghurs and Han Chinese in Shaoguan in the southern province of Guangdong. On July 5, hundreds, perhaps thousands, of Uyghurs riot in Urumqi after security forces move in on a protest over the Shaoguan incident. On July 7, nearly 200 people, mostly Han Chinese, are killed in the unrest, with more than 1,600 injured and hundreds arrested. Eventually, at least 26 are reportedly sentenced to death. On September 2, Han residents of Urumqi protest for days over a wave of syringe stabbings, which the government eventually says kill nearly 500 victims, blaming "ethnic separatist forces."

2010: On March 9, the National Conference on Paring-aid to Xinjiang is held. On April 19, the central government decides to select 19 provinces and municipalities to provide aid to Xinjiang. The seventh batch of paring-aid cadres, coming from 19 provinces and cities, with its number more than that of the past 10 years, arrives in Xinjiang. On May 17, the Central Work Conference on Xinjiang is held. On June 1, the Ministry of Finance and State Taxation Administration issue "Notification concerning the oil and gas resources tax reform in Xinjiang." On August 19, a Uyghur man, using a three-wheeled vehicle, detonates explosives in a crowd of police and paramilitary guards in Aksu. The bombing eventually results in at least seven deaths and 14 injuries. The assailant targets police officers in the area, and most of the victims are also Uyghurs.

2011: The Golmud-Korla Railway is announced. This railway is 1,182 km long and runs across the northwest Qinghai and via Ruoqiang and Weili counties of Bayingolin Mongol autonomous prefecture of Xinjiang. From May 27 to 29, the "Second National Work Conference on the Paring-aid to Xinjiang" is held. On July 18, Uyghur demonstrators attack a police station in Hotan, southern Xinjiang, killing one officer. Police kill 20 protesters in clashes. From July 31 to August 1, two attacks by alleged terrorists leave 13 people dead in a Han-Chinese community of Kashgar, and police kill eight suspected

Uyghur separatists. On September 15, courts in Xinjiang sentence to death four Uyghurs over the July incidents. On December 28, police in Pishan kill seven Uyghurs in a hostage standoff that leaves one officer dead. State media call them terrorists engaged in a "holy war."

2012: On February 28, rioters armed with knives kill at least 10 people in Yecheng, and police shoot two of the attackers dead. One man is later sentenced to death. On October 20, the construction of the 500-km Golmud-Dunhuang Railway line is announced. This single-track electrified rail line will run from Dunhuang (in Gansu province) to the Yinmaxia Station on the Qinghai–Tibet Railway north of Golmud.

2013: On April 23, gunfights in Bachu leave 15 police and community workers and six attackers dead. Two men are later sentenced to death. On June 26, at least 35 people are killed when "knife-wielding mobs" attack police stations and other sites in Lukqun town, Shanshan county, before security personnel open fire. Three people are later sentenced to death. On August 20, a Chinese policeman is killed in Yecheng county, Kashgar. On October 28, three members of the same Xinjiang family crash their car into tourists in Tiananmen Square in Beijing, killing two people (including a woman from the Philippines) and injuring 40 (including one from Japan) before setting the car on fire and dying. On November 17, two policemen and nine attackers are killed at a police station in Serikbuya. On December 16, 14 Uyghurs and two police officers are killed in Shufu county. On December 30, an assault on a police station in Yarkand leaves eight attackers dead.

2014: On January 15, a Uyghur economics lecturer in Beijing is detained by police and later charged with separatism. On January 25, a total of 12 people are killed in Xinhe, six in explosions and six shot dead by police. On February 14, a total of 11 people die in an attack on police in Wushi, with officers shooting eight dead and three blowing themselves up, authorities say. On March 1, a total of 33 people (including 29 civilians) are killed and more than 140 wounded by knife-wielding assailants at Kunming train station in Yunnan province, more than 1,600 km (1,000 miles) from Xinjiang. On April 30, a gang with knives attacks people at the exit of the South Railway Station of Urumqi and sets off explosives, leaving three dead, including two suspects, and 79 injured. On May 8, Chinese police shoot dead an assailant and arrest one more who attacked a police vehicle with knives in Aksu city of Xinjiang, with one policeman wounded. On May 20, courts in Xinjiang sentence 39 Uyghurs to prison for crimes, including organizing and leading terrorist groups, inciting ethnic hatred, ethnic discrimination, and the illegal manufacture of guns. On May 22, there are multiple explosions at the morning market near the Cultural Palace in Urumqi, killing 39 people (including four of the alleged assailants) and wounding more than 90. On May 23, Xinjiang and the Chinese authorities announce a 1-year campaign against militant violence. It has also been the toughest measure that China has taken to fight terrorism after the May 22 attack. As of May, police have detained more than 200 terrorist suspects in 23 groups and found more than 200 explosive devices in Hotan, Kashgar, and Aksu prefectures in southern Xinjiang, where terrorism and religious extremism are active. In June, 13 people are executed for Xinjiang linked terrorist attacks. On July 28, 37 civilians (including 35 Hans and 2 Uyghurs) are killed, and 13 civilians are wounded in an attack on a police station and government offices in Shache county (or Yarkand in the Uyghur language) in Kashgar prefecture, in which more than 30 police cars are also damaged or destroyed. Police shoot dead 59 Uyghur attackers and arrest 215 suspects. On July 30, a head of the Id Kah mosque in Kashgar, the largest in China, is killed after leading morning prayers. Jume Tahir, the Uyghur imam of the 600-year-old Id Kah mosque in the city of Kashgar, is murdered by three thugs who were influenced by religious extremist ideology. On August 1, police shoot dead nine suspected terrorists and capture one in Moyu county, Kashgar prefecture. On August 6, authorities of Karamay, the northwestern city of Xinjiang, prohibit five types of passengers (i.e., those who wear veils, head scarves, a loose-fitting garment called a jilbab, clothing with the crescent moon and star, and those with long beards) from boarding buses. The rules are intended to help strengthen security through August 20 during an athletic event. On August 23, China executes eight people for "terrorist attacks" in Xinjiang, with one or more of the condemned convicted for a suicide car crash at Tiananmen Square in Beijing.

Chinese-style development in Xinjiang: Narrative

2

Quasi-militaristic development zones

Xinjiang production and construction corps

The Xinjiang Production and Construction Corps (XPCC, or known as *Bingtuan* in Chinese for short) was founded in 1954. The stated goals of the XPCC are to develop frontier regions, promote economic development, ensure social stability and ethnic harmony, and consolidate border defense. As a unique semi-military governmental organization and located in Xinjiang Uyghur autonomous region, the XPCC has administrative authority over six medium-sized cities (i.e., Aral, Beitun, Kuitun,[1] Shihezi, Tumushuke, and Wujiaqu) as well as settlements and farms all across Xinjiang. It has its own administrative structure, fulfilling governmental functions such as healthcare and education for areas under its jurisdiction. The Government of Xinjiang Uyghur autonomous region does not usually interfere in the administration of these areas.

The XPCC draws from the traditional Chinese *tuntian* system, a policy of settling military units in frontier areas so that they become self-sufficient in food, and similar policies in the Qing dynasty. Construction corps had been set up for several sparsely populated frontier regions, including Heilongjiang, Inner Mongolia, and Xinjiang. In the early 1950s, the newly founded PRC had the problem of what to do with many former non-Communist soldiers who had been removed from economic production for many years. Ideas about settling such soldiers on the land had been common in China for many years. The Chinese government formed the XPCC from soldiers from the People's Liberation Army (PLA) First Field Crop, former Kuomintang (KMT) soldiers, and soldiers from the local Ili National Army (Rossabi, 2005, pp. 157–158).

When the XPCC was founded in October 1954, it only comprised 175,000 military personnel based in Xinjiang. The XPCC was initially set to settle, cultivate, and develop sparsely populated areas, such as the fringes of the Taklimakan Desert and Gurbantunggut Desert. It also served as a reserve force for the military in Xinjiang during the early years of the PRC. The ranks of the XPCC were also joined by many youths, including middle school graduates, both male and female, from other parts of China (e.g., Gansu, Henan, Hubei, Hunan, Shanghai, Jiangsu, Tianjin, and Shandong provinces) to balance out its sex ratio and include members with better education backgrounds. By the end of 1960, the XPCC had a total population of

[1] Note that Kuitun as a city has not been administrated by the XPCC since 1975.

China's Spatial (Dis)integration.

724,100, or 4.1 times that in 1954.[2] In 2010, its population increased to 2.61 million (*Bingtuan Daily*, December 29, 2011).

In 1962, after the Sino–Soviet split, rioting occurred in Yining, and 60,000 ethnic minorities living across the border fled to the Soviet Union. At that time, the Chinese government feared that the Soviet Union was trying to destabilize China and start a war (O'Neill, April 13, 2008; Rossabi, 2005, pp. 157–158). The XPCC, together with many other governmental and party organizations, was severely damaged by the chaos of the Cultural Revolution. In 1975, it was abolished completely, with all of its powers transferred to the government of Xinjiang Uyghur autonomous region and the local authorities thereof. After the Soviet Union invaded Afghanistan in 1979, the Chinese government, fearing of Soviet encirclement and Islamic fundamentalism, reopened the XPCC in December 1981.

Organization of the Xinjiang production and construction corps

The XPCC is administered by both the Chinese central government as well as the government of Xinjiang Uyghur autonomous region. It has subprovincial powers on par with subprovincial ranking municipalities (Shenyang, Nanjing, and Guangzhou, to name but three), and its economic and social development are administered separately from those of Xinjiang. Officially, the XPCC's land area and population are generally included in those of Xinjiang's, but sometimes other statistical data of the XPCC are reported separately.

The XPCC is headquartered at Urumqi, capital of Xinjiang Uyghur autonomous region. The XPCC is now consisting of 14 reclamation areas called "divisions" (Table 2.1), which are then subdivided into 174 regimental agricultural and stockbreeding farms; 4,391 industrial, construction, transport, and commercial enterprises; and well-run social undertakings covering scientific research, education, culture, health, sports, finance, and insurance, as well as judiciary organs, scattered throughout Xinjiang, mostly in previously unpopulated or sparsely populated areas.[3] Each XPCC division corresponds to a prefecture-level administrative division of Xinjiang and is in itself subprefectural in rank.

The XPCC—as well as each individual division thereof—is headed by two leaders, a political commissar and a commander. The role of political commissar of the XPCC is filled by a member of the Chinese Communist Party (CCP) Xinjiang Standing Committee, and the rank of the political commissar of each XPCC division is similar to that of the CCP secretary in each of the corresponding prefecture-level divisions. At the end of the 20th century, the military role of the XPCC has been diluted, being given instead to the Xinjiang Military District. The latter is part of the Lanzhou Military Region that is in charge of all military affairs of northwestern China. At present, the military personnel of the XPCC are mostly reservists or militia.

The XPCC has built six medium-sized cities (Aral, Beitun, Kuitun, Shihezi, Tumushuke, and Wujiaqu) during its history and now controls five of them

[2] See the website of the XPCC (http://www.xjbt.gov.cn/zjbt/btgk/26100.htm. Accessed April 20, 2013).
[3] Ibid.

Table 2.1 **Divisions of the Xinjiang production and construction corps***

Division	Founded	Area(s) covered	Headquarters	Population (2010)
No. 1	1953	Aksu P	Aksu, Aral	284,627
No. 2	1953	Bayingolin Mongol AP	Korla	190,369
No. 3	1966	Kashgar P	Kashgar, Tumushuke	213,329
No. 4	1953	Southern Ili Kazakh AP	Yining	214,077
No. 5	1953	Bortala Mongol AP	Bortala	113,162
No. 6	1953	Changji Hui AP	Wujiaqu	301,438
No. 7	1953	Western Karamay PM	Kuitun, TND	213,861
No. 8	1953	Eastern Karamay PM	Shihezi	636,240
No. 9	1962	Tacheng P; Ili Kazakh AP	Emin County	72,889
No. 10	1959	Altay P; Ili Kazakh AP	Beitun	77,608
No. 11	1953		Urumqi	53,636
No. 12	1982	Urumqi PM	Urumqi	72,234
No. 13	1982	Kumul P	Kumul	85,345
No. 14	1982	Hotan P	Hotan	7,898

AP, Autonomous prefecture; *P*, prefecture; *PM*, prefectural-level municipality; *TND*, Tianbei New District.
*Except No. 11 Division, which specializes in construction engineering, all of the other divisions are agricultural.
Sources: McMillen (1981), Becquelin (2000), and *Bingtuan Daily* (December 29, 2011).

Table 2.2 **Cities governed by the Xinjiang production and construction corps**

City (New area)	Population (2010)	Founded	Governing period(s)
Aral	166,205	2002	1953–1975, 1980–
Beitun	76,300	2011	2002–
Kuitun	166,261	1975	1953–1975
Shihezi	635,582	1976	1953–1975, 1980–
Tianbei New Area	26,221	2002	2002–
Tumushuke	147,465	2002	1966–1975, 1980–
Wujiaqu	72,613	2002	1953–1975, 1980–

Sources: O'Neill (2008), State Council (2003), and author.

(Table 2.2). The governments of these cities are combined entirely with the division that controls them. For example, the division headquarters is the same entity as the city government, the division political commissar is the same person as the city committee secretary, the division commander is the same person as the city's mayor, and so forth. Five XPCC-administered cities are nominally listed as "county-level cities" of Xinjiang Uyghur Administrative Region, but the government of Xinjiang is usually not involved in the administration of these cities.

Although dozens of ethnic groups are represented in the XPCC, the largest of them are the Han, Uyghur, Hui, Kazakh, and Mongol. Because most of the Han people have no religious beliefs, Muslims are the largest religious group represented, but there also exist smaller populations of Buddhists, Protestants, and Catholics. Although the Han have been the largest group of XPCC workers, their relative numbers have been declining. For example, in 1980, the Han membership represented 90% (Rossabi, 2005, pp. 157–158); in 2010, according to the Sixth National Population Census, it only accounted for 85.5%.

Functions of the Xinjiang production and construction corps

The XPCC is currently focused on economic development as its stated primary goal. With the continued opening up of the economy, the XPCC has created many publicly traded subsidiary companies involved in the production and sale of a variety of products. When involved in such economic activities, the XPCC uses the name "China Xinjian Group." The primary economic activity of the XPCC remains agriculture, including cotton, fruit, vegetables, food crops, vegetable oils, sugar beets, and so forth. Important products are cotton, tomatoes, ketchup, Korla pears, Turpan grapes, wine, and so forth. The XPCC has a mix of factory farming and smaller farms.

The XPCC is also involved in a variety of tertiary industries, including trade, distribution, real estate, tourism, construction, even insurance. In its 60-year history, the XPCC has built farms, towns, and cities and provided land and work for disbanded military units. During its history, the XPCC established a large amount of mining and mining-related industries, most of which have subsequently been handed over to the Xinjiang government. Currently, the XPCC is primarily engaged in food- and agriculture-related industries. It also participates in economic activities and is known as the China Xinjian Group. At present, the group has 11 traded subsidiaries:

- Xinjiang Baihuacun Co., Ltd: primarily information technology
- Xinjiang Tianye Co., Ltd.: primarily plastics
- Suntime International Economic-Trading Co., Ltd.: primarily international trade
- Xinjiang Talimu Agriculture Development Co., Ltd.: primarily cotton
- Xinjiang Yilite Industry Co., Ltd.: primarily alcohol
- Xinjiang Chalkis Co., Ltd.: primarily tomatoes and related industries
- Xinjiang Tianhong Papermaking Co., Ltd.: paper manufacturing
- Xinjiang Tianfu Thermoelectric Co., Ltd.: electricity
- Xinjiang Guannong Fruit & Antler Co., Ltd.: fruits and animal husbandry
- Xinjiang Qingsong Cement Co., Ltd.: cement
- Xinjiang Sayram Modern Agriculture Co., Ltd.: primarily cotton

At present, the XPCC is playing the most important role in Xinjiang's social and economic development. It has one sixth of Xinjiang's population and one fourth of its arable land. The XPCC has its own separate education system covering primary, secondary, and tertiary education. It currently has two universities,

Shihezi University and Tarim University. The XPCC has its own official daily newspaper, the *Bingtuan Daily*, as well as TV stations at both the XPCC and its division levels.

Large construction projects

Exploitation of natural resources

In its long history, Xinjiang has been noted for producing salt, soda, borax, gold, and jade. Because Han-Chinese culture has had a strong attachment to jade, for thousands of years, jade has been exploited in Xinjiang and supplied to ancient Chinese dynasties. Known reserves of iron ore are put at 730 million tons; those for salt are 318 million tons; mirabilite, 170 million tons; and natron saltpeter, more than 2 million tons. With its deposits of more than 70 nonmetallic minerals, the region is well known for its muscovite, gemstones, asbestos, and Hotan (Hetian) jade. In addition, estimates put its coal reserves at more than one third of the national total. Petroleum and natural gas reserves are estimated at 30 billion tons and account for more than 25% of the national total (Guo, 2013a, p. 321).

Recently, Xinjiang has become one of the most important energy producers in China. Although the discovery of natural resources has certainly been a boost for the province, these remain scattered about an uninhabited and undeveloped landscape. Development in the areas of production and transportation will be necessary to maximize the region's economic growth. In 2009, Xinjiang produced more natural gas than any other province, the fourth most crude oil in China, and a large amount of coal.

The latest round evaluation of oil and gas resources, conducted by the Geological and Mineral Bureau of Xinjiang, shows that Xinjiang contains 20.9 billion tons of oil resources and 10 trillion cubic meters of natural gas resources, which account for about 25% and 28% of China's total onshore oil and gas reserves, respectively. At the beginning of 2012, PetroChina (China's largest oil producer) proposed the building of three large oil and gas fields, with the production capacities equivalent to 50 billion tons of oil by 2015 (Xiong, July 7, 2012). Recently, the Geological and Mineral Bureau of Xinjiang has made important progress in the exploration of coal, iron, nickel, gold, lead and zinc ores, and coal, with 15 new mineral fields being found 15 (of which 7 are large ones). It is expected that by the end of the 12th 5-year plan (2011–2015), Xinjiang will have completed ten 10-million ton, five 30-million, and two 50-million ton scales of coal enterprise groups, with the total annual outputs of 400 million tons of coal and of 100 billion cubic meters of natural and coal gas (Zhang, January 16, 2013).

Thanks to its abundant reserves of coal, crude oil, and natural gas, on the one hand and China's western development policy introduced by the State Council in the late 1990s on the other, Xinjiang has achieved rapid economic development

Table 2.3 **Demographic and socioeconomic profile: Xinjiang***

Indicator		2000		2010	
		Xinjiang	% of China	Xinjiang	% of China
Population (million persons)		19.25	1.52	21.85	1.63
Illiterate rate of population age 15 years and older (%)		5.56	82.74	2.36	57.84
GRP (billion yuan)		136.44	1.40	543.75	1.24
Composition of GRP (%)	Primary sector	21.1	138.18	19.8	213.59
	Secondary sector	43.0	91.30	47.7	94.74
	Tertiary sector	35.9	95.40	32.5	80.51
Fixed asset investment (billion yuan)		61.04	1.85	342.32	1.23
Foreign trade (million U.S. dollar)	Export	1,147	0.46	12,555	0.80
	Import	1,439	0.64	8,809	0.63
Per capita income of urban residents (yuan)		5,645	89.89	13,644	71.40
Engle's coefficient (%)		36.38	92.85	36.23	101.57
Per capita net income of rural residents (yuan)		1,618	71.81	4,643	78.44
Engle's coefficient (%)		31.05	73.93	40.32	101.56
Number of patent per million persons	Inventions	3.43	70.29	8.65	14.54
	Utility models	24.68	57.42	92.08	36.08
	Designs	9.14	33.39	16.52	6.95

GRP, gross regional product.
*All monetary values are measured at current prices.
Sources: Xinjiang Bureau of Statistics (2001 and 2011) and National Bureau of Statistics (2001 and 2011).

during the past decade. Its gross regional product was quadrupled from 2000 and 2010. However, its share of China's total gross domestic product declined from 1.40% in 2000 to 1.24% in 2010 (Table 2.3).

The West-East gas Pipeline

In July 2002, China began to construct the West-East Gas Pipeline. The project, which starts in the Tarim Basin of the Xinjiang Uyghur autonomous region in northwest China and ends in the east China coastal city of Shanghai, is part of the efforts of the country to make full utilization of the rich resources in the western part of the country and ease energy hunger in the economically developed eastern part.

The project includes the following lines:[4]

- The first pipeline, crossing 10 provincial regions, has transferred more than 138 billion cubic meters of gas since 2004. It starts from Xinjiang and ends in Shanghai.
- The second pipeline, measuring around 8,700 km, can transfer 30 billion cubic meters of gas annually. It runs from Xinjiang to Guangdong province in the south.
- The third pipeline is a key project, consisting of one trunk line and eight branch lines. The trunk line (from Horgos in Xinjiang and end at Fuzhou, capital city of Fujian) measures 5,000 km. The project is expected to be completed before 2015. Around 25 billion cubic meters of gas will come from central Asian countries each year, and five billion cubic meters of gas will come from Xinjiang.
- The fourth and fifth pipelines are under planning. China aims to build a nationwide natural gas network that connects with overseas resources in future.

Socioeconomic implications

Xinjiang's development has been quite spatially imbalanced, especially between its southern and northern parts. Even though there are many other reasons behind this kind of south–north difference, including the one that most of the XPCC's activities have been conducted in northern vis-à-vis southern Xinjiang), geographical location (southern Xinjiang is farther from the Chinese inland than northern Xinjiang), physical environment, and social and cultural issues (to be discussed in Chapter 5), the large-scale energy exploitation activities in northern Xinjiang should also have played a role. For example, the oil and gas extraction industry in Aksu and Karamay is booming; and the oil and petrochemical sector accounts for 60% of the local economy (Guo, 2013a, p. 323). However, because most of the exploitation activities have been conducted by large, state-owned enterprises, local residents cannot expect to obtain any substantial benefits from them.

Through the West-East Gas Pipeline, China is now able to increase the share of natural gas in its primary energy consumption and boost balanced development between regions. However, the major beneficiary is not Xinjiang itself; neither are the local communities and residents there. Even though this project has provided job opportunities for a few of people (mostly the Han Chinese), most of the others (especially the Uyghurs and other non–Han Chinese) have rarely benefited from it. Even worse, they may suffer from unexpected environmental and ecological damages stemming from the operations of this project.

Pairing-aid programs

Historical evolution

The pairing-aid (or "duikou zhiyuan" in Chinese) program stems from the idea that economic leading provinces and cities help economically backward areas. It started as early as the 1950s. From the 1950s to the early 1960s, Shanghai dispatched tens of thousands

[4] Sources: China Central Television (March 8, 2004) and China Radio International (October 16, 2012).

of cadres, workers, and intellectuals in finance, construction, textile, electrics, mechanics, and higher education to Shaanxi, which have played an important role in Shaanxi's economic development and social progress (Huang, February 9, 2011).

In 1979, the pairing-aid program was officially established by the Chinese central government as a national policy in its No. 52 Central Document. In the "National Frontier Defense Work Meeting" held in April 1979, Ulanhu, then Chief of the Central United Front Work Department presented in the General Assembly a report titled "National People Unite and Struggle to Build a Thriving Frontier and Consolidate Border Defense." In the report, China pledged to increase the input of capital and materials to and organize the inland provinces and municipalities to support border areas and ethnic minority areas.[5] Later on, this policy expanded to three patterns corresponding to different objectives: for economic development of the minority-inhabited border areas, for grand infrastructure construction projects, and for disaster relief and recovery.

After decades of practical operations, China's central government has accumulated rich experience for applying the pairing-aid idea by mobilizing the whole country. The representative example of pairing aid for grand infrastructure construction is the huge emigration of the areas affected by the Three Gorges Dam from the early 1990s until the 2000s, in which 22 provinces have involved. The pairing-aid program for disaster relief and recovery of the Sichuan Earthquake in 2008 was another trial of this idea and showed the advantage in postdisaster reconstruction work.

Progress and achievements

Pairing the more-developed provinces and municipalities in the east with the impoverished regions in the west in poverty reduction is a policy adopted by the Chinese government in its efforts to achieve common prosperity. Since 1996, the government has made arrangement for more than a dozen economically more developed provinces and municipalities in the east to help the remaining, less developed provinces (autonomous regions and municipalities directly under the central government) in the west to get rid of poverty. The basic framework of this east-help-west cooperation is mainly composed of government assistance, enterprise cooperation, social aid and human resource support. According to a report released by the Chinese government:

> *From 2003 to 2010, some 2,592 cadres were sent from the east to the west to hold temporary leading posts there, and 3,610 were sent from the west to the east for the same purpose. About 4.44 billion yuan-worth of assistance funds was provided and 5,684 enterprises were recommended by governments of the eastern regions for cooperation in this regard, resulting in 249.76 billion yuan actually ploughed in and 1.42 billion yuan in social donations, in addition to 226,000 technical personnel trained and 4.672 million people from the poverty-stricken areas providing labor services elsewhere.*[6]

[5] Source: State Ethnic Affairs Commission (2008).

[6] Cited form Xinhua (November 16, 2011).

Table 2.4 China's East-West Pairing-aid programs, 2001 to 2010*

East province (municipality)	West province (municipality, autonomous region)
Beijing M	Inner Mongolia AR
Dalian SPM of Liaoning P	Guizhou P
Fujian P	Ningxia Hui AR
Guangdong P	Guangxi Zhuang AR
Jiangsu P	Shaanxi P
Liaoning P	Qinghai P
Ningbo PM of Zhejiang P	Guizhou P
Qingdao PM of Shandong P	Guizhou P
Shandong P	Xinjiang Uyghur AR; Chongqing M (after June 2010)
Shanghai M	Yunnan P
Shenzhen SPM of Guangdong P	Guizhou P
Tianjin M	Gansu P
Xiamen SPM of Fujian P	Chongqing M (before June 2010); Linxia Hui AP of Gansu P (after June 2010)
Zhejiang P	Sichuan
Zhuhai PM of Guangdong P	Chongqing M (before June 2010); Liangshan Yi AP of Sichuan P (after June 2010)

AR, Autonomous region, *AP*, autonomous prefecture, *M*, municipality directly under the central government, *P*, province, *PM*, prefectural-level municipality, *SPM*, subprovincial level municipality.
*Tibet and Xinjiang, which are entitled to receive multilateral pairing-aid programs, are not shown here.
Sources: Xinhua (November 16, 2011) and miscellaneous news clippings.

From 2001 to 2010, except for Tibet and Xinjiang (which are entitled to receive pairing aid from all the eastern, richer provinces and municipalities), China's East-West pairing-aid programs are shown in Table 2.4.

Pairing aid to Xinjiang

China's pairing-aid programs started in Xinjiang from as early as the 1950s, when the XPCC was established there. In the national pairing-aid work meeting, held in Beijing on March 30, 2010, a total of 19 pairing-up Xinjiang programs were scheduled from 2011 to 2020. The aid programs include the following provinces and municipalities:

- Anhui province (pairing with Hotan prefecture): scheduled to provide technical and financial assistance to Pishan county
- Beijing municipality (pairing with Hotan prefecture): Five demonstration projects, including (i) first phase of the community reconstruction project in Hotan city, (ii) construction of earthquake-resistant housing and the new rural construction plan, (iii) construction of the agricultural infrastructure in Moyu county, (iv) construction of a patient building for the People's Hospital of Luopu county, and (v) the construction of a processing base for the No. 14 Agricultural Division of the XPCC
- Fujian province (pairing with Changji Hui autonomous prefecture): scheduled to provide assistance to Changji city, and Manasi, Hutubi, Qitai, Jimusar, and Mulei counties, focusing on employment, education, and housing

- Guangdong province (pairing with Kashgar prefecture): scheduled to provide assistance to Shufu county, Jiashi county, and Tumushuke city of the No. 3 Agricultural Division of the XPCC
- Hebei province (pairing with Bayingolin Mongol autonomous prefecture: scheduled to provide technical and financial assistance to the No. 2 Agricultural Division of the XPCC
- Heilongjiang province (pairing with Altay prefecture): scheduled to provide technical and financial assistance to Fuhai, Fuyun, and Qinghe counties and the No. 10 Agricultural Division of the XPCC, focusing on the industrialization of agricultural production and the joint exploration and exploitation of mineral resources
- Henan province (pairing with Kumul prefecture): scheduled to provide assistance to the No. 13 Agricultural Division of the XPCC
- Hubei (pairing with Bortala Mongol autonomous prefecture): scheduled to provide assistance to Bole city and Jinghe and Wenquan counties and the No. 5 Agricultural Division of the XPCC
- Hunan province (pairing with Turpan prefecture): scheduled to provide assistance to construct a few of key projects
- Jiangsu province (pairing with Kizilsu Kirgiz and Ili Kazakh autonomous prefectures): scheduled to provide assistance to Artux city and Wuqia county of Kizilsu Kirgiz autonomous prefecture and Huocheng county, the No. 66 Regiment of the No. 4 Agricultural Division of the XPCC, Yining county and Chabucharxibo autonomous county of Ili Kazakh autonomous prefecture, focusing on educational development and campus construction. In addition, Jiangsu will also provide support for students to study in Jiangsu's middle schools and universities.
- Jiangxi province (pairing with Kizilsu Kirgiz autonomous prefecture): scheduled to, after 5 years of pairing assistance, triple the gross economic output, financial revenue, and the urban size of Arctao county, reaching the average level of Jiangxi's counties (cities)
- Jilin province (pairing with Altay prefecture): scheduled to provide assistance to Altay city and Habahe, Burjin, and Jimunai countries
- Liaoning province (pairing with Tacheng prefecture): scheduled to complete the housing construction for the disaster-hit areas before the winter of 2010
- Shandong province (pairing with Kashgar prefecture): scheduled to provide assistance to Shule, Yingjisha, Maigaiti, and Yuepuhu counties, focusing on the improvement of local residents' living standard and self-enhancing abilities of development
- Shanghai municipality (pairing with Kashgar prefecture): scheduled to provide assistance to Bachu, Shace, Zepu, and Yecheng counties, focusing on the improvement of local residents' living standard and sustainable development
- Shanxi province (pairing with Changji Hui autonomous prefecture): scheduled to provide technical and financial assistance to Wujiaqu city of the No. 6 Agricultural Division of the XPCC and Fukang city
- Shenzhen municipality of Guangdong province (pairing with Kashgar city and Tashikurkan county): to be determined
- Tianjin municipality (pairing with Hotan prefecture): Ten measures will be taken for the new round of paring-aid programs to Minfeng, Cele, and Yutian counties
- Zhejiang province (pairing with Aksu prefecture): scheduled to provide assistance to one city and eight counties (of Aksu prefecture) and Aral city (of the No. 1 Agricultural Division of the XPCC)[7]

[7] Source: The National Work Conference on the Pairing Aid to Xinjiang, Beijing, March 29–30, 2010.

The major events relating to China's interprovincial pairing-aid-to-Xinjiang programs can be found in the Annex.

Inland middle school classes

Motivation

Since September 2000, the central government has set up classes for students from Xinjiang in 13 senior middle schools of Beijing, Shanghai, and other economically developed cities. These classes are called *neidi gaozhong ban* in Chinese, or *neigao ban* for short. The initiative of the *neigao ban* program had two major tasks for Xinjiang: (i) to speeded up the educational development of poor, rural areas and (ii) to promote interethnic exchange and unity.

The numbers of enrolled students were 1,000 persons per year for the first 2 years, of whom 90 percent were non-Han ethnic minorities (mainly the Uyghur, Kazak, and Hui). In 2002, the total number of the enrolled students increased to 1,540. In the meantime, the XPCC was permitted to send 70 junior middle school graduates—of whom 50 percent were ethnic minorities—to the inland middle schools to pursue a further study. In 2005, the number of cities to host students from Xinjiang increased to 25, with a total number of 35 middle schools involved in the "inland middle school classes for Xinjiang" program.[8]

In 2010, according to the requirements of the Ministry of Education, the enrollment continues to incline toward the southern (poorer) Xinjiang area and toward the children of farmers and herdsmen therein, with farmers' and herdsmen's children accounting for more than 80% of the total students enrolled. In addition, from 2011 onward, secondary vocational classes were also opened in some inland schools, which have been recruiting 3,000 junior middle school graduates from Xinjiang annually (Table 2.5).

Organization

The neigao ban program is organized through a period of 4 years (including 1 year of preparatory class). Regardless of their ethnic grouping, all students are required to use Chinese language textbooks. In the preparatory stage, the training of Chinese language, mathematics, physics, and chemistry is prepared for those who have not reached the general level of the inland junior middle school graduates. In the following 3 years of senior middle school classes, all teaching activities are run according to the plan designed by local education authorities.

The funds that are used to run the neigao ban are divided into lump-sum and regular funds. The lump-sum funds are mainly provided by the National Development and Reform Commission (NDRC) and the Ministry of Finance (MOF), although the regular funds, with an annual average of more than

[8] Data source: CPPCC Daily (August 19, 2010).

Table 2.5 Statistics of Xinjiang's students enrolled in Inland provinces' middle and vocational schools (in person), 2000 to 2014

Year	Whole Xinjiang area		Xinjiang UAR*		XPCC†	
	Senior class	Vocational	Senior class	Vocational	Senior class	Vocational
2000	1000	—	1000	—	—	—
2001	1000	—	1000	—	—	—
2002	1540	—	1470	—	70	—
2003	1540	—	1470	—	70	—
2004	1540	—	1470	—	70	—
2005	3075	—	2920	—	150	—
2006	3990	—	3840	—	150	—
2007	5000	—	4850	—	150	—
2008	5518	—	5368	—	150	—
2009	5500	—	5350	—	150	—
2010	6378	—	6178	—	200	—
2011	7090	3300	6860	3000	230	300
2012	8330	3300	8030	3000	300	300
2013	9122	3300	8792	3000	330	300
2014	9880	3300	9530	3000	350	300

UAR, Uyghur Autonomous Region; *XPCC*, Xinjiang Production and Construction Corps.
*Ethnic minority (mainly the Uyghur) students account for 90% of the total numbers.
†Ethnic minority (including Uyghur, Kazak, Hui, and so on) students account for 50% of the total numbers.
Source: Author based on miscellaneous news clippings.

6,000 yuan per student, are supplied by the municipal governments of the respective cities in which the neigao ban are located. In addition, the government of Xinjiang autonomous region also bears the responsibility of an annual average 2,700 yuan for each student to cover his or her transport fees as well as the subsidies for part of the learning, living, and medical expenses. Students enrolled in the neigao ban are classified into three categories according to their family economic conditions: "extremely poor," "poor," and "not poor." All living costs and tuitions are exempted for the "extremely poor" students, and those who are classified as "poor" and "not poor" are only charged 450 yuan and 900 yuan per year, respectively, for their living costs and tuition.[9]

From 2014 onward, the central government began to provide free middle school education for all students from the four prefectures of Aksu, Hotan, Kashgar, and Kizilsu in southern Xinjiang. As a result, this policy has also applied to all the neigao-ban students from these prefectures.

The expenditure of the inland secondary vocational classes for Xinjiang comes from three sources. First, the NDRC provides a lump-sum subsidy on the construction of new infrastructures (e.g., Muslim canteens). Second, the MOF provides funds for the purchase of teaching equipment, books, and living and learning

[9] Data source: http://www.833200.com/Item.aspx?id=3253. Accessed January 9, 2014.

appliances, with the standard of the annual average subsidies of 5,000 yuan for each student to cover his or her living expenses, accommodation fees, textbook fees, medical care fees, material fees in experiment, and others. Third, the host provinces and cities and Xinjiang autonomous region each also provide transport and living and medical care subsidies.[10]

Performance

Since 2000, the inland middle schools and classes have expanded annually, with the total number of host cities being from 12 in 2000 to 45 in 2014. At present, the host cities are Beijing, Shanghai, Tianjin, Harbin, Changchun, Shenyang, Dalian, Xi'an, Zhengzhou, Ji'nan, Qingdao, Yantai, Weihai, Weifang, Yancheng, Xuzhou, Huaian, Zhenjiang Yangzhou, Nanjing, Taizhou, Suzhou, Hangzhou, Wuxi, Ningbo, Wenzhou, Jiaxing, Suqian, Haining, Lianyungang, Wuhan, Xiamen, Guangzhou, Shenzhen, Zhuhai, Jiangmen, Dongguan, Zhaoqing, Changle, Fuqing, Taizhou, Zibo, Longyan, Putian, and Jining. As of 2014, there are a total number of 91 inland middle schools to host the junior middle school graduates from Xinjiang.[11]

After graduation, all students are able to attend the university entrance exams in the inland middle schools, with much higher probability of entering into prestigious universities than the Han students from inland provinces. As of January 2014, nearly 29,000 students have graduated from the inland middle schools, 95 percent of whom have been accepted by universities.[12] Obviously, this has also benefited from China's preferential policy toward Xinjiang. For example, the minimum scores for Xinjjang's students at the inland middle schools to enter Chinese universities were set in 2012 as the following: (i) 415 (both liberal arts and sciences) for ethnic Han students to enter Han-dominated universities, (ii) 330 (liberal arts) and 315 (sciences) for ethnic-minority students to enter Han-dominated universities, and (iii) 310 (liberal arts) and 300 (sciences) for ethnic-minority students to enter minority-dominated universities. However, these minimum scores are still much lower than those for students from the inland provinces (Table 2.6).

The success of the inland middle school classes has been always a positive factor contributing to social and economic improvements of the non-Han ethnic population living in poor, rural areas in Xinjiang. In the meantime, it has also provided a bridge for all ethnic groups concerned to enhance exchange and cooperation. For example, in China, the Uyghurs are generally stereotyped as happy ethnic dancers; curbside kebab-sellers; or, increasingly, Islamist militants. By contrast Abdulhabir Muhammad—a 24-year-old chief operating officer of an educational consulting company and a Muslim who prays at a mosque every Friday—epitomizes the

[10] Source: Ibid.
[11] Source: http://www.xjyledu.gov.cn/articles/2014/03/03/4389.htm. Accessed January 9, 2014.
[12] Source: Ibid.

Table 2.6 A comparison of college entrance criteria between Inland China and Xinjiang*

<table>
<tr><th rowspan="2">Type</th><th colspan="2">Scores (Liberal arts)</th><th colspan="2">Scores (Sciences)</th></tr>
<tr><th>Inland China</th><th>Xinjiang</th><th>Inland China</th><th>Xinjiang</th></tr>
<tr><td>Specially planned colleges</td><td>557 (H), 537 (M)</td><td rowspan="4">415 (H), 330 (MH), 310 (MM)</td><td>540 (H), 520 (M)</td><td rowspan="4">415 (H), 315 (MH), 300 (MM)</td></tr>
<tr><td>Regular colleges I</td><td>557 (H), 537 (M)</td><td>540 (H), 520 (M)</td></tr>
<tr><td>Regular colleges II</td><td>509 (H), 489 (M)</td><td>481 (H), 461 (M)</td></tr>
<tr><td>Regular colleges III</td><td>447 (H), 427 (M)</td><td>391 (H), 371 (M)</td></tr>
<tr><td>Junior/technical/ vocational colleges</td><td>360 (H), 340 (M)</td><td>305 (H), 300 (MH), 284 (MM)</td><td>300 (H), 280 (M)</td><td>290 (H), 284 (MH), 280 (MM)</td></tr>
</table>

H, Han students; *M*, minority students; *MH*, minority students to enter Han-dominated universities; *MM*, minority students to enter minority-dominated universities.
*Data are as of 2012. College entrance criteria vary from province to province in inland China, and this table uses Henan province as reference.
Sources: Department of Education of Henan province and the College Entrance Leading Group for the Tibet and Xinjiang Students in Inland Provinces, the Ministry of Education, Beijing, China.

authorities' preferred vision of Xinjiang's future. The following is reported by an AFP (French Press Agency) correspondent:

> *His father was a poor wheat farmer who rose to own a chain of supermarkets in the region, and Abdulhabir has come further still.*
>
> *Aged 15, he was accepted into a Beijing high school where he mastered Chinese and English, and then earned a degree in accounting from Binghamton University in New York state, followed by an MBA in entrepreneurship.*
>
> *Now his company, which helps Chinese study abroad, has around 20 employees, 15 of them Han, China's dominant ethnic majority, and his business partner is a Manchu woman.*
>
> *Telegenic and confident, Abdulhabir has been featured in state media along with other young business people as positive examples of Uyghur identity.*
>
> *"You know the reason I'm in the media is because I am a good Uyghur," he says. "And I want other Uyghurs to see me as a good Uyghur as well."*[13]

Unresolved issues

This chapter gives a critical analysis of China's past policies toward Xinjiang in general and the Uyghurs in particular. Among all the ethnic groups of Xinjiang, the Uyghur and the Han are the largest. For a long time, Uyghurs and the mostly Han has disagreed on which group has greater historical claim to the Xinjiang

[13] Cited from Olsen (August 28, 2014).

region: Uyghurs believe their ancestors were indigenous to the area, but government policy considers present-day Xinjiang to have belonged to China since around 200 BC (Gladney, 2004b, pp. 63–98). Nevertheless, according to James A. Millward (professor of Chinese and Central Asian History at Georgetown University), foreigners often mistakenly think that Urumqi (capital city of Xinjiang) was originally a Uyghur city and that the Chinese destroyed its Uyghur character and culture. In reality, Urumqi was founded as a Chinese city by Han and Hui (Tungans), and the Uyghurs are new to the city (Millward, 1998, pp. 133–134).

Although China's current minority policy has reinforced a Uyghur ethnic identity that is distinct from the Han population, some scholars argue that Beijing unofficially favors a monolingual, monocultural model that is based on the majority crackdown on any activity that appears to constitute separatism.[14] These policies, in addition to the long-standing cultural differences, have sometimes resulted in "resentments" between Uyghur and Han citizens. On the one hand, as a result of Han immigration and government policies, Uyghurs' freedoms of religion and of movement are curtailed, but most Uyghurs argue that the government deliberately downplays their history and traditional culture. On the other hand, some Han citizens view the Uyghurs as benefiting from special treatment, such as preferential admission to universities and exemption from the one-child policy, and as harboring separatist aspirations.

China has invented various approaches to promote Xinjiang's economic development and social stability. But Xinjiang, after more than 60 years of socialist construction with Chinese characteristics, is still a politically fragile region. As will be discussed in greater detail in Chapter 5, China's development programs in Xinjiang are not successful, at least compared with those in Tibet. Among the negative effects that China's development programs have yielded in Xinjiang during the past decades are the interregional and interethnic economic disparities.

Without good reason, the above-mentioned interregional and interethnic economic disparities should have been responsible to most, if not all, of the growing frequencies of ethnic unrest related to Xinjiang (see Chapter 3 for the detailed narratives of the Uyghur unrest from the 1980s to the 2010s). Most of the terrorists involved in recent attacks are young men or women in their 20s or 30s, indicating that basic education and employment in Xinjiang need to be strengthened. In May 2014, as the Chinese government vowed to crack down on separatists and terrorists, major measures relating to the stability of Xinjiang were announced:

- According to the statement released after a meeting of the Political Bureau of the CCP Central Committee, chaired by its general secretary, Xi Jinping from May 29 to 30, 2014, steps will be taken to boost local education in Xinjiang, including speeding up the building of boarding schools in agricultural, pastoral areas, and remote areas and offering free education for senior middle school students (i.e., those from school years 10 to 12) in Xinjiang's southern regions, mainly inhabited by ethnic Uyghurs.[15]

[14] See Dillon (2003, p. 51), Dwyer (2005, p. 2), and Bovingdon (2005, p. 19) for more detailed analyses in this regard.

[15] Source: http://news.xinhuanet.com/english/china/2014-05/28/c_133366222.htm. Accessed June 1, 2014.

- According to a new regulation issued by the government of Xinjiang Uyghur autonomous region on May 31, 2014, no less than 70 percent of the newly employees offered by all enterprises, including state-owned enterprises, in Xinjiang must come from local Xinjiang. To achieve this target, Xinjiang will establish a special fund for the development of labor-intensive industry. Specific measures include (i) to heavily invest in textile and apparel sectors, (ii) to implement large-scale employment programs, and (iii) to create "fast track" projects in southern Xinjiang by cultivating private enterprises to improve local employment.[16]

Are these policies or measures toward Xinjiang too late (or not enough) to prevent the Han—Uyghur unrest? Let us open our eyes to watch what will happen in Xinjiang.

Annex: Major interprovincial events relating to the Pairing-Aid-to-Xinjiang programs[17]

Anhui: On September 3, 2010, during the "Urumqi Foreign Economic and Trade Fair," the delegations of Anhui province and Xinjiang Uyghur autonomous region hold a "cooperation-enhancing meeting." On June 7, 2011, the Tourism Bureaus of Xinjiang Uyghur autonomous region and Anhui province hold the "Meeting of Assisting Xinjiang" in Hefei, Anhui province and sign a "Tourist Cooperation Agreement." From June 16 to 19, 2011, the "Meeting of Strategic Cooperation of Construction Sector between Anhui province and Xinjiang autonomous region" is held in Urumqi, Xinjiang Uyghur autonomous region, aiming to deepen the strategic cooperation of construction industry between Anhui and Xinjiang. On October 27, 2011, the Anhui provincial officials meet, in Hefei, Xinjiang's prefectural level officials enrolled in the Party School of the Chinese Communist Party Central Committee, aims to further strengthen the exchange and cooperation between and to promote the economic and social development of Anhui and Xinjiang.

Beijing: On July 20, 2010, the Beijing municipal government, the Economic Cooperation Team of Beijing Pairing Aid Department, and the 14th Division of the XPCC establish the Headquarters of the Beijing-Xinjiang Pairing Aid Department in Hotan. On September 8, 2010, the Associations of Science and technology of Beijing Municipality and of Hotan city of Xinjiang Uyghur autonomous region sign an agreement on pairing aid. 2011, the Beijing provincial government offers a total of 33 industrial projects to Xinjiang; 16 well-known enterprises such as Beijing Jinyu Building Materials, Beijing Gas Group have investments in Hotan, whose projects cover the energy, trade, and logistics industries. On May 8, 2012, Beijing Normal University and Xinjiang Normal University build a cooperative relationship, aiming to expand the pairing aid work. On May 14, 2012, the Xinjiang Forestry Department and the Beijing Gardening and Greening Bureau sign a

[16] Source: http://news.sina.com.cn/c/2014-05-31/172330271192.shtml (in Chinese). Accessed Jun 1, 2014.

[17] Source: Collected and compiled by author with assistance by Luc Guo (data are as of 2012).

pairing-aid agreement. On July 2, 2012, the signing ceremony of the "2012 Beijing-Xinjiang Industrial Assistance Cooperation Agreement" is held in Xinjiang, in which Beijing will invest 16 projects (with a total amount of 6 billion yuan) in Xinjiang.

Chongqing: On September 1, 2010, the Bureaus of Human Resource and Social Security of Chongqing and of Xinjiang Uyghur autonomous region and the Bureau of Labor and Social Security of the XPCC meet in Urumqi, Xinjiang autonomous region to carry out labor cooperation, and Chongqing and Xinjiang sign a long-term cooperative framework agreement aiming to further strengthen the labor cooperation between two places. On October 31, 2010, the Chongqing Municipal Transportation Commission and Xinjiang Department of Transportation sign a strategic cooperation agreement, aiming to accelerate the strategic cooperation between Chongqing and Xinjiang. On December 18, 2010, the Government of the Xinjiang autonomous region sign, in Chongqing, a strategic energy cooperation agreement between Xinjiang and Chongqing. The Chongqing Energy Group will construct a coal mine, with the total production capacity of 50 million tons per year, in Hami during the "12th Five-Year" period. On October 25, 2011, a delegation of Karamay city (Xinjiang autonomous region) holds an investment promotion meeting in Chongqing Municipality. The delegation brings 15 investment projects, with a total amount of more than 6 billion yuan, involving petroleum and petrochemicals, new materials, equipment manufacturing, tourism, and other fields.

Fujian: On September 28, 2003, the Bureaus of Township Enterprises of Xinjiang autonomous region and of Fujian province sign an agreement concerning the establishment of their long-term relations. Some cooperative projects between the two provinces' enterprises have also been signed, with a total investment of more than 3.5 billion yuan, mainly involving mineral and energy developments. On February 4, 2010, the Changji prefecture government of Xinjiang autonomous region and the Fujian Provincial Tourism Bureau reach an agreement on pairing aid in seven fields, aiming to accelerate the tourist development of the two places. On September 10, 2010, the "Promotion Meeting Concerning the Economic and Trade Cooperation between Xinjiang and Fujian" is held in Xiamen city, Fujian province. On June 3, 2011, the "Tourist Promotion of Beautiful Xinjiang" is held in Fujian province. The Tourism Bureaus of the Fujian and Xinjiang sign a strategic cooperation agreement and an agreement on the arrangements of special trains and chartered flights between the two places.

Gansu: On June 23, 2011, Xinjiang Uyghur autonomous region and Gansu province pledge to enhance comprehensive cooperation in coal mining, labor export, oil pipeline maintenance, and so on. From June 9 to 11, 2012, Gansu province and Xinjiang Uyghur autonomous region agree to (i) enhance economic and technological cooperation; (ii) deepen cultural and tourist cooperation; and (iii) strengthen cooperation and exchange in the fields of nonferrous metals, petrochemicals, coal, and other traditional industries as well as wind power, solar power, new energy and equipment manufacturing. On June 18, 2012, Xinjiang and Gansu begin to develop the largest copper mine in Xinjiang (namely, the Hudehe Copper Mine), with an annual output of 6 million tons of copper minerals. The proven reserves of copper metal content are 362,500 tons (vision reserves are 1 million ton) with a total investment of 1.466 billion yuan. This project has yielded 800 million yuan of revenue per year and provided nearly 1000 jobs.

Guangdong: On April 2, 2008, the China Nuclear Power Group of Guangdong and Xinjiang Uyghur autonomous region sign a strategic cooperation framework agreement concerning the exploitation of uranium resource and the construction of power projects. On June 28, 2010, the "Sixth Kashi Commodity Fair" opens. Guangdong and Xinjiang (Kashgar) sign a total of 42 trade and economic cooperation projects, with a total investment of 10.2 billion yuan. On August 10, 2010, the Bureaus of Overseas Chinese of Huizhou (Guangdong) and of Hami (Xinjiang) become a friendly paring-aid partnership. On December 1, 2010, the Intellectual Property Office of Guangdong and Kashgar prefecture of Xinjiang sign the "Agreement of Intellectual Property Pairing Cooperation." On April 28, 2011, Guangdong province and the Xinjiang Uyghur autonomous region hold a cooperation symposium in Guangzhou city, aiming to jointly promote the in-depth pairing-aid work. On June 27, 2012, the Cotton Industry Group Co., Ltd. of Xinjiang signs a strategic cooperation agreement with the Guangdong Materials Corporation, hoping to deepen the cooperation in the fields of cotton circulation and deep processing, modern logistics, the development of mineral resources, and the trade of bulk production materials (trucks, coal, iron and steel, petrochemical products, and so on). On August 22, 2012, a cooperation meeting organized by the government of Guangzhou is held in Urumqi city of Xinjiang autonomous region. Forty cooperative projects are secured in this meeting, with a total investment of 25.76 billion yuan.

Guangxi: On March 31, 2011 the Tianye Group of Xinjiang Uyghur autonomous region and the Agriculture Department of Guangxi sign, in Nanning city of Guangxi, a cooperation framework agreement concerning the promotion of drip irrigation technology in Xinjiang. On July 20, 2011, the Poverty Alleviation Offices of Xinjiang and Guangxi sign, in Urumqi, a friendly cooperation agreement, aiming to strengthen the exchange and cooperation in interprovincial antipoverty work. On August 3, 2011 the Inspection and Quarantine Bureaus (IQBs) of Guangxi and Xinjiang sign, in Urumqi, an agreement concerning the strengthening of pairing aid and exchange and the promotion of common prosperity and stability of their respective frontier regions. The two bureaus will implement the national arrangement of the pairing aid to Xinjiang, which is assigned by the General Administration of Quality Supervision, Inspection and Quarantine of the PRC. On November 20, 2011, the Entry-Exit IQBs of Xinjiang and Guangxi sign a memorandum of cooperation to strengthen the collaborative supervision of and the joint promotion of fruit and vegetable trade via the Pingxiang and Dongxing ports of Guangxi to Southeast Asia.

Guizhou: On October 24, 2008, the People's Government of Guizhou province and the XPCC sign a comprehensive economic and trade cooperation agreement, aiming to jointly build a demonstration base of agricultural machinery. On November 9, 2010, the XPCC, the Management Committee of the Southern Xinjiang Area and Shihezi University sign a strategic cooperation framework agreement of production and research with the Shenqi Group of Guizhou province. The Shihezi University and the Shenqi Group will carry out a comprehensive cooperation in the development of Tibetan medicine, the joint training of nursing professionals, the exploration of cooperation education mode, and so on. On August 3, 2012, a Guizhou Provincial government and the XPCC pledge strengthen cooperation in the fields of agriculture, machinery manufacturing, aiming to strengthen exchange and cooperation to benefit from mutually complementary advantages and to achieve common development.

Hainan: On January 26, 2007, a delegation of the No .1 Prison of the Xinjiang Uyghur autonomous region pays an inspection to the Meilan Felony Prison of Hainan province. The two sides sign a "Friendly Prison Cooperation Agreement," aiming to exchange experiences in the management of felony prisoners. On December 19, 2008, the Hainan United Mining Co., Ltd. and the Xinjiang Hongshan Mining & Metals Co., Ltd. sign a joint venture agreement. According to the agreement, the Hainan Mining Company will acquire a 70% stake in the Hongshan Mining Company. On December 18, 2012, Karamay Municipal People's Government of Xinjiang and the Hainan Airlines Group sign a cooperation agreement in Haikou city. Under the agreement, the Hainan Airlines will participate in the construction and management of the Karamay Airport. This cooperation will not only improve the air traffic situation in Karamay, but it will also accelerate the economic and social development and promote the economic and cultural linkages between Hainan and Xinjiang.

Hebei: On June 19 and 20, 2010, the Hebei and Xinjiang Chambers of Petroleum Commerce hold, in Urumqi of Xinjiang Uyghur autonomous region, an exchange and cooperation seminar. On August 21, 2012, the agricultural sectors of Xinjiang Uyghur autonomous region hold, in Shijiazhuang city of Hebei province, a promotion meeting, aiming to increase the sales of Xinjiang's special agricultural products in Hebei. On September 24, 2012, Bayingolin Mongol autonomous prefecture of Xinjiang and Hebei province carry out pairing aid and cooperation. Since the start of the new round of pairing aid, Hebei and Bazhou have signed 50 cooperation agreements, with a total investment of more than 80 billion yuan in Bayingolin, of which 20 projects (with a total investment of 21.6 billion yuan) either have been completed or are under construction.

Heilongjiang: On April 14, 2009, the Reclamation Science Institute of Xinjiang and the Agricultural Machinery and Engineering Research Institute of Heilongjiang sign a cooperation framework agreement, aiming to promote agricultural development in Xinjiang. On May 30, 2011, the Tourism Bureaus of Heilongjiang and Xinjiang hold, in Harbin city, an aid work forum. The two sides decide to jointly build an air-ticket subsidy mechanism, aiming to promote the tourism development in Xinjiang. On June 1, 2011, the Xinjiang Tourism Bureau and Harbin city of Heilongjiang sign five cooperation agreements, including four tourist cooperation agreements and one strategic cooperation agreement between the two provincial bureaus. In addition, the two sides also reach a consensus on the issues of regular bilateral cooperation and the increase of chartered trains and flights. On May 2012, the Fisheries Research Institute of Heilongjiang and the Aquatic Bureau of Altay prefecture, the Aquatic Bureau of Fuhai county of Altay prefecture and the aquatic sector of the No. 10 Agriculture Division of the XPCC become cooperative partners, aiming to jointly develop the aquatic and fishery market in Northwest China. The Heilongjiang province has invested 150 million yuan in Xinjiang in 2011. On June 20 and 21, 2012, Heilongjiang province and Xinjiang Uyghur autonomous region hold a pairing-aid symposium in Altay city of Xinjiang.

Henan: On August 8, 2007, the Coal Chemical Industry Corporation of Henan and the Tianfu Company of Xinjiang jointly develop a salt and coal chemical project. On March 22, 2011, Erqi District of Zhengzhou city and Hami city of Xinjiang establish pairing-aid partnerships. On July 8, 2011, Ruoqiang county of Xinjiang and Xinzheng city of Henan sign a cooperation framework agreement concerning the establishment of a high-tech agricultural demonstration park. From July 11 to 15, 2011, Henan province and the No. 13 Division of the XPCC and sign a strategic energy cooperation agreement. On April 9, 2012, the Henan Coal Chemical Group Xinjiang Branch signs a coal mining cooperation framework agreement with the government of Kizilsu Kirgiz autonomous prefecture of Xinjiang. On July 17, 2012, the Xinjiang and Henan Branches of the Bank of China sign a strategic cooperation agreement with Henan's enterprises involved in the pairing-aid-to-Xinjiang programs. On March 28, 2012, the tourist promotion of Xinjiang Uyghur autonomous region is held in Zhengzhou. The Tourist Bureaus of Henan and Xinjiang sign a cooperation framework agreement on the joint launching of the "10,000 People Tour Xinjiang" activity. On September 25, 2012, Henan province and the No. 13 Division of the XPCC sign 33 cooperation agreements on coal, wind power, chemical industry, and machinery manufacturing, with a total investment of 10.4 billion yuan.

Hubei: On June 2011, the Jinbo Seed Industry Center of the Fifth Agricultural Division of the XPCC becomes a pairing-aid partnership of the Jingchu Seed Industry Co., Ltd. of Hubei. From July 19 to 26, 2011, Xinjiang and a number of Hubei based companies sign cooperation agreement in livestock investment. On September 1, 2011, at the 1st China-Asia-Europe Expo, Bortala Mongol autonomous prefecture of Xinjiang Uyghur autonomous region and the Front Headquarters of Aiding-Xinjiang Team of Hubei province hold a signing ceremony of cooperation projects. The two sides sign a total of 13 projects, with a total investment of more than 50 billion yuan. On December 13, 2011, the Supply and Marketing Cooperatives of Hubei province and the Fifth Agricultural Division of the XPCC sign, in Wuhan city, a cooperation agreement of cotton industrialization. On June 13, 2012, the Energy Group of Hubei signs an investment agreement with the Power Company of Fifth Agricultural Division of the XPCC. The two sides will carry out cooperation in wind power and coal production. On July 13, 2012, the Intellectual Property Offices of Hubei and Bole city of Xinjiang hold a pairing-aid cooperation forum.

Hunan: On November 26, 2011, the Nonferrous Metals Authority of Hunan and the No. 13 Division of the XPCC hold, in Changsha city, a signing ceremony of strategic cooperation. On July 23, 2012, the Public Security Bureau of Dongkou county (Shaoyang city, Hunan province) and the Urumqi police of Xinjiang conduct a joint action against criminal activities. On September 2, 2012, in the "2nd China-Asia-Europe Expo" which is held in Urumqi city, Hunan province and Xinjiang Uyghur autonomous region, sign two major cooperation agreements, which are the Xinjiang Hunan-Xinjiang Investment Fund Project and the project of strategic cooperation between Hengyang city of Hunan and the Xinjiang Tebian Electric Apparatus Stock Co., Ltd. On September 4, 2012, the Economic and Trade Office of Hunan province holds a forum with the Xinjiang Bureau of Investment and Development, aiming to strengthen the aiding-Xinjiang work. On October 16, 2012, the symposium of aiding-Xinjiang through tourism, sponsored by the Tourism Bureaus of Hunan province and Xinjiang Uyghur autonomous region, is held in Urumqi city. The two sides sign a framework cooperation agreement.

Inner Mongolia: On June 29, 2004, the Chairman of Xinjiang Uyghur autonomous region welcomes the delegation of Inner Mongolia autonomous region during the celebration of the 50th anniversary of Bayingolin Mongol autonomous prefecture of Xinjiang; he acknowledges the support and aid from Inner Mongolia. On December 27, 2008, Inner Mongolia and Tortala Mongol autonomous prefecture of Xinjiang establish an education pairing-aid relationship; the affiliated Hospital of Inner Mongolia University and the Bortala Mongol Autonomous Prefectural Hospital also establish a pairing-aid relationship. On October 4, 2009, Xinjiang Uyghur autonomous region signs a strategic cooperation framework agreement with four Inner Mongolia enterprises (i.e., the Yitai Group, Ordos Investment Holding Group, Dongda Mongol King Group, and Gaofeng Group). The four enterprises will invest 100 billion yuan in Ili autonomous prefecture of and the Turpan-Hami area of Xinjiang to exploit coal resources for a time period of six to eight years. Inner Mongolia's enterprises in Xinjiang are mainly engaged in the development of mineral resources, the deep processing of agriculture and animal husbandry products and other industrial activities. On August 18, 2011, the Inspection and Quarantine Bureaus of Inner Mongolia and Xinjiang sign a memorandum of cooperation to deepen the joint prevention and control mechanisms and to ensure the health security in the China–Russian border area.

Jiangsu: In 2011, the Jiangsu and Xinjiang governments sign two agreements concerning the further strengthening of strategic energy cooperation and the deepening of clean energy cooperation between the two places. On April 16, 2011, 100 pairing-aid projects relating to the livelihood construction and industrial development of Yili Kazakh autonomous prefecture (Xinjiang) are officially launched, with a total investment of 2.655 billion yuan (of which 0.96 billion yuan is voluntarily provided by Jiangsu). The two sides also draft the pairing-aid plans from 2011 to 2015. On December 3, 2011, Xinjiang and Jiangsu sign an agreement concerning the strengthening of cooperation in construction industry. On December 27, 2011, Jiangsu and Xinjiang sign a cooperation agreement and pledge to strengthen cooperation in economy and trade, science, education, and culture. On April 9, 2012, in the "Jiangsu-Xinjiang Clean Energy Strategic Cooperation Project Promotion," Jiangsu and Xinjiang sign 26 project agreements, with a total investment of 5.18 billion yuan. On June 19, 2012, the Transportation and Communication Departments of Jiangsu and Xinjiang sign a framework cooperation agreement relating to highway maintenance, personnel training, technology introducing, and so on.

Jiangxi: On June 3, 2011, The Tourism Bureaus of Jiangxi and Xinjiang hold a forum and sign an agreement concerning tourist cooperation and development. On September 25, 2011, the Jiangxi Vocational College of Applied Technology and the Xinjiang Bureau of Geology and Mineral Resources Exploration sign a production and research cooperation agreement. On December 25, 2011, the Jiangxi Provincial Higher People's Court and the Kizilsu Kirgiz autonomous prefecture Court of and the Artux county Court of Xinjiang sign a pairing-aid agreement. From April 25 to 27, 2011, a government delegation of Xinjiang pays an inspection to Jiangxi province. The Xinjiang delegation hopes to strengthen cooperation with Jiangxi in energy development, modern agriculture and animal husbandry, and tourism development; Jiangxi proposes Artux county as its pairing-aid target and donates 310.2 million yuan (including 16 new projects).

Jilin: In October 2010, the governments of Jilin province and Xinjiang Uyghur autonomous region sign a cooperation framework agreement concerning Jilin's pairing aid to Xinjiang through talent introduction. The two sides will base their cooperation and development strategies on Xinjiang's advantageous natural resources and economic specialties, mainly focusing the research and development and application of oatmeal cultivation, natural pig breeding, blueberry production, and white thorn cultivation. In February 2011, Jilin and Xinjiang sign the "Plan of the Jilin province Pairing Aid to the Altay prefecture of Xinjiang." On June 1, 2011, the Tourism Bureaus of Xinjiang and Jilin sign a strategic cooperation agreement. Both sides will rely on their featured tourist resources and carry out cooperation in tourist product development, marketing promotion, investment, personnel training, and others; they decide to launch the "10,000 Jilin People Visit Xinjiang" and "10,000 Xinjiang People Visit Jilin" activities and to cooperate in providing discounted air and rail tickets. On June 16, 2011, the Communist Youth League Committees of Altay and Jilin sign an aid cooperation agreement. Jilin donates books to Altay. On February 25, 2012, the Agricultural Bureau of Moyu county of Hotan prefecture (Xinjiang) and the Bureau of Commerce of Changchun city (Jilin) hold a jujube fair.

Liaoning: On April 27, 2011, the "Tacheng-Liaoning Industrial Cooperation Project Promotion" is held in Shenyang city. The two sides sign agreements in financial support, and technological and industrial cooperation, with a total value of more than 14 billion yuan. On May 3, 2011, the Inspection and Quarantine Bureaus of Liaoning and Xinjiang sign, in Dalian city of Liaoning, a pairing-aid cooperation agreement. On May 31, 2011, the Petroleum and Chemical Planning and Design Institute of Liaoning province establishes a branch in Wusu city of Xinjiang, mainly responsible for the design of the development of petrochemical industrial project and the special development planning of petrochemical, coal chemical and natural gas chemical projects. On June 3, 2011, the Tourism Bureaus of Xinjiang and Liaoning sign an agreement on pairing aid by tourism. The two sides decide to promote the "10,000 People Tour Xinjiang" and the "10,000 People Tour Liaoning" activities. On July 24, 2011, the Forestry Department of Liaoning and Tacheng prefecture of Xinjiang sign a forestry cooperation framework agreement. On September 7, 2011, the Human Resource and Social Security Departments of Liaoning province and the No. 9 Division of the XPCC sign a pairing-aid framework agreement concerning the employment and social security in the No. 9 Division. On July 1, 2012, the Food and Drug Administrations of Yumin county of Xinjiang and of Jinzhou city of Liaoning sign an agreement on pairing-aid work.

Ningxia: On December 1, 2010, a 2.5-MW wind turbine, which is jointly developed by the Tianjing Group of Ningxia and the Jinfeng Science & Technology Co., Ltd. of Xinjiang, is completed. The two sides decide to enhance the annual production of the 2.5-MW wind power generators to 1,000 units, with a total investment of 40 million yuan. From April 14 to 18, 2011, the Drug Control Commission (also Drug Control Office) and the Public Security Bureau of Xinjiang visit Ningxia and sign a drug control cooperation agreement. On April 23, 2011, at the "Ningxia-Beijing Trade and Economic Cooperation Promotion," Ningxia announces its willingness to cooperate with Xinjiang. The "Xinjiang-Ningxia Coal Cooperation" strategy is designed to use the convenient rail transport and the land and water advantages of Zhongwei city of Ningxia to develop rich coal resources in Xinjiang, with a total investment of 300 billion yuan. On September 1, 2011, a delegation of Ningxia holds, in Urumqi city of Xinjiang, a trade and investment promotion. The two autonomous regions pledge to strengthen cooperation in energy, chemical industry, new materials, machinery manufacturing, agricultural and sideline products, halal products, and so on.

Qinghai: On April 29, 2006, the Western Mining Co., Ltd. of Qinghai and the International Border Trade Mall Industries Co., Ltd. of Tacheng city of Xinjiang agree to cooperatively develop tin ore in Kyrgyz Republic. The total investment of the project is $US 24.64 million. The Ming Company's annual ore processing capacities reach 330,000 tons, producing 2,746 tons and 920 tons of purified tin ores and purified copper ores, respectively. On April 17, 2008, Qinghai province and the XPCC reach a consensus on labor cooperation. Qinghai's emigrated labors to Xinjiang are mainly engaged in agriculture, including about 50,000 flowers-picking workers and about 5000 seasonal agricultural workers. In September 2009, Xinjiang autonomous region and Qinghai province sign a framework agreement on the strengthening of regional economic and technological cooperation. Both sides reach a consensus on coal resource exploitation, infrastructure, and industrial park constructions. On September 16, 2012, the "Xinjiang-Qinghai Exchange Forum for Economic and Social Development" is held in Xinjiang city. The two sides sign a comprehensive cooperation agreement, aiming to strengthen exchange and cooperation in the development and utilization of energy resources, traffic channel construction, and cultural tourism. On October 12, 2012, the Lianglike Copper Company of Menyuan county (Qinghai) and the Xinjiang Nonferrous Materials Company sign a strategy cooperation agreement of purified copper mineral supply from 2013 to 2017.

Shaanxi: On August 1, 2011, the No. 1 Topographic Survey Team of National Bureau of Surveying and Mapping of Shaanxi and the No. 1 Institute of Surveying and Mapping of Xinjiang sign, in Urumqi city, a bilateral cooperation framework agreement. On September 7, 2011, Xi'an Jiaotong University and other 10 universities which are directly under the PRC Ministry of Education hold, in Xinjiang University, the Annual Work Meeting of Pairing Aid to Xinjiang University. On November 4, 2011, the Inspection and Quarantine Bureaus of Xinjiang and Shaanxi sign a memorandum of cooperation. From August 10 to 13, 2011, the "Shaanxi (Urumqi) Specialties Fair and the Shaanxi-Xinjiang Industrial Cooperation Promotion" is held in Urumqi city of Xinjiang. The two sides pledge to strengthen cooperation in energy, chemical industry, equipment manufacturing, textile and clothing, energy saving and environmental protection, and the comprehensive utilization of natural resources. On October 12, 2012 the Automobile Group Co., Ltd. of Shaanxi and the Guanghui Industrial Investment (Group) Co., Ltd. of Xinjiang sign a strategic cooperation framework agreement. The Shaanxi Company will provide logistical and transport solutions to specific energy projects of the Xinjiang Company.

Shandong: On December 28, 2010, a cement-clinker production line, which is developed by the Yingjisha Shanshui Cement Co., Ltd. of Shandong, operates in Sixian county of Kashi prefecture (Xinjiang), offering 400 jobs. The project has a total investment of 820 million yuan, with expected annual profits of more than 80 million yuan. On April 13, 2011, the Public Security Bureaus of the XPCC and Shandong sign a cooperation agreement. Twenty police officers of the XPCC will be invited to Qingdao, Zaozhuang, Laiwu, Dezhou, Liaocheng, and Qidu Cities for 3 months of training. On June 2, 2011, the Tourism Bureaus of Xinjiang and the Shandong province sign, in Ji'nan, a strategic cooperation and development agreement. The travel agencies of Shandong sign a cooperation agreement with the Xinjiang Travel Agency. These enterprises will carry out the "Mutual Delivery of 10,000 Tourists" activity as well as cooperation in charter trains and discounted tickets. On May 19, 2012, the Yongheng Mining Co., Ltd. of Xinjiang and the Southern Shandong Geological Engineering Investigation Institute sign, in Korla city of the Bayingolin Mongol autonomous prefecture (Xinjiang), a strategic cooperation agreement concerning the prospecting of mineral resources. On September 3, 2012, the Standardization Institutes of Shandong and Xinjiang hold, in Urumqi city, a signing ceremony of strategic cooperation.

Shanghai: On February 12, 2009, the Shanghai Intellectual Property Administration and the Aksu prefecture delegation of Xinjiang hold, in Shanghai, a pairing-aid symposium and sign cooperation project agreements. Shanghai will provide 200,000 yuan to support the construction of information platform and of the personnel training of intellectual property services in Aksu. On September 6, 2011, Shanghai and Xinjiang's Federations of Trade Union, the Communist Youth Leagues and the Women's Federations sign the "12th Five-Year Plan" cooperation framework agreements. Under the agreement, the Shanghai Trade Union will establish a 50 million yuan special aid fund, the Communist Youth League of Shanghai will construct at least 1,000 health care stations in Xinjiang, and the two Women's Federations will jointly host educational aid activities. On November 12, 2011, the friendly cooperation agreement between the Shanghai and the Xinjiang is held in Shanghai. The agreement includes the joint governance of public security in

Xinjiang, the development of the Kashi Special Economic Zone, pairing-aid work, personnel exchange, and cooperation among enterprises. On May 11, 2012, Shanghai and Xinjiang sign, in Urumqi city of Xinjiang, three aid agreements, involving health and education. Shanghai hopes to improve medical care and education in Xinjiang.

Shanxi: On July 28, 2007, Xinjiang and the Lu'an Mining Co., Ltd. of Shanxi sign an agreement concerning the comprehensive development of the coal resources in Xinjiang. On October 20, 2009, the Xinjiang government and the Shanxi Coking Coal (Group) Co., Ltd. sign, in Urumqi city, a strategic cooperation agreement. Under the agreement, the Shanxi Coking Coal Group will invest 100 billion yuan to construct a large-scale coal and chemical base, with a total processing capacity of 100 million tons. On June 3, 2011, the Tourism Bureaus of Xinjiang Uyghur autonomous region and Shanxi sign a strategic cooperation agreement. The Tourism Bureaus of and relevant sectors of Changji (Xinjiang) Hui autonomous prefecture and Shanxi sign agreements on pairing aid, mutual delivery of tourists, charter and special trains, and others. On December 5, 2011, Fukang city of Xinjiang and Datong city of Shanxi sign a cooperation agreement concerning the pairing-aid programs. From July 19 to 22, 2012, a delegation, led by the Director of the Shanxi Department of Science and Technology, pays an inspection to the No. 6 Agricultural Division (Wujiaqu city) of the XPCC. The two sides' companies sign two aiding-Xinjiang agreements on the technological integration and industrialization of vegetable production and on the construction of a 33-MW power plant that uses coal and gas. On November 28, 2012, the Shanxi Department of Culture and the No. 6 Agricultural Division of the XPCC sign, in Wujiaqu city of Xinjiang, the "Cooperation Framework Agreement of Cultural Development."

Sichuan: On July 1, 2008, Sichuan University and Xinjiang Uyghur autonomous region sign a comprehensive cooperation agreement, marking the start of the 5-year comprehensive cooperation between Xinjiang and the University. On September 5, 2012, at the "2nd Asia Europe Expo," Sichuan and Xinjiang sign a framework agreement to further strengthen business and trade cooperation. Both sides will also cooperate in customs, entry–exit inspection and quarantine and port and regional clearance. On September 27, 2012, the Merchants Bureau of Xinjiang and the Investment Bureau of Sichuan sign, in Chengdu, an economic cooperation agreement. Both sides agree to strengthen investment cooperation and support the development of each others' key enterprises. On November 11, 2012, Sichuan and Xinjiang begin to jointly construct a ±1100-kv power line that sets out to transmit electricity from Xinjiang to Sichuan. This project is included by the State Grid in China's power network, aiming to upgrade West China's power transmission.

Tianjin: On July 14, 2007, the China Steel Group Xinjiang Company and the Tianjin Institute of Geological Research of the China Steel Group sign, in Tianjin, a cooperation agreement on investment and exploitation of resources. According to the agreement, the Tianjin Institute will send two geological professionals to help the Xinjiang Company to establish a technological department in Xinjiang. On September 2, 2007, the Xinjiang-Tianjin Science and Technology Park (the Liaison Office of the Tianjin municipal government in Urumqi city) is established in the

Xinjiang Science Building. On August 11, 2010, the "Tianjin-Xinjiang Regional Trade and Economic Cooperation Forum" is held in the Urumqi Customs Conference Center, as well as in Korla, Aletai, Tacheng, Huoerguosi, Kashi, and Alashankou. The Customs Associations of Tianjin and Xinjiang sign a memorandum of cooperation. On August 20, 2010, the Tianjin Chamber of Commerce in Xinjiang Uyghur autonomous region is established, aiming to further implement aiding-Xinjiang work. On June 27, 2011, Tianjin Vocational Normal University and Xinjiang sign a cooperation agreement of joint education. According to the agreement, the school will provide tuitions, living expenses, and scholarships for the students from Xinjiang.

Xinjiang-Tibet: On August 29, 2003, the National Nature Reserve Management Office of Aerjin Mountain of Xinjiang, the National Nature Reserve Management Bureau of Qiangtang of Tibet, and other two National Nature Reserve Management Bureaus (Kekexili and the water source of the three rivers of Yangtze, Yellow, and Mekong) jointly sign a memorandum of information exchange and cooperation of Tibetan antelopes protection, aiming to strengthen the protection of the Tibetan antelope; to strengthen supervision and enforcement of the crime activities, such as smuggling and sales of Tibetan antelope products; and to effectively curb illegal and criminal activities in the protected areas. On April 10, 2006, the Geological Exploitation Bureaus of Tibet and Xinjiang autonomous regions and the China Geological Survey Bureau sign an agreement of wild workstation management, aiming to strengthen the safety of scientific investigation activities in wild areas. On November 11, 2010, the Customers' Committees (or Associations) of Xinjiang and Tibet jointly hold a conference on the protection of consumers' rights and sign an agreement. According to the agreement, the Consumers' Committee of any side which receives the complaints from other five sides should promptly investigate, handle, and report the treatment progress or suggestions to the complaint side as soon as possible.

Yunnan: On June 6, 2011, Yunnan and Xinjiang sign, in Kunming city, a strategic cooperation framework agreement. Both sides reach consensuses on traffic construction, economic and trade cooperation, development of tourism, industrial cooperation, ecological construction and environmental protection, establishment of intergovernment exchange mechanism, and so on. On December 2, 2011, at the "First Xinjiang Tea Culture Exhibition," Yunnan, as a major tea producer, promotes its black tea and Pu'er tea. The companies from Yunnan and Xinjiang pledge to jointly develop tea market in Xinjiang, which is already one of the largest five Pu'er tea's market in China. From 2009 to 2011, the total number of tea enterprises and tea bars in Urumqi city of Xinjiang has increased from some 400 to more than 800. On September 17, 2012, Xinjiang releases an announcement in which graduates from Yunnan's universities are invited to apply for employment opportunities. Xinjiang will employ a total number of 500 university graduates from Yunnan and other provinces and autonomous regions to work as village carders in Xinjiang.

Zhejiang: On March 13, 2010, Xinjiang and Zhejiang sign a strategic energy cooperation agreement. On September 25, 2010, the Zhejiang Materials Group and Aksu prefecture sign an agreement on the construction of the "Southern Xinjiang

Logistics Park." On October 12, 2010, the Civil Affairs Departments of Zhejiang and Xinjiang sign an agreement on pairing-aid programs. On November 17, 2010, the Zhejiang Construction Group and the Aksu prefecture of Xinjiang sign a cooperation agreement concerning the construction of roads and housing in the prefecture. On November 17, 2010, Zhejiang and the No. 1 Division of the XPCC in Aral city (Xinjiang) sign an agreement on cotton and rice planting, with a total value about 10 billion yuan. On May 7, 2012, the Jiaxing Electric Power Bureau of Zhejiang and the Bazhou Electric Power Company of Xinjiang sign a cooperation framework agreement on grid construction. On June 9, 2012, Zhejiang and Kuche county of Aksu prefecture (Xinjiang) sign 27 project agreements, including the 600,000-ton PVC project (with a total investment of 2 billion yuan), the Ningbo Plaza in Guici (with a total investment of 500 million yuan), and the 300-MW solar photovoltaic power project (with a total investment of 4.5 billion yuan). On August 13, 2012, the No. 6 Agricultural Division of the XPCC and the Rifa Holdings Group of Zhejiang sign a cooperation agreement on lamb industry, with a total investment of 3.06 billion yuan. On October 20, 2012, the Xinjiang Basic Geographic Information Center and the Zhejiang Geographical Information Center sign a technological cooperation agreement.

Uyghur unrest and Xinjiang: Narrative

3

Unorganized unrest (1986–1989)

From 1986 to 1989, Xinjiang experienced a series of spontaneous social and political unrest. The Han–Uyghur unrest before the mid-1980s was either dormant or on a much smaller scale. This might largely result from China's political situation. For example, during the Cultural Revolution period (1966–1976), the suppression of religious freedoms in China reached the highest extent. Alongside the political framework deployed to proscribe the freedom of expression, there were also various forms of curtailments of cultural self-determination in Xinjiang.

In 1986, a group of Uyghurs in Xinjiang marched through the streets of Urumqi protesting against a wide range of issues, including the environmental degradation of the Zungharian plain, nuclear testing in the Taklimakan, increased Han immigration to Xinjiang, and ethnic insults at Xinjiang University. In October 1989, Muslims throughout China protested against a children's book that portrayed Muslims, particularly their restriction against pork, in a derogatory fashion. In each case, the Chinese government responded quickly with a promise to meet most of the Muslims' demands by condemning the publications and arresting the authors and closing down the printing houses (Gladney, 2003, p. 155).

Urumqi protests (1989)

The Urumqi unrest took place on May 19, 1989. It began when Muslim protesters marched and finally escalated into violent attack against the Chinese Communist Party (CCP) Xinjiang Committee tower at People's Square in Urumqi, capital of Xinjiang. They carried out beating, smashing, and looting activities on a large scale against the autonomous region Party Committee and the Regional People's Congress, Advisory Commission, and Discipline Inspection Commission. During this turmoil, more than 40 saloon cars were destroyed, and more than 150 members of the armed police forces, public security policemen, and governmental functionaries were injured (Dillon, 2003, p. 61).

The immediate cause was a book titled *Sexual Customs* published in 1987, which purported to describe the sexual lives of Muslims and provoked some Hui people from Gansu, Ningxia, and Xinjiang. The protesters, mainly the Uyghur and the Hui, initially conducted an orderly march in the days and demanded that the government destroy *Sexual Customs* and punish the book authors. However, the protest ended up rioting, and nearly 2,000 rioters overthrew cars, smashed windows, and some

China's Spatial (Dis)integration.

attacked staff at the CCP Xinjiang Committee. The government dispatched 1,000 policemen and 1,200 armed police soldiers to disperse the crowd, and 173 people were arrested (Ma, 2002, p. 254).

Organized unrest (1990s)

Baren riot (1990)

The Baren township riot or uprising was an armed confrontation that took place in Baren township, Akto county of Xinjiang's Kizilsu Kirgiz autonomous prefecture. On April 4, 1990, Zeydun Yusup, head of the East Turkistan Islamic Party that was secretly established in Baren township in 1989, led 200 or more men to protest against the 250 forced abortions enforced by the government upon the local Uyghur women. They marched to the local government office and demanded an end to the mass immigration of Han Chinese into Xinjiang. They also demanded that the forced abortions be stopped, that the Han Chinese be stopped, and that the Han Chinese leave Xinjiang (Castets, 2003).

The initial response of the Chinese government was to send in troops to stop the demonstrations. The major events relating to the Baren uprising are reported as the following:[1]

> *On April 4, at 6:30pm, a group of two to three hundred Uyghurs began to attack the gate of the township government office. At 9:09pm, a detachment of armed police, composed of 130 men, arrived at the site of turmoil, but were attacked immediately by the Uyghur fighters. Six policemen were killed, 13 were wounded and five were captured, with rifles and rounds of ammunition being captured. The police arrested 19 Uyghur fighters.*
>
> *On April 5, at 0:00am, the Uyghur fighters offered an exchange of the captured men, while the police only agreed a dialogue with their representatives. At 4:10am, the Uyghurs began to throw grenades and shoot, injuring three policemen, while the police also began to shoot. At 4:44am, one, Zeydun Yusup, who was also the leader of the Uyghur fighters, was killed. At 5:00am, the No. 6 armed police detachment of Kashgar prefecture (composed of over 100 soldiers) and a border defence army of Kizilsu Kirgiz autonomous prefecture (composed of 40 soldiers) arrived at the site of turmoil; at the same time, more People's Liberation Army (PLA) soldiers were ordered to march towards Baren township. At 5:23am, the Uyghur fighters proposed another negotiation and an exchange of captured men; however, since the captured Uyghurs did not want to return back, this round of negotiation failed. At 8:15am, the PLA soldiers, together with two militia companies (of the No. 41 regiment of the No. 3 Agricultural Division and of the*

[1] Based on an internal report written in Chinese. The anonymous author was a senior government official of Xinjiang's Kizilsu Kirgiz autonomous prefecture and participated in the whole process of fighting against the Baren township riot.

Kashgar Cotton Mill) arrived. The Uyghur fighters began to escape. At 9:50am, the rebellion was put down, with six Uyghur fighters being killed and most of the others surrendered. From the morning of April 5 to the early morning of the next day, 23 escaped Uyghur fighters were captured.

On April 8, at 11:00am, the PLA pursuit troop found and besieged 16 escaped Uyghur fighters (of whom six were killed and three were captured).

On April 9, when the PLA continued pursuing and attacking the escaped Uyghur fighters, one PLA guide (who was also an interpreter) was killed and two other PLA men were wounded. Three Uyghur fighters were killed.

On April 10, at 3:30am, four Uyghur fighters were captured.

The conflict ended on April 10, 1990, with a total of 23 people killed and 21 wounded and the eventual capture of 232 Uyghur fighters.[2]

Yining incident (1997)

The Yining (or called Ghulja in Uyghur) incident was the culmination of a series of Uyghur demonstrations in the city of Yining (Ghulja) of Ili Kazakh autonomous prefecture beginning in early February 1997.

The protests were sparked by the news of the execution of 30 Uyghur independence activists as well as the crackdown on attempts to revive elements of traditional Uyghur culture, including traditional gatherings known as meshrep. On February 5, 1997, after 2 days of protests during which the protesters had marched shouting: "Allah [the God] is great" and "Independence for Xinjiang" and had reportedly been dispersed using clubs, water cannons, and tear gas, the demonstrations were crushed by the People's Liberation Army (PLA) using gunfire. Official reports put the death toll at nine, but dissident reports estimated the number killed is much larger (Global Security, 2008).

According to dissident sources, as many as 1,600 people were arrested on charges of intending to split the motherland, conducting criminal activity, fundamental religious activity, and counterrevolutionary activities after the crackdown. A report by Amnesty International documented that as many as 190 executions were carried out in the years immediately after the incident in Xinjiang, overwhelmingly against Uyghurs.[3]

Rebiya Kadeer, a witness to the incident, went on to become leader of the World Uyghur Congress (WUC), an anti-China, pro-Xinjiang independence organization located in Germany.

[2] There are also reports in which the actual numbers of casualties are much larger. For example, according to Global Security (2008), 1,600 Uyghur fighters and Chinese soldiers were killed in the conflict, and more than 7,900 Uyghurs were arrested after the crackdown on "criminal activities of ethnic separatists and other criminal offenders."

[3] Based on an article by Global Security (2008).

Unrest from dormancy to activation (2000s)

Xinjiang raid (2007)

On January 5, 2007, the Chinese police in Xinjiang carried out a raid against a suspected East Turkestan Islamic Movement (ETIM) training camp in Akto county in the Pamir plateau near the border with Afghanistan and Pakistan. A spokesperson for the Xinjiang Public Security Department said that 18 terror suspects were killed and 17 captured. The raid also resulted in the death of one Chinese paramilitary officer and the injury of another. Police seized 22 hand grenades and more than 1,500 that were still being made (BBC, January 8, 2007).

In reaction, exiled Uyghur leaders, including Rebiya Kadeer, claimed that the Chinese government has yet to produce evidence to substantiate the camp's connections to terrorism, calling for an independent United Nations (UN) investigation into the raid. In response, Zhao Yongchen, vice head of the Xinjiang counterterrorism forces, reiterated the reality of the camp's terrorist threat.[4]

The ETIM was found in 1997 by Hasan Mahsum, who was the student of Abdul Hakeem, founder of the Hizbul Li-Turkistan (Turkistan Islamic Movement or Islamic Party of Turkestan) that was created in the 1940s. On September 11, 2002, the ETIM was at the UN Security Council list of entities associated with Al-Qaeda and the Taliban. In 2007, the ETIM emerged renamed as Turkestan Islamic Party (TIP) years after Abdul-Haq al Turkistani (Maimaitiming Maimaiti) allegedly took over the leadership of the group in 2003 after Mahsum's death (Rodríguez, 2013, pp. 143–144).

Kashgar (2008) attack

The 2008 Kashgar attack occurred in the morning of August 4, 2008, in the city of Kashgar in Xinjiang. According to Chinese government sources, it was a terrorist attack perpetrated by two men with suspected ties to the Uyghur separatist movement. The men reportedly drove a truck into a group of approximately 70 jogging police officers and proceeded to attack them with grenades and machetes. This attack resulted in the deaths of 16 policemen and another 16 being hurt.

Two attackers were involved in the incident near the western city of Kashgar. The Xinhua News Agency said the attack happened at about 8:00 AM (local time). One of the men drove a dump truck into a group of border patrol police officers as they were jogging on a street. The attacker then got out of the truck and start attacking other officers with homemade explosives. The explosives went off prematurely and blew off one of his arms. The other attacker threw improvised explosive devices at a nearby police office. He then went into the building with a knife but

[4] Based on http://www.taipeitimes.com/News/world/archives/2007/01/10/2003344141 (accessed March 19, 2013).

was subdued by police officers inside the complex. Both perpetrators were captured during the raid. The attackers were later identified as two men a, including a 28-year-old taxi driver and a 33-year-old vegetable vendor. They are members of the Uyghur ethnic group, and it was suspected that the attack was supported by Eastern Turkistan separatists.[5]

The Chinese government claimed that the incident was a terrorist attack. Furthermore, the police claimed that the design of these explosives was very similar to the explosives made by the militant ETIM when Chinese police raided their training facility in January 2007 (see the section on the Xinjiang Raid [2007]). Xinjiang's regional public security department also claimed that it had received intelligence that the ETIM planned to carry out terrorist attacks during the week before the opening ceremonies of the Beijing Olympic Games. This incident happened 4 days before the Beijing Olympics after repeated warnings in recent months from the Chinese government that militants from the restive Xinjiang region were planning to stage attacks to disrupt the Games (Delabroye and Sébastien, August 4, 2008).

Shaoguan incident (2009)

The Shaoguan incident was a civil disturbance that took place in Shaoguan, Guangdong province, China. A violent dispute erupted between migrant Uyghur and Han workers at a toy factory in Shaoguan as a result of allegations of the sexual assault of a Han woman. Overnight on June 25 to 26, 2009, tensions flared at the factory, leading to a full-blown ethnic brawl between Uyghurs and Han. As a result of the fighting, two Uyghurs died, and 118 people (of which 79 were Uyghurs and 39 were Hans) were injured; 400 police and 50 anti-riot vehicles were mobilized (Pomfret and Tarrant, June 26, 2009; Xinhua, June 27, 2009). The rioting was sparked by allegations of sexual assault on Han women by Uyghurs and rumors of an incident in which two female Han workers were sexually assaulted by six Uyghur coworkers at the factory. Police said that their investigations found no evidence that a rape had taken place (Beattie, July 8, 2009).

The factory where the incident took place is the Xuri ("early light") Toy Factory, owned by the Hong Kong based Early Light International (Holdings) Ltd. The company's factory in Shaoguan employs some 16,000 workers. At the behest of the Guangdong authorities, it hired 800 workers from Kashgar, in Xinjiang, as part of an ethnic program that relocated 200,000 young Uyghurs since the start of 2008 amid continuing labor shortages (Zhai, September 13, 2009). Most workers signed a 1- to 3-year contract and then travelled to factory dormitories in the south; in addition to their salaries ranging from 1,000 to 1,400 yuan a month, many got free board and lodging. Most of these Kashgars were away from home to work for

[5] Cited from Xinhua (March 25, 2008), Avery (August 4, 2008), and Delabroye and Sébastien (August 4, 2008).

the first time, and these young workers often lacked even basic Chinese language skills and found it difficult to fit in with the dominant Han culture (McLaughlin, July 17, 2009).

At a trial on October 10, 2009, at the Shaoguan Intermediate People's Court, two Han Chinese were sentenced to death (for being the "principal instigator" of the violence) and to a life sentence (for manslaughter), respectively; three other people were sentenced to 7 to 8 years for assault. On the same day, the People's Court of Wujiang District, Shaoguan, jailed three more Han and three Uyghur workers for participating in the brawl; they were sentenced to 5 to 7 years' imprisonment. The event was widely cited as the trigger event for the Urumqi riots in 2009 (see the next section).

Urumqi riots (2009)

The Urumqi riots were a series of violent riots over several days that broke out on July 5, 2009, in Urumqi. The first day's rioting, which began as a protest but escalated into violent attacks that mainly targeted ethnic Han Chinese. People's Armed Police were deployed, and 2 days later, hundreds of Han people clashed with both police and Uyghurs. People's Republic of China (PRC) officials said that a total of 197 people died, with 1,721 others injured and many vehicles and buildings destroyed (Hu & Lei, 2009; Yan et al., July 18, 2009). On the other hand, Uyghur exile groups say the death toll was higher (Bristow, October 21, 2009). Rioting began when the police confronted the march, calling for a full investigation into the violent incident in Shaoguan, a brawl in southern China several days earlier in which two Uyghurs were killed (see Shaoguan Incident [2009]).

When the riots began, communications were immediately cut off. In the weeks that followed, official sources reported that more than 1,000 Uyghurs were arrested and detained; mosques were temporarily closed. By November 2009, more than 400 individuals faced criminal charges for their actions during the riots. Nine were executed in November 2009, and by February 2010, at least 26 had received death sentences.[6] How the demonstrations became violent is unclear. The government's official line was that the violence was initiated by the protesters and had been premeditated and coordinated by Uyghur separatists abroad. Demonstrations began on the evening of July 5 with a protest in the Da Bazaar (in Uyghur, meaning "big market"), a prominent tourist site (Figure 3.1). The demonstration began peacefully, and official and eyewitness accounts reported that it involved about 1,000 Uyghurs (Epstein, July 5, 2009). The first day's rioting consisted mainly of "Han stabbed by marauding gangs of Uyghurs" (Macartney, July 7, 2009).

Although the majority of rioters were Uyghur, not all the Uyghurs were violent during the riots; there were accounts of Han and Uyghur civilians helping each other to escape from the violence and hide (*Shanghai Daily*, July 9, 2009).

[6] Data are cited from Cui (December 5, 2009), Sainsbury (January 2, 2010), and Yu (January 26, 2010).

Figure 3.1 The Da Bazaar, central Urumqi, Xinjiang.
Source: Wikipedia Commons.

According to the official count released by the Chinese government in August 2009, 134 of the 156 civilian victims were the Han, and the remaining were Hui (11 persons), Uyghur (10 persons), and Manchu (1 person), with 627 vehicles and 633 constructions being damaged (Xinhua, July 12, 2009; August 5, 2009). About 1,000 police officers were dispatched; they used batons, live ammunition, tasers, tear gas, and water hoses to disperse the rioters and set up roadblocks and posted armored vehicles throughout the city (Branigan and Watts, July 5, 2009).

On July 7, there were large-scale armed demonstrations in Urumqi. This time, they were conducted by ethnic Han. Conflicting estimates of the Han demonstrators' numbers were reported by the Western media and varied from "hundreds" to as high as 10,000 (BBC, July 7, 2009; Foster, July 7, 2009). The *Times* reported that smaller fights were frequently breaking out between the Uyghurs and the Hans and that groups of Han citizens had organized to take revenge on "Uyghur mobs" (Macartney, July 7, 2009). Police used tear gas and roadblocks in an attempt to disperse the demonstration and urged Han citizens over loudspeakers to "calm down" and "let the police do their job" (Foster, July 7, 2009).

Mass protests had been quelled by July 8, although sporadic violence was reported. In the days after the riots, thousands of Han people tried to leave the city, and the price for bus tickets rose as much as fivefold (Clem & Choi, July 14,

2009). The following reports the experiences of a Harvard PhD student who stayed at central Urumqi when the riots occurred:

> *On July 4, 2009, I flew from Beijing to Urumqi to visit a high-school friend of mine, Qian, who lived in the central district of the city. After lunch, we took bus to the Da Bazaar where I, for the first time in my life, enjoyed a marvelous collection of Islamic culture in Xinjiang, including Uyghur-style architecture, entertainment, commerce, and food. I still remember that on our way back home, we planned another visit to the market before my flight back to Beijing.*
>
> *In the evening of the following day, when Qian and I, together with her mum, were watching TV at home, their relative called to see if all of the Qian's family members were at home and safe. By then, we could hear noises in the nearby street—it was at that moment that we realized something must have gone wrong in Urumqi. Soon after, the Internet and mobile phone text message services were cut off. In the following week, Qian and I spent our time at home anxiously, without any information about what had actually happened in Urumqi. On July 8, the local government began to supply vegetables and other necessities to our residential area....*
>
> *On my way to the airport for Beijing, Qian's father drove me to the place in which the most horrible attack occurred. He pointed to a bridge and told me that many people were forced to fall down from it. After seeing blood on the ground and many armed policemen who were still being dispatched to guard on both sides of the street, I guessed that there must have been sporadic riots in recent days.*
>
> *Only at that moment, a question suddenly emerged from my mind: "Will Qian and I be able to have a reunion at the Da Bazaar?"*[7]

On July 10, city authorities closed Urumqi mosques. Large crowds of Uyghurs gathered for prayer anyway, demonstrating over people detained after the riot, but were dispersed by riot police, with five or six people arrested (Buckley, July 10, 2009). By the end of August, hundreds of individuals were reported arrested in connection with the riots. Xinjiang authorities later announced that arrest warrants had been issued to 196 suspects, of which 51 had already been prosecuted. Police also requested that the procuratorate approve the arrest of a further 239 individuals and detention of 825 more (*China Daily*, September 4, 2009). In early December, 94 "fugitives" were arrested (BBC, December 9, 2009).

In the aftermath of the July 2009 Urumqi riots, Urumqi experienced a period of unrest in September 2009. Late August and early September saw a series of syringe attacks on civilians. In response to the attacks, thousands of residents held protests for several days, resulting in the deaths of five people. By February 2010, the number of death sentences issued had increased to at least 26, including at least one Han and one female Uyghur (Yu, January 26, 2010). Nine of the individuals sentenced were executed in November 2009; based on previous government statements, eight were Uyghur, and one was Han (Barriaux, November 9, 2009).

[7] This text was provided by Miss Xiaoxuan Lu in her e-mail of August 18, 2014.

Attacks in which hundreds of individuals claim to have been stabbed with hypodermic needles began as early as on August 17 (Xinhua, September 4, 2009). On September 2, posters appeared around Urumqi saying that 418 people had reported being stabbed or pricked, referring to the attacks as a "serious terrorist crime," although the government had so far not produced evidence of any terrorist link. A six-person PLA medical review panel announced at a press conference: "In the patients we have seen in the last couple of days, there are many which we believe were not actually punctured with needles." They believed the false reports were caused by widespread fear and lack of medical knowledge (Fan, September 6, 2009). Witnesses say those who had been attacked include the Hans as well as the Uyghurs (CCTV, September 7, 2009).

In response to both the concern about the attacks and the dissatisfaction over the government's slowness in prosecuting people involved with the July riots, protesters took to the streets. Official media CCTV (September 7, 2009) and the BBC (September 4, 2009) reported tens of thousands marching in the city center in the morning of September 3. The police dispersed the crowd with tear gas; five people died during the protests and 14 were injured.

On September 4, 2009, the CCP Urumqi Committee Chief, Li Zhi, was removed from his post, along with the police chief, Liu Yaohua. After the latest protest, the government announced a ban on all unlicensed marches, demonstrations, and mass protests. On September 9, state media *China Daily* (September 9, 2009) reported a further 77 syringe attacks from the previous 2 days.

More unrest and attacks (2010–2014)

Aksu bombing (2010)

At about 10:30 on August 19, 2010, a Uyghur man, using a three-wheeled vehicle, detonated explosives in a crowd of police and paramilitary guards in Aksu, Xinjiang. The bombing eventually resulted in at least seven deaths and 14 injuries. The assailant targeted police officers in the area, and most of the victims were also Uyghurs (Chang, August 20, 2010).

Before the 2010 Aksu bombing, Xinjiang Governor Nur Bekri was quoted as saying that "Xinjiang faces a long and fierce and very complicated struggle" because "Separatism in Xinjiang has a very long history, it was there in the past, it is still here now and it will continue in the future" (Bristow, August 19, 2010). The site of the explosion, Aksu, is about 650 km west of Urumqi and just 60 km from the border with Kyrgyzstan. According to a report by the Associated Press, two attackers drove a three-wheeled motorbike into a crowd and threw explosives from it. The attack was carried out by a man, who was arrested on the spot and whom Xinjiang government spokeswoman Hou Hanmin stated is Uyghur, and a woman who died during the attack (Chang, August 20, 2010).

Of the seven victims died, at least five were local security officers. An anonymous Radio Free Asia source claims that officers in the targeted police station had commonly booked Uyghurs with beards or traditional head coverings and brought them to the police station for political education (Radio Free Asia, August 19, 2010). Chinese police stated that it was an intentional act and that a suspect was detained at the scene after incurring injuries himself. According to Xinjiang government spokesperson, the four detained suspects were part of a "violent gang of six people" (Associated Press, August 25, 2010).

Hotan attack (2011)

The 2011 Hotan attack was a bomb-and-knife attack that occurred in Hotan, Xinjiang on July 18, 2011. The men occupied a police station on Nuerbage Street at noon, killing two security guards with knives and bombs and taking eight hostages. Fourteen of the attackers were killed, and four were detained. Six of the hostages were rescued alive, and two were killed in the attack. Local and national governments said the attack was organized terrorism motivated by religious extremism and found that two of the attackers have links to the militant ETIM.

According to a subsequent investigation, a group of 18 antigovernment "religious extremists" arrived in Hotan from Kashgar on July 16; they brought "several dozen different knives including cleavers, axes and switchblades" with them (Olsen, July 19, 2011). After killing the guard, the men shouted slogans in Uyghur denouncing the government's campaign against the Islamic veil in what onlookers described as Kashgar and Aksu accents (Choi, July 22, 2011). The men proceeded to storm the police building wielding molotov cocktails, knives, and grenades. Shouting jihadist slogans such as "Allah is the only god!" and "Holy war!" (Olsen, July 19, 2011), they broke into the police station, wherein they took police hostages, smashed computer hardware and furniture, and set fires. Two Uyghur women submitting forms inside the police office were trapped inside a smoky room before being rescued through the windows by street vendors (Shao, July 21, 2011).

Hotan is a city of 360,000 people (of which more than 90% are Uyghurs) in Hotan prefecture, Xinjiang. Hotan prefecture is a predominantly agricultural county and the poorest in Xinjiang, so it is a frequent source of migrant workers to wealthier Xinjiang cities such as Urumqi. Uyghurs tend to have less wealth than their Han counterparts; as a result, many Uyghurs are unemployed and subsist on Chinese social welfare benefits (Hille, July 25, 2011).

The Xinjiang regional government called the incident an organized, long-planned terrorist attack. On July 19, a spokesperson for China's Ministry of Public Security announced that two of the 18 attackers had links to ETIM (Rajan and Ashok, July 29, 2011). Citing the deaths of Uyghur civilians in the attack, a government spokesperson said that the attack was apparently not ethnically motivated (Krishnan, July 21, 2011). But the environment in the city after the attack bore signs of interethnic tensions. Many Han residents of the city feared for their lives, recalling recent violent crimes against Han people by Uyghurs in Hotan. Many businesses owned by Han shut down, and both local and visiting Han are said to have "almost disappeared in the Uyghur-dominated areas" (Choi, July 25, 2011; Hille, July 21, 2011).

The WUC said that the cause of the violence was a clash between police and protesters (Yu, July 20, 2011). However, the *Financial Times* interviewed local Han and Uyghur residents, and none of them had any knowledge of a demonstration before the attack (Hille, July 21, 2011). A local government spokesperson also denied that there was a mass protest before the attack. The WUC spokesperson Dilxadi Rexiti (also known as Dilxat Raxi) accused the authorities of lying, rhetorically asking, "If the attack was premeditated, why didn't the police take precautions?" (Olsen, July 19, 2011).

Several security analysts claimed that Pakistani-based terror groups were linked to the attack (Krishnan, July 21, 2011). Both the director of the Institute of Central Asia at the Xinjiang Academy of Social Sciences and Chinese counterterrorist expert Li Wei alluded to the influence of foreign terrorist organizations in the attack without mentioning any specific country, which the *Times of India* claimed referred to Pakistan. However, the Chinese government, which has good relations with Pakistan, and the WUC did not give any remarks on the alleged connection to terrorists based in Pakistan (Rajan & Tiku, July 29, 2011; Dasgupta, July 20, 2011). On September 8, the Search for International Terrorist Entities (SITE)—a United States–based terrorist monitoring organization that tracks the online activity of terrorist organizations—reported on a video made by ETIM leader Abdul Shakoor Damla claiming responsibility for the July Hotan and Kashgar attacks on behalf of his group (BBC, September 8, 2011).

On September 14, six men were tried for their involvement in the Hotan and Kashgar attacks. Four were given death sentences, and two were given 19-year jail terms for charges including "leading and organizing a terror group, manufacturing illegal explosives, intentional homicide, [and] arson" (Olsen, September 4, 2011). Xinjiang authorities have unveiled a package of policy responses to the attacks to placate Muslim Uyghurs, which include increasing quotas for Uyghur participation in local government and increasing government subsidies for local schools.

Yecheng attack (2012)

On February 28, 2012, a serious attack occurred in Yecheng, a remote town on Xinjiang's border with Pakistan. According to China's official reports and court documents, a group of eight Uyghur men led by religious extremist Abudukeremu Mamuti attacked pedestrians with axes and knives on Happiness Road. Local police fought with the attackers. Chinese officials characterized the event as a "terrorist attack."

The oasis city of Yecheng (also known as Kargilik), in Kashgar prefecture, has proximity to China's border with Pakistan. Chinese border police have had difficulty in asserting control over its border towns with Pakistan because militants cross the porous border in between attacks. Despite its strategic location, Yecheng has long been remote and isolated from the rest of Xinjiang. Compared with the other cities of Xinjiang, Yecheng is an impoverished place. Generally, Chinese authorities trace these attacks to Muslim hardliners who want independence from China, trained indigenously or in Pakistan (Blanchard & Buckley, February 29, 2012). Yecheng is located between two cities (Aksu of Kashgar and Hotan) that have seen Uyghur militant attacks in 2011 (see Aksu Bombing [2010] and Hotan Attack [2011], respectively).

According to subsequent trial documents, at 6:00 PM on February 28, 2012, the group of nine started stabbing people in a crowd on the Happiness Road (Xingfu Lu), which is mostly populated by ethnic Han, and most of the victims were Han, although some victims were Uyghur. Thirteen pedestrians were killed immediately, and 16 were injured, two of whom died later from their injuries. Responding police shot seven of Mamuti's group dead and fatally injured another attacker while sustaining one death and four injuries of their own (China Radio International, February 28, 2012).

On March 26, 2012, the Intermediate people's court of Kashgar prefecture convicted Mamuti of "organizing and leading a terrorist group, and intentional homicide," and sentenced him to death with possibility of appeal (Reuters, March 27, 2012). The pro-Xinjiang independence WUC described the attack as Uyghurs "using primitive fighting methods" to fight "China's systematic repression"; however, the Chinese foreign ministry said that the assailants deliberately targeted civilians and called them "terrorists" (Al Jazeera, February 29, 2012).

Bachu raid (2013)

On April 23, 2013, violent clashes between armed men and officials and police occurred in Bachu county of Kashgar prefecture in the southwestern part of Xinjiang. The confrontation involved axes, knives, and at least one gun and ended with the burning down of a house.

The county of Bachu—known as Maralbexi to Uyghurs—is strategically located on the borders between China and Afghanistan, Pakistan, and other Central Asian countries, where Islamic separatists want to establish an independent East Turkestan Republic. The Chinese government spokeswoman said that it was a "terrorist attack" in which a total of 21 people were killed, including 15 community workers and police (10 Uyghurs, three Han Chinese, and two Mongols) and six suspects (all were Uyghurs). In addition, two other community workers were wounded, and eight Uyghur suspects were detained.

According to the Chinese official source, at 1:30 PM local time on Tuesday, three community workers were conducting regular checks in a neighborhood of Bachu county in Kashgar prefecture. After they found that there were suspicious people and a number of knives in a private house, one of the three used a mobile phone to call for help. This immediately resulted in their being kept as hostages; all of them were killed later on by the Uyghur rioters in the house. Several police (only one police officer was armed with a gun), and other community workers came in different groups to the home where the Uyghurs used axes and large knives to slash the police officers and workers. The battle ended with the gang members burning down the house, killing the rest of the people there.

Chinese officials blame that such attacks were conducted by Muslim militants who had connections with overseas terrorist entities. According to the Chinese official source, the terrorist suspects were found by the local community workers to watch the videocassette recorder (VCR) of overseas terrorist attacks.[8] The WUC, an exiled Uyghur activist group in Germany, rejected China's claims of terrorism. The WUC says the violence started after Chinese "armed personnel" shot dead a young Uyghur during inspection raids (Reuters, April 24, 2013). In addition, many Western sources, including the U.S. Department of State, have defined this incident as "violence" instead of "terrorist attack."

This violence just followed the Boston Marathon bomb attacks on April 15, 2013. The Boston bombing has been confirmed to be conducted by Chechen separatists. This has resulted in some complains in China that the United States holds "double standards" over terrorism. For example, *Wen Wei Po*, a Beijing-backed Hong Kong newspaper, urged the United States to "learn a lesson" and not harbor Muslim separatists in Xinjiang (Anonymous, April 25, 2013).

As of April 28, 2013, Xinjiang police had nabbed all 19 suspects from Kashgar prefecture, Bayingolin Mongolian autonomous prefecture, and Urumqi. According to a report by the Xinhua News Agency, the terrorist group, headed by Qasim Muhammat, was founded in September 2012. The group members watched video clips advocating religious extremism and terrorism and attended illegal preaching ceremonies. Since early December 2012, they had regularly gathered at the house of Muhanmetemin Barat (a group member) to do physical training and to practice killing skills they had learned from the terrorist video clips. Vice Minister of Public Security Meng Hongwei said on April 29 that police had tracked down a batch of homemade explosives, lethal weapons, and flags of "East Turkistan" terrorists after the April 23 clash. Meng warned of the "prolonged and complicated" nature of the antiterror fight in Xinjiang. During the clash, the terrorist suspects brutally killed law enforcement personnel and innocent residents, disregarding their gender or ethnic group (Xinhua, April 30, 2013).

Shanshan riots (2013)

On June 26, 2013, riots happened at about 6 AM in Lukqun township, Shanshan county in Turpan prefecture, which is about 250 km from Urumqi, the capital city of Xinjiang Uygur autonomous region. Knife-wielding men attacked the township's police stations, the local government building, and a construction site, stabbing people and setting fire to police cars.

According to the Xinhua News Agency (a Chinese state-run media), the gang, formed by religious extremists and led by Ahmatniyaz Sidiq, had raised funds, purchased knives and gasoline, and researched the sites since mid-June to prepare for the attack. Fearing their plot might be revealed after one gangster was arrested on Tuesday (June 25, 2013), 16 rioters on Wednesday morning attacked the township's police stations, a local government building, a construction site, a private store, and a hair salon and set fire to police cars. A total of 24 people, including two police officers, were killed by the knife-wielding rioters. Twenty-one police officers and

[8] Source: http://www.farmer.com.cn/xwpd/jsbd/201304/t20130426_835796.htm. Accessed April 26, 2013.

civilians were also injured in the attack. The police shot and killed 11 rioters and captured four others who were injured at the scene; one managed to escape but was captured later (Xinhua, June 30, 2013).

The incident happened 2 months after a deadly attack by suspected terrorists in Bachu county, Kashgar prefecture (see Bachu Raid [2013] for details). The Shanshan rioting shows that attackers have turned to eastern Xinjiang, which has long been peaceful, after security was strengthened in southern Xinjiang, where several similar attacks occurred in recent years. Police investigations into similar cases have found that the attackers in Xinjiang usually receive training and instructions from separatist forces abroad (Jia & Wang, June 27, 2013).

According to CNN, the WUC, a German-based Uyghur advocacy group, said it had tried to gather more information about the events, but "all Uyghur telecommunications have been shut down" in Turpan, the prefecture. The WUC called on authorities "to independently investigate the incident and its root causes, and to alleviate the legitimate concerns of Uyghurs so as to avert such incidents in the future." In the meantime, the Uyghur American Association urged "the international community to exercise caution over details" of the events (Mullen, June 27, 2013).

The Shanshan incident was the second deadliest attack in Xinjiang. A riot that broke out in the regional capital, Urumqi, on July 5, 2009, killed 197 people. Unlike the latter, which was a clash between the Hans and the Uyghurs, the Han Chinese were not the only target in the Shanshan attack. Also, among the 24 victims, 16 were from the Uygur ethnic group. One of the Uyghur victims was reported in a Chinese official media:

> *Memetjon Nimar, 43, who owned the Unity Hotel opposite the police station, was killed as he attempted to help the injured. He pleaded with the gang to stop, according to his brother, Ahmet. "My brother tried to pull a man, who had blood streaming down his face, into the hotel, but was stopped by the attackers. He urged them to stop, but he was killed right in front of my eyes," said Ahmet, tears filling his eyes. "They wouldn't listen to my brother or anyone else. They've been brainwashed." Adalathan Yiminiaz, 34, Memetjon's widow, is now faced with the prospect of raising four children on her own. Her stepson, who is in his 20s, was also wounded as he tried to help his father. "I can't describe how much I hate them (the attackers). My family is destroyed and I cannot see any future," cried Adalathan Yiminiaz, holding her 3-year-old son.*[9]

Tiananmen attack (2013)

Ethnic rioting and clashes have caused hundreds of deaths in Xinjiang. The Tiananmen attack, which occurred on October 28, 2013, however, marks the first time in the modern era that violence purportedly associated with the Xinjiang clashes has reached China's capital. The ETIM claimed responsibility for the attack

[9] Cited from Cui (July 5, 2013).

at the Tiananmen square. Tiananmen Square was built as a symbol of Mao's power. He proclaimed the founding of the PRC from the Tiananmen Gate in 1949. The square was the site of major prodemocracy protests in 1989.

In a statement by the Beijing Municipal Public Security Bureau, the crash that killed five people (including a woman from the Philippines and a man from South China's Guangdong province) and injured 40 (including one from Japan) was identified as a "rigorously planned, organized, premeditated, violent terrorist attack." According to the official statement, the vehicle, which contained gasoline, machetes, iron rods, and "flags with extreme religious content," careened along a pedestrian walkway in front the square's famed gate tower and exploded in flames after it hit the Jinshui Bridge, killing three occupants and two tourists. The driver had set gasoline on fire after crashing the vehicle to blow up the car in front of the Tiananmen Gate, a crowded tourist attraction.

The driver is identified as Usmen Hasan who is from the Uyghur minority group, an ethnic Turkic Muslim group native to the western Xinjiang region. The two other passengers were his mother Kuwanhan Reyim and his wife Gulkiz Gini. Ten hours after the incident, five suspects were arrested in a night raid. The suspects who were arrested told police during their interrogation that they knew Hasan and had "schemed to carry out the violent terrorist act" with him. Police said they found flags calling for "jihad" and long knives when the men were taken into custody. Police identified the men as Husanjan Wuxur, Gulnar Tuhtiniyaz, Yusup Umarniyaz, Bujanat Abdukadir, and Yusup Ahmat.

One Uyghur group expressed immediate doubts about the police investigation, citing its lack of transparency. "The Chinese government will not hesitate to concoct a version of the incident in Beijing, so as to further impose repressive measures on the Uyghur people," said WUC President Rebiya Kadeer in a statement from Washington on October 29, 2013. "Today, I fear for the future of East Turkestan and the Uyghur people more than I ever have." A spokesman for the WUC said the organization's members in China say police have arrested 93 Uyghurs since the crash, not just the five suspects whose detention has been announced. "There were no reasons given for the arrests," said Dilxat Raxit, indicating that it could mark the start of escalated repression (Wan, October 30, 2013).

Kunming attack (2014)

On March 1, 2014, a terrorist attack occurred in the city of Kunming, Yunnan province. The incident, targeted against civilians, left 29 civilians and 4 perpetrators dead with more than 140 others injured.

At around 9:20 PM local time, a group of eight knife-wielding Uyghurs began attacking passengers at the Kunming Railway Station. Both male and female attackers, who dressed in black clothes, rushed into the square and ticket lobby of the railway station and started to attack people indiscriminately. At the scene, police killed four assailants and captured one injured female.

Police initially attempted to subdue the attackers using tear gas shells but were unable to do so, before shooting four suspects and arresting one. A wounded female suspect was detained at the scene and sent to a hospital. China News Service quoted Mr. Tan, who remembered seven to eight attackers indiscriminately slashing people regardless of age, even stabbing the wounded on the floor until they were dead. He also saw a police officer carrying a child of about 5 years of age, with slashed pants and blood streaming down the legs.[10]

The UN Secretary-General Ban Ki-moon and the Security Council separately both strongly condemned the attack (UN, March 1, 2014). On the afternoon of March 3, police announced that this terrorist group had been neutralized after the arrest of three remaining suspects.

In the aftermath of the attack, heavy police presence was noted in Dashuying, a low-income ghetto that houses many of Kunming's Uyghurs. Kunming police interrogated members of the small local Uyghur Chinese community, questioning them at gunpoint. After the deadly Kunming attack, the government began sending Uyghurs back to their hometowns. Many people in Kunming worry that this type of ethnic isolation may only make matters worse. Because anyone with darker looks, a beard, or other features is regularly mistaken for hailing from Xinjiang, some foreign residents have been taking precautions in Kunming. This was observed by a Western foreigner as the following (Smith, March 16, 2014):

> *When I visited the station a few days after the attack, I noticed heavily armored trucks and soldiers strategically placed around the entrance. Two local men were giving out white flowers for the visitors to place at the memorial site, under the iconic statue of a golden bull at the main gate. . . .*
>
> *A crowd had gathered around to watch mourners come and go, while many people were walking around taking photos. Nonetheless, it was business as usual at the station, albeit with fewer travelers. "Are you travelling?" one man asked me. "Yes," I lied, so as to not draw too much suspicion to myself. After all, I too was taking photographs and was the only foreigner there at that moment. Surprisingly, I wasn't confronted by anyone else and I left the scene quietly.*
>
> *The next evening, I was cooking dinner at home with my girlfriend when I heard a loud knock at my apartment door.*
>
> *Standing outside were two security guards, a policeman and a soldier. Stern but polite, they asked to see our passports and checked our visas. Once they had verified that everything was in order, they pointed at the bag of garbage that was sitting outside my door, reminded us to take it downstairs and left. Ten minutes before the knock, my girlfriend had stepped out to buy some water and was followed by one of the guards. We speculated that she may have racially profiled as Uyghur because of her dark features. . . .*

Mong Cai clash (2014)

Five Chinese civilians and two Vietnamese border guards died on April 18, 2014, in a gun battle between the guards and illegal migrants at a remote frontier crossing

[10] Cited from http://www.chinanews.com/fz/2014/03-02/5898969.shtml. Accessed April 14, 2014.

(Mong Cai city of Quang Ninh province) in northeast Vietnam, which borders China's Guangxi Zhuang autonomous region.

The clash began after the Vietnamese guards detained 16 Chinese citizens, including 10 men, four women, and two children, and were to return them to the Chinese authorities. Some detainees seized an AK-47 assault rifle from the guards and began firing. Despite warnings from the Vietnamese side to surrender their weapons, including knives taken by the women, the detainees continued to fight (Zhang, April 21, 2014).

In a statement made by the Quang Ninh provincial government in Vietnam, while Vietnamese authorities were attempting to repatriate them, some Chinese men in this group seized guns from Vietnamese border guards and shot at them. Vietnamese media has reported that the Chinese citizens were from China's far western Muslim Xinjiang, where some human rights groups say that there has been persecution of local ethnic Uighurs (McDonell, April 19, 2014).

Urumqi attacks (2014)

At around 7:10 PM local time on April 30, 2014, a gang with knives attacked people at the exit of the South Railway Station of Urumqi and set off explosives. Three people (including two of the alleged assailants) were killed, and 79 were wounded in the attack. The station reopened around 2 hours after the attack under heavy police presence. It was not clear if Chinese President Xi Jinping was still in Xinjiang at the time of the attack, at the end of his 4-day visit to the region during which he stressed tough policing to fight terrorists.

Exiles and some rights groups say the cause of unrest in the resource-rich and strategically important region is heavy-handed conduct by authorities, including curbs on Islam and the culture and language of its Muslim Uyghur people. Dilxat Raxit, spokesman for the Germany-based WUC exile group, said he feared the incident would lead to a new round of repression against Xinjiang's Uyghurs (Blanchard, April 30, 2014). The TIP—formerly called the Turkestan Islamic Movement (ETIM), which was at the UN Security Council list of entities associated with Al-Qaeda and the Taliban—claimed responsibility for this attack.

The SITE said that the TIP had released a 10-minute video in the Uygur language showing the construction of a briefcase bomb that was used in the station attack. It said the video had been produced by the TIP's Islam Awazi Media Center and was posted on its website on May 11, 2014 (*Shenzhen Daily*, May 16, 2014). On May 14, seven fleeing suspects were captured by police in Xinjiang. All of these suspects arrested by police were found "on a farm of the town of Changji, in the district of Jimsar, not far from Urumqi." Police had earlier identified one of the suspected attackers, Sedirdin Sawut, 39, originally from the south of Xinjiang. Two of Sawut's brothers, together with his wife and one of his cousins, were among those arrested.[11]

[11] Source: http://www.stcn.com/2014/0517/11425199.shtml. Accessed May 18, 2014.

At about 7:50 AM on May 22, 2014, there were multiple explosions at the morning market near the Cultural Palace in Urumqi. Attackers in two SUVs plowed through crowds of shoppers in a busy street market, setting off explosives, killing 39 people (including four of the alleged assailants) and wounding more than 90. One alleged assailant was caught later in Bayingolin Mongol autonomous prefecture, southern Xinjiang. The May 22 attack was the deadliest in a series of recent attacks linked to Xinjiang, where unrest over Beijing's iron rule appears to have exploded into a wave of Islamist violence launched by separatists from the mostly Uyghur Muslim region. According China's state media, the SUVs carried no numbered plates but flew two small black flags carrying writing in the local Uyghur language.

On May 20, just 2 days before the attack, courts in Xinjiang sentenced 39 Uyghurs to prison for crimes including organizing and leading terrorist groups, inciting ethnic hatred, ethnic discrimination, and the illegal manufacture of guns. However, many of the victims caught in the blasts were elderly—both the Han and the Uyghur—people who regularly visited the morning market. The international community, including the UN, has condemned this terrorist attack. The U.S. government announced that the attack was a despicable and outrageous act of violence against innocent civilians and that the United States resolutely opposes all forms of terrorism (Denyer, May 22, 2014).

A few days after the last—and the deadliest—attack in Urumqi, Xinjiang and the Chinese authorities announced a 1-year campaign against militant violence. It has also been the toughest measure that China has taken to fight terrorism after the May 22 attack. As of May 2014, police have detained more than 200 terrorist suspects in 23 groups and found more than 200 explosive devices in Hotan, Kashgar, and Aksu prefectures in southern Xinjiang, where terrorism and religious extremism are active (*China Daily*, May 26, 2014).

Further implications

Most of the attacks in Xinjiang were ethnically motivated by the Uyghur residents. Unlike some other ethnic minorities, the Uyghurs have retained a distinctly separate culture, speaking a Turkic language that has no relation to Chinese and following Muslim traditions similar to those of Central Asia. The Xinjiang region has been part of China for centuries, but its people have a long history of rebellion against foreign rule. Since the founding of Xinjiang Uyghur autonomous region in 1955, the Xinjiang government has made various efforts to keep Xinjiang's peripheral, non-Han areas under its effective control. However, until now, the costs spent have been quite high and the outcomes achieved have been rarely encouraging, especially in southern Xinjiang. (See Table 3.1 for a brief summary of the interethnic clashes in Xinjiang.)

A brief review of the interethnic clashes during the past decades reveals that the reasons behind the Han–Uyghur unrest are quite dependent in Xinjiang. Some

Table 3.1 Statistics of selected Han–Uyghur unrest cases, from 1989 to August 2014

No.	Date(s)	Place	Casualties	Arrested
1	May 19, 1989	Urumqi city, NX	150 wounded	173
2	April 5–10, 1990	Baren township, Akto county, SX	23 dead; 21 wounded*	232*
3	February 5, 1997	Yining (Ghulja) city, NX	>9 dead	1,600
4	January 5, 2007	Akto county, SX	18 dead	17
5	August 4, 2008	Kashgar city, SX	16 dead; 16 wounded	2
6	June 25–26, 2009	Shaoguan city, Guangdong	2 dead; 118 wounded	8
7	July 5, 2009	Urumqi city, SX	197 dead; 1,721 wounded	1,000
8	August 2010	Aksu city, SX	>7 dead; 14 wounded	
9	July 18, 2011	Hotan city, SX	16 dead; 4 wounded	4
10	February 28, 2012	Yecheng city, SX	23 dead; 15 wounded	
11	April 23, 2013	Bachu county, Kashgar prefecture, SX	21 dead	8
12	June 26, 2013	Shanshan county, Turpan prefecture, NX	35 dead; 25 wounded	5
13	October, 28, 2013	Tiananmen, Beijing	5 dead; 40 wounded	5
14	March 1, 2014	Kunming, Yunnan	33 dead; 143 wounded	4
15	April 18, 2014	Mong Cai city, Quang Ninh province, Vietnam	7 dead	11
16	April 30, 2014	Urumqi city, NX	3 dead; 79 wounded	7
17	May 22, 2014	Urumqi city, NX	39 dead; 94 wounded	1
18	July 28, 2014	Shache county, Kashgar prefecture, SX	96 dead; 13 wounded	215
19	August 1, 2014	Moyu county, Kashgar prefecture, SX	9 dead	1

NX, Northern Xinjiang; *SX*, southern Xinjiang.
*It was also said that 1,600 Uyghur fighters and Chinese soldiers were killed in the conflict and more 7,900 Uyghurs were arrested after the crackdown on "criminal activities of ethnic separatists and other criminal offenders" (Global Security, 2008).
Source: Annex at the end of Chapter 3.

violent events were either accidental (e.g., the Shaoguan incident in 2009, which was actually a common civil case) or preventable (e.g., the Urumqi unrest in 1989, which should have been effectively precontrolled by the Chinese government). Even though most of these cases have been deeply rooted at the long-standing distrusts and cultural and religious differences between the Han and the Uyghur populations in Xinjiang, some of them cannot be merely defined as being "Uyghur–Han clashes." For example, in the two cases that occurred in Bachu county of Kashgar prefecture in the southwestern part of Xinjiang on April 23, 2013 (see Bachu Raid [2013]) and in Lukqun township, Shanshan county in Turpan prefecture on June 26, 2013 (see Shanshan Riots [2013]), the Uyghurs—not the Han Chinese—were the major victims, and the case that occurred in Mong Cai city of Quang Ninh province in northeast Vietnam on April 18, 2014 (see Mong Cai Clash [2014]) has nothing to do with the Han Chinese.

On June 24, 2014, Chinese government released a television program about online terrorism by the ETIM. According to the documentary, terror audio and videos are directly linked to terrorism and violence, including the attacks in Urumqi on April 30 at a railway station that killed three and on May 22 that took 39 lives (see Urumqi Attacks [2014]). From 2010 to 2014, the amount of audio and video materials put online by the ETIM has been increasing (Figure 3.2). The recordings were matched by a surge in attacks. Besides promoting terrorism, ETIM videos also offer tutorials on how to make explosives and how to use weapons, according to the documentary. The documentary indicates that the videos are produced outside

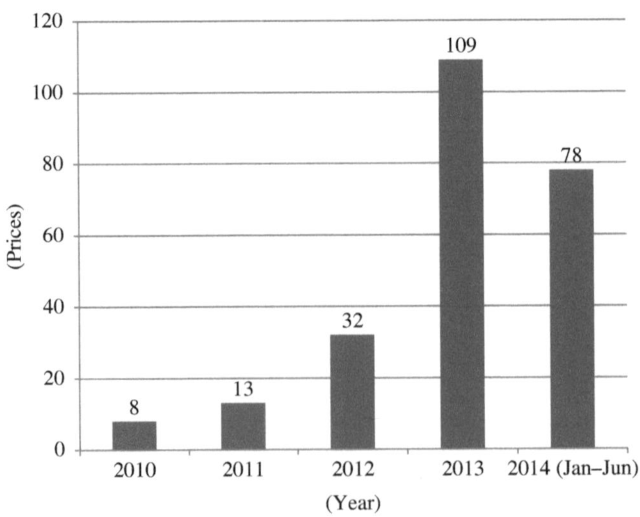

Figure 3.2 Pieces of terror-related audio and video content produced by the East Turkestan Islamic Movement.
Source: http://news.cntv.cn/2014/06/24/ARTI1403575644096677.shtml (accessed June 25, 2014).

China. The Chinese government has vowed to prevent terrorist materials produced overseas from being spread in China, delete such information online, punish website servers violating rules, and urge Internet companies to meet their responsibilities. To this end, more than 30 websites, including Sina, Tencent, Baidu, and Taobao, signed a letter of commitment on June 20, 2014, to meet their responsibilities regarding antiterrorism and deleting terror information.

The increasing frequency with which various violent incidents occurred in Xinjiang illustrates the PRC's reticence to address the root causes of the tensions that are escalating. China's administration of its minority-based, peripheral regions has been a challenging task, particularly when ethnicity is at times a volatile issue and separatist movements are feared. Located on China's northwestern border where at least four distinct cultures—Buddhism, Islam, Eastern Orthodox, and Han Chinese—meet, Xinjiang is one of China's most strategically important regions. Uyghur separatists, on the other hand, have been demanding that Xinjiang become an independent state, which is thought to have seriously affected China's national unity and territorial integrity.

In short, the evolution of Xinjiang's unrest reflects the separation between the Han and the Muslim sections. In Urumqi, for example, the Han residents congregated in the city's north, where there are new real estate developments, leaving the south area dominated by Muslim Uyghurs. The following were reported by two Associated Press correspondents:

> *The latest attacks [May 22, 2014] have left Urumqi's ethnic [Han] Chinese on edge about their Muslim neighbors. At a convenience store on a street near the vegetable market, the operator spoke of heightened alert whenever a Uyghur steps in. "If it is a Uyghur man, we follow him in the store in case he could place something here, like an explosive," Jiang Lulu said. "We have been told by the government to take extra precautions here." Longtime Han residents say their relationship with Uyghur friends is changing. "We are speaking less with each other, and they don't trust us," said a Xinjiang-born Han resident, who asked not to be identified by name. "Now, there is something between us."*
>
> *A Han taxi driver grumbled when a visitor asked to be taken to the Da Bazaar in a Uyghur neighborhood and urged her to get out quickly when they arrived. A Han vendor in the bazaar explained that drivers are worried they might pick up potential attackers there. Drivers said no male passenger is allowed to sit in a taxi's front seat after 10 p.m. but must sit in the back, separated by metal bars.*
>
> *A Uyghur woman complained that a grade school Han classmate called her daughter "livestock" repeatedly in class without being stopped by their Han teacher. "We are living on our own land," said the woman, who refused to give her name, "but we feel like we are foreigners."*[12]

[12] Cited from Tang and Watt (May 26, 2014).

Annex: Timeline of unrest related to Xinjiang (1986–2014)

1986: Uyghurs in Xinjiang march through the streets of Urumqi protesting against a wide range of issues, including the environmental degradation of the Zungharian plain, nuclear testing in the Taklimakan, increased Han immigration to Xinjiang, and ethnic insults at Xinjiang University.

1987: A book titled *Sexual Customs* is published that purports to describe the sexual lives of Muslims and provokes the Hui people in Gansu, Ningxia, and Xinjiang.

1989: On May 19, Muslim protesters march and finally escalate into violent attack against the CCP Xinjiang Committee tower at People's Square in Urumqi. During this turmoil, more than 40 saloon cars are destroyed, and more than 150 members of the armed police forces, public security policemen, and governmental functionaries are injured. In October, Muslims throughout China protest against a children's book that portrays Muslims, particularly their restriction against pork, in a derogatory fashion. In each case, the Chinese government responds quickly with a promise to meet most of the Muslims' demands by condemning the publications and arresting the authors and closing down the printing houses.

1990: On April 4, Zeydun Yusup, head of the East Turkistan Islamic Party, leads 200 or more men to protest against the 250 forced abortions enforced by the government upon the local Uyghur women. On April 10, the conflict ends with the eventual capture of hundreds of Uyghur fighters.

1997: On February 5, protesters in the city of Yining (Ghulja) of Ili Kazakh autonomous prefecture are dispersed using clubs, water cannons, and tear gas; the demonstrations are crushed by the PLA using gunfire. Official reports put the death toll at nine.

2007: On January 5, the Chinese police in Xinjiang carries out a raid against a suspected ETIM training camp in Akto county in the Pamir plateau near the border with Afghanistan and Pakistan, with 18 terror suspects killed and 17 captured. The raid also results in the death of one Chinese paramilitary officer and the injury of another.

2008: On August 4, a separatist group of approximately 70 Uyghurs attacks police officers in the city of Kashgar. This attack results in the death of 16 policemen and another 16 being hurt.

2009: On June 25, two Uyghur factory workers are killed and 118 people (including 79 Uyghurs) injured in the ethnic brawl between Uyghurs and Han Chinese in Shaoguan, in the southern province of Guangdong. On July 5, hundreds, perhaps thousands, of Uyghurs riot in Urumqi after security forces move in on a protest over the Shaoguan incident. On July 7, nearly 200 people, mostly Han Chinese, are killed in the unrest, with more than 1,600 injured and hundreds arrested. Eventually, at least 26 are reportedly sentenced to death. On September 2, Han residents of Urumqi protest for days over a wave of syringe stabbings, which the government eventually says included nearly 500 victims, blaming "ethnic separatist forces."

2010: On August 19, a Uyghur man, using a three-wheeled vehicle, detonates explosives in a crowd of police and paramilitary guards in Aksu, Xinjiang. The bombing eventually results in at least seven deaths and 14 injuries. The assailant targets police officers in the area, and most of the victims are also Uyghurs.

2011: On July 18, Uyghur demonstrators attack a police station in Hotan, southern Xinjiang, killing one officer. Police kill 20 protesters in clashes. On July 31 and August 1, two attacks by alleged terrorists leave 13 people dead in a Han-Chinese community of Kashgar, and police kill eight suspected Uyghur separatists. On September 15, courts in

Xinjiang sentence to death four Uyghurs over the July incidents. On December 28, police in Pishan kill seven Uyghurs in a hostage standoff that leave one officer dead. State media call them terrorists engaged in a "holy war."

2012: On February 28, rioters armed with knives kill at least 10 people in Yecheng, and police shoot two of the attackers dead. One man is later sentenced to death.

2013: On April 23, gunfights in Bachu leave 15 police and community workers and six attackers dead. Two men are later sentenced to death. On June 26, at least 35 people are killed when "knife-wielding mobs" attack police stations and other sites in Lukqun town, Shanshan county before security personnel open fire. Three people are later sentenced to death. On August 20, a Chinese policeman is killed in Yecheng county, Kashgar. On October 28, three members of the same Xinjiang family crash their car into tourists in Tiananmen Square in Beijing, killing two people (including a woman from the Philippines) and injuring 40 (including one from Japan) before setting it on fire and dying. On November 17, two policemen and nine attackers are killed at a police station in Serikbuya. On December 16, 14 Uyghurs and two police officers are killed in Shufu county. On December 30, an assault on a police station in Yarkand leaves eight attackers dead.

2014: On January 15, an Uyghur economics lecturer in Beijing is detained by police and later charged with separatism. On January 25, a total of 12 people are killed in Xinhe, six in explosions and six shot dead by police. On February 14, a total of 11 people die in an attack on police in Wushi, with officers shooting eight dead and three blowing themselves up, authorities say. On March 1, a total of 33 people (including 29 civilians) are killed and more than 140 wounded by knife-wielding assailants at Kunming train station in Yunnan province, more than 1,600 km (1,000 miles) from Xinjiang. On April 30, a gang with knives attacks people at the exit of the South Railway Station of Urumqi and sets off explosives, leaving three dead, including two suspects, and 79 injured. On May 8, Chinese police shoot dead an assailant and arrested one more who attack a police vehicle with knives in Aksu city of Xinjiang, with one policeman wounded. On May 20, courts in Xinjiang sentence 39 Uyghurs to prison for crimes including organizing and leading terrorist groups, inciting ethnic hatred, ethnic discrimination, and the illegal manufacture of guns. On May 22, there are multiple explosions at the morning market near the Cultural Palace in Urumqi, killing 39 people (including four of the alleged assailants) and wounding more than 90. On May 23, Xinjiang and the Chinese authorities announce a 1-year campaign against militant violence. It has also been the toughest measure that China has taken to fight terrorism after the May 22 attack. As of May 2014, police have detained more than 200 terrorist suspects in 23 groups and found more than 200 explosive devices in Hotan, Kashgar and Aksu prefectures in southern Xinjiang where terrorism and religious extremism are active. On June, 13 people are executed for Xinjiang linked terrorist attacks. On July 28, 37 civilians (including 35 Hans and 2 Uyghurs) are killed, and 13 civilians are wounded in an attack on a police station and government offices in Shache county (or Yarkand in the Uyghur language) in Kashgar prefecture, in which more than 30 police cars are also damaged or destroyed. Police shoot dead 59 Uyghur attackers and arrest 215 suspects. On July 30, a head of the Id Kah mosque in Kashgar, the largest in China, is killed after leading morning prayers. Jume Tahir, the Uyghur imam of the 600-year-old Id Kah mosque in the city of Kashgar, is murdered by three thugs who are influenced by religious extremist ideology. On August 1, police shoot dead nine suspected terrorists and captured one in Moyu county, Kashgar prefecture. On August 23, China executes eight people for "terrorist attacks" in Xinjiang, with one or more of the condemned convicted for a suicide car crash at the Tiananmen Square in Beijing.

Determinants of spatial (dis)integration: A model[1]

4

Literature review

Past studies of the determinants of spatial economic interdependence seem controversial, or at least incomplete. According to the Heckscher-Ohlin theorem, if the two factors of production are capital and labor, countries with dissimilar levels of per capita income (or, more precisely, dissimilar capital-to-labor ratios) will trade more than countries with similar levels (Heckscher, 1919; Ohlin, 1933). However, a number of empirical results indicate that the inclusion of income level as a determinant of trade contradicts the assumptions of traditional Heckscher-Ohlin theory (e.g., Linder, 1961; Deardorff, 1998, p. 15). To fill up this gap, economists have put forward new theories that base international trade on, among others, economies of scale, market imperfections, and cross-national differences in technology (e.g., Markusen, 1986; Helpman, 1987; Krugman, 1995).

However, past studies have raised more questions than they have answered. For example, the effects of geographical proximity on trade have not been shown to fall over time. Rather, these effects have been shown to strengthen over time for 1950 to 1988 (Boisso and Ferrantino, 1997) and 1965 to 1992 (Frankel et al., 1997a).[2] Similarly, using panel data from 1970, 1980, and 1990, Rauch (1999) finds little evidence that the effects of distance-related barriers declined from 1970 to 1990. Clearly, this provides no evidence that as a result of technological innovation, declining distance-related transactions costs should have led to increased trade flows. One possibility is that these analyses exclude important explanatory variables, thereby biasing the estimates. To clarify related issues, it is necessary to isolate the influences of all distance-related variables on trade. In particular, the inclusion of some relevant cultural variables might allow us to gain a better understanding of the black box containing the distance-related transactions costs that affect spatial economic activities.

China has officially identified, except other unknown ethnic groups and foreigners with Chinese citizenship, 56 ethnic groups. Although the majority of China's

[1] The first sections of this chapter are largely based on my paper (Guo, forthcoming).

[2] In their analyses of the negative correlation between distance-related costs and the interdependence for sovereign countries, Frankel et al. (1997a) use the data from the 1980s and obtain slightly larger coefficients ($\approx 0.5-0.6$) on distance compared with Eichengreen and Irwin's (1995) interwar estimates ($\approx 0.3-0.6$) based on data from the 1930s.

population is of the Han nationality (which accounts for more than 90 percent of China's total population), the non-Han ethnic groups have a population of more than 100 million. Thanks to the easing migration policy that has been implemented since the 1980s, China's interprovincial labor flows have increased dramatically. It is noteworthy that these flows have also been conducted by people coming from the inland ethnic minority areas and moving into the coastal, Han-majority areas. Consequently, China's interprovincial ethnic networks have been enhanced. As of 2010 when the Sixth National Population Census of the People's Republic of China (PRC) was conducted, each of China's 31 provinces has become home to almost all ethnic groups. How have these growing ethnic networks contributed to (or impeded) China's interprovincial economic cooperation and integration?

Cultural influences on trade

There is a widely held view that easily observable impediments, such as transportation costs, do not adequately capture transactions costs in international trade. Trade is also reduced by hidden transaction costs associated with unobserved trade barriers.[3] In addition, some studies use international panel data and find that cultural distance or dissimilarity—as proxied by, among other things, the ethnic/linguistic and religious differences across national populations—is a robust determinant of the volume of international trade (see, for example, Rauch and Trindade, 2002; Noland, 2005; Guiso et al., 2006; and Guo, 2009, pp. 77–102).

Since the 1990s, numerous quantitative studies have examined the role that cultural factors play in international trade (e.g., Havrylyshyn and Pritchett, 1991; Foroutan and Pritchett, 1993; Frankel and Wei, 1995; Frankel et al., 1997a; Rauch, 1999). These studies used linguistic links as one or more explanatory variables. The estimated results suggest that countries that are linguistically similar to one another have been more likely to trade with each other in the postwar period. In other words, there is evidence of linguistic barriers to trade. However, linguistic variables have been highly simplified in these studies. Using the cross-sectional data of East Asia, in which linguistic and religious factors are treated as continuous variables, Guo (2007b) finds that religion tends to have more significant influences on intraregional trade than language, but language tends to exert more significant influences on interregional trade than religion.

In this context, the analysis then turns to how cultural variables may affect trade. The emphasis on the role of cultural linkage in economic activities may be traced back to biologic analyses showing that cooperation among animals is influenced by

[3] These trade barriers take a number of forms, including legal and institutional differences (Anderson and Marcouiller, 2002; Linders et al., 2005; Combes et al., 2005; and Guiso et al., 2006), ethnic/linguistic networks (Rauch, 2001; and Rauch and Trindade, 2002) and linguistic/religious dissimilarities (Guo, 2004).

genetic similarity. In general, four aspects of differences in cultural behavior are relevant:

(i) feelings of superiority (and occasionally inferiority) toward people who are perceived as being very different;
(ii) fear of and lack of trust in such people;
(iii) communication difficulties resulting from differences in language and accepted civil behavior; and
(iv) lack of familiarity with the assumptions, motivations, relationships, and social practices of other people (Huntington, 1996, p. 129).

Trade and economic cooperation may also be affected by cultural dissimilarities because it is easier and more efficient for people with the same cultural identity (ethnicity, language, religion, or any other cultural element) to trust and communicate each other than for those with different cultural identities. In this chapter, our particular interest is to test how ethnic differences have influenced China's interprovincial trade and economic cooperation. Even though language is an effective tool of communication and that religion can provide insights into the characteristics of a culture, we would rather select ethnicity as the explanatory variable. The rationale is that most, if not all, of China's ethnic groups are identified in terms of either linguistic or religious traditions. Another reason lies in the fact that in China, it is more difficult, if not impossible, to collect interprovincial panel data on linguistic and religious groups than those on ethnic groups.

Analytical framework

Gravity model

The gravity model is most commonly used by international and regional economists to study trade.[4] The classic early application of the model was by Linnemann (1966), who continued work first reported in Tinbergen (1962) and then in Pöyhönen (1963). Some of the most recent work on the application of the model was Frankel et al. (1997a, 1997b), Rauch (1999), and Rose (2004), among others. Generally, a gravity model assumes that the volume of trade between any two economies will be directly proportional to the product of their economic masses (measured by gross domestic product [GDP] or gross national product [GNP]) and inversely proportional to the distance between them. Per capita incomes (measured by product of per capita GDPs or GNPs) have become a standard covariate in the gravity models of, for example, Eaton and Tamura (1994), Frankel et al. (1997a, 1997b), and Rauch (1999).

[4] The earliest application of the gravity model can be traced back to the 1940s (see, e.g., Zipf, 1946; Stewart, 1948).

In addition to "distance," "adjacency" (i.e., the country pair shares a common land border) and "cultural links" also influence trade (see, e.g., Rauch and Trindade, 2002; Noland, 2005; Guiso et al., 2006; and Guo, 2009, pp. 77–102). The basic form of the gravity model to be used in our empirical analysis of interprovincial trade is as the following:

$$\ln(\mathrm{TRADE}_{ij}) = \alpha_0 + \alpha_1 \ln(\mathrm{GDP}_i\mathrm{GDP}_j) + \alpha_2 \ln(\mathrm{GDPPC}_i\mathrm{GDPPC}_j) + \alpha_3 \ln\mathrm{DISTANCE}_{ij} + \alpha_4 \mathrm{ADJACENT}_{ij} + \alpha_5 \mathrm{ETHNIC56}_{ij} \tag{4.1}$$

In Equation 4.1, ln represents natural logarithm; TRADE_{ij}, measured in thousand tons, is the total freight exchange between provinces i and j. $\mathrm{GDP}_i\mathrm{GDP}_j$ is the product of GDP (in Chinese currency) of the ith and jth provinces. $\mathrm{GDPPC}_i\mathrm{GDPPC}_j$ is the product of GDP per capita (in Chinese currency) of the ith and jth provinces. $\mathrm{DISTANCE}_{ij}$ represents the distance between the geographical centers of gravity of the ith and jth provinces (in kilometers). $\mathrm{ADJACENT}_{ij}$ is a dummy variable, which takes the value of 1 for provinces i and j to have a common border and 0 otherwise. $\mathrm{ETHNIC56}_{ij}$ represents the extent to which the ith and jth provinces are ethnically linked each other (details about the measurement are discussed in Equation 4.6).

Note that because ETHNIC56 is a comprehensive index for all of China's 56 ethnic groups, it can only be used to derive a general pattern of correlation between interprovincial trade and ethnic linkage. If we want to examine the role that each ethnic group plays, the gravity model can be now written as the following:

$$\ln(\mathrm{TRADE}_{ij}) = \alpha_0 + \alpha_1 \ln(\mathrm{GDP}_i\mathrm{GDP}_j) + \alpha_2 \ln(\mathrm{GDPPC}_i\mathrm{GDPPC}_j) + \alpha_3 \ln\mathrm{DISTANCE}_{ij} + \alpha_4 \mathrm{ADJACENT}_{ij} + \sum_{k=1}^{37} \beta_k \mathrm{ETHNIC}_{ijk} \tag{4.2}$$

In Equation 4.2, ETHNIC_{ijk} represents the extent to which the kth ethnic group is linked between the ith and jth provinces (details about the measurement will be discussed in Equation 4.5). We only include 37 ethnic variables in this equation.[5]

Of China's 56 officially recognized ethnic groups, 19 ethnic groups (Achang, Baonan, Deang, Derung, Ewenki, Gaoshan, Hezhe, Jing, Jino, Lhoba, Monba, Nu, Oroqen, Pumi, Russian, Tajik, Tatar, Uzbek, and Yugur) have the smallest populations. Each of these ethnic groups, as of 2010, has a population of less than 100,000 (see Annex 4.1 for more detailed information). Therefore, they are assumed to have much weaker, if any, interprovincial economic influences than the 37 ethnic groups selected in this chapter.

[5] The corresponding names of these 37 ethnic groups are shown in Table 4.2.

Nonlinear ethnic influences

Theoretically, cultural (ethnic) dissimilarity can result in both social transactions costs (a factor directly impeding trade) and "economic complementarity" (an important factor directly facilitating trade) simultaneously. As a result, the relationship between trade and cultural (ethnic) similarity may follow a nonlinear pattern (Guo, 2004; 2009, pp. 96–101). Our interest now goes to the clarification of specific ethnic groups that may have different types of influences on trade with provinces differing in income levels. To go further, we use a new explanatory variable: $\ln(\text{GDPPC}_i\text{GDPPC}_j)\text{ETHNIC56}_{ij}$. Consequently, we obtain a modified form of gravity model:[6]

$$\ln(\text{TRADE}_{ij}) = \alpha_0 + \alpha_1\ln(\text{GDP}_i\text{GDP}_j) + \alpha_2\ln\text{DISTANCE}_{ij} + \alpha_3\text{ADJACENT}_{ij} + \alpha_4\ln(\text{GDPPC}_i\text{GDPPC}_j)\text{ETHNIC56}_{ij} + \sum_{k=1}^{37}\beta_k\text{ETHNIC}_{ijk} \tag{4.3}$$

In Equation 4.3, ethnicity variable is now entered into the gravity model linearly and as a product with the natural log of per capita GDPs. Thus, the effect of an ethnic group on interprovincial trade is now allowed to exist separately and to depend on the levels of trading partners' economic development, measured by the natural log of their per capita GDPs. As a matter of fact, because ETHNIC56_{ij} can be written as $\text{Ethnic}_{ij1} + \text{Ethnic}_{ij2} + \ldots + \text{Ethnic}_{ijk} + \ldots + \text{Ethnic}_{ij56}$, the nonlinear effects of some, if not all, ethnic variables on interprovincial trade may be derived from Equation 4.3.

Specifically, as for the *k*th ethnic group ($k = 1, 2, \ldots, 37$), if the estimated coefficients on Ethnic_{ijk} (i.e., β_k) and on $\ln(\text{GDPPC}_i\text{GDPPC}_j)\text{ETHNIC56}_{ij}$ (i.e., α_4) have different signs (e.g., $\alpha_4 < 0$ and $\beta_k > 0$ or $\alpha_4 > 0$ and $\beta_k < 0$) and are statistically significant in Equation 4.3, we obtain a threshold value ($\ln(\text{GDPPC}_i\text{GDPPC}_j)^*_k$) by letting the first-order differential of the dependent variable—$\ln(\text{TRADE}_{ij})$—with respect to Ethnic_{ijk} be zero, that is:

$$\ln(\text{GDPPC}_i\text{GDPPC}_j)^*_k = -\beta_k/\alpha_4 > 0\,(\text{with } \alpha_4 < 0 \text{ and } \beta_k > 0;\ \text{or } \alpha_4 > 0 \text{ and } \beta_k < 0). \tag{4.4}$$

As for the case of $\alpha_4 < 0$ and $\beta_k > 0$, we have

(i) If $\ln(\text{GDPPC}_i\text{GDPPC}_j)_k$ is smaller than $\ln(\text{GDPPC}_i\text{GDPPC}_j)^*_k$, the *k*th ethnic group has a positive effect on the trade between the *i*th and *j*th provinces.
(ii) If $\ln(\text{GDPPC}_i\text{GDPPC}_j)_k$ is larger than $\ln(\text{GDPPC}_i\text{GDPPC}_j)^*_k$, the *k*th ethnic group has a negative effect on the trade between the *i*th and *j*th provinces.

[6] We have also tried other forms of gravity models. But after running their regressions, we found that they could more easily result in multicollinearity than Equation 4.3.

Interprovincial variables and data

Ethnic linkage index

Interprovincial ethnic linkage (or similarity) indexes can be constructed in different ways. The simplest method is to introduce a dummy that uses 1 for provinces to be ethnically linked with each other and 0 otherwise. Although it has been applied in a number of studies[7], this method cannot precisely measure the extent to which provinces are ethnically linked to each other, particularly when the provinces have two or more ethnic groups. In this chapter, a more comprehensive method is used to construct interprovincial ethnic linkages. Suppose that there are k ethnic groups in both provinces i and j. If the ith and jth provinces' population shares for the kth ethnic group are expressed by x_k (it ranges between 0 and 1) and y_k (it ranges between 0 and 1), respectively, the kth ethnic group's linkage index between provinces i and j can be measured by the following formula:

$$\text{ETHNIC}_{ijk} = \min(x_k, y_k), \text{ where } x_k \in (0, 1) \textit{ and } y_k \in (0, 1). \tag{4.5}$$

In Equation 4.5, min (•) denotes the minimization of the variables within parentheses. The data on the population shares (x_k and y_k) are calculated by the author based on the data released by the Fifth and Sixth National Population Census of the PRC (conducted at 0:00 AM on November 1 of 2000 and 2010, respectively).

Because there are 56 ethnic groups in China, the overall ethnic linkage between provinces i and j can be measured by the following formula:[8]

$$\text{ETHNIC56}_{ij} = \text{ETHNIC}_{ij1} + \text{ETHNIC}_{ij2} + \ldots + \text{ETHNIC}_{ij56} = \sum_{k=1}^{56} \min(x_k, y_k) \tag{4.6}$$

In Equation 4.6, min (•) denotes the minimization of the variables within parentheses. For all k, $x_k \in (0, 1)$, $y_k \in (0, 1)$, and $\sum x_k = \sum y_k = 1$. Consequently, ETHNIC56_{ij} ranges between 0 and 1. In the extreme cases, when $\text{ETHNIC56}_{ij} = 1$, provinces i and j have a common ethnic structure (i.e., for all k, $x_k = y_k$); when $\text{ETHNIC56}_{ij} = 0$, the two provinces do not have any ethnic linkage with each other (i.e., for all k, x_k (or y_k) $= 0$). In other words, greater values of ETHNIC56_{ij} indicate greater degrees of ethnic linkages between the two provinces. This formula has been used in Guo (2004; 2009, p. 89) and Noland (2005). Several other methods

[7] See, for example, Havrylyshyn and Pritchett (1991), Foroutan and Pritchett (1993), Frankel and Wei (1995), and Frankel et al. (1997a).

[8] In addition to China's 56 ethnic groups, other unknown ethnic groups and foreigners with Chinese citizenship also exist in China. However, because these ethnic identities are still not known and there are no specific statistical data on the nationalities of these foreigners for each province, these populations are be included in the measurement of interprovincial ethnic linkages.

can also be used.[9] However, Equation 4.6 can prevent the index of interprovincial ethnic linkages from further reduction when the values of x_k and y_k are small.

The data on the interprovincial ethnic linkages are provided in Annex 4.2 at the end of this chapter.

Other variables

Interprovincial trade

The data on interprovincial trade are cited from the *China Communications Yearboo*k (2000 and 2010, edited by China Association of Communications and Transportation and the National Development and Reform Commission of the PRC and published by China Communications Yearbook Press in 2001 and 2011, respectively) (see Table 4.1 for a brief description). The data on the freight exchange via local or privately owned railways are not considered in this table. Notice that "re-exports" may exist in China's interprovincial trade. They are generated by either the unavailability of or the inconvenient access to national railways. For example, in 2000, the freight exchange between Anhui and Hainan provinces may have possibly been conducted via railway from Anhui to Guangdong and via other land/sea route from Guangdong to Hainan. In this case, the amount of the freight exchange should not be included (as either the "export" or the "import") in the "Anhui–Guangdong" entry for the year 2000. Unfortunately, we are not able to identify such kind of "re-exports" in this research.

Gross domestic product and per capita gross domestic product

In China, the GDP reported by each province is also called gross regional product (GRP). In this chapter, the terms GDP and GRP are used interchangeably. China's 2000 and 2010 provincial GDP and per capita GDP data are from *China Statistical Yearbooks* (National Bureau of Statistics, 2001 and 2011).

Distance

Unlike those of many Western democratic economies, China's provincial capitals usually are also the economic centers of these provinces. To this end, we use the following terms to express China's interprovincial geographical proximity. "Distance between capitals" is represented by the distance (in kilometers) between two provinces' capitals via national railway. The data on "distance between capitals" are calculated by the author based on the data released by the Ministry of Railways of the PRC. If there are two or more rail lines between two provinces' capitals, our calculations are based on the following rules: (i) if both freight and passenger rail lines exist, only freight lines are considered, and (ii) if two or more freight (or passenger) rail lines exist, only the shortest distance is considered.

[9] Boisso and Ferrantino (1997), for example, use $\sum x_k y_k$ as the construct of similarity index.

Table 4.1 **Changes in China's domestic and interprovincial trade from 2000 to 2010***

Provincial economy	Domestic trade (thousand tons)			Ratio of interprovincial trade (%)		
	2000	2010	Change (%)	2000	2010	Change (%)
Anhui	6,087	12,092	98.65	56.84	47.93	− 8.91
Beijing	2,612	1,571	− 39.85	72.21	95.23	23.02
Chongqing	1,613	2,197	36.21	56.79	65.95	9.16
Fujian	2,475	3,704	49.66	46.22	53.48	7.26
Gansu	3,236	6,186	91.16	52.10	61.27	9.17
Guangdong	4,521	7,505	66.00	74.70	79.72	5.02
Guangxi	2,815	6,109	117.02	67.10	75.82	8.72
Guizhou	3,585	7,991	122.90	69.29	82.98	13.69
Hainan	311	542	74.28	NA	10.89	NA
Hebei	11,399	16,481	44.58	60.61	56.09	− 4.52
Heilongjiang	12,701	16,888	32.97	54.47	49.19	− 5.28
Henan	9,655	13,374	38.52	78.92	71.53	− 7.39
Hubei	3,937	5,698	44.73	62.81	66.57	3.75
Hunan	4,668	5,783	23.89	65.62	61.27	− 4.35
Inner Mongolia	9,171	37,698	311.06	69.55	77.00	7.46
Jiangsu	4,076	6,372	56.33	63.67	85.75	22.08
Jiangxi	2,959	5,376	81.68	57.92	51.95	− 5.97
Jilin	5,630	7,674	36.31	60.55	69.53	8.98
Liaoning	12,520	18,118	44.71	34.03	29.94	− 4.09
Ningxia	1,782	4,414	147.70	73.12	86.45	13.33
Qinghai	647	3,096	378.52	81.14	61.66	− 19.48
Shaanxi	3,280	8,836	169.39	65.95	69.09	3.15
Shandong	10,585	18,285	72.74	52.24	62.67	10.43
Shanghai	1,054	959	− 9.01	89.56	93.53	3.97
Shanxi	28,469	60,812	113.61	91.96	92.76	0.80
Sichuan	5,516	7,389	33.96	46.79	51.59	4.80
Tianjin	2,004	7,240	261.28	81.64	54.46	− 27.18
Tibet	NA	30	NA	NA	100.00	NA
Xinjiang	3,353	6,775	102.06	73.67	74.05	0.39
Yunnan	2,882	5,209	80.74	59.51	67.92	8.41
Zhejiang	1,929	3,806	97.30	62.10	41.59	− 20.51
All	165,472	308,210	86.26	65.53	69.06	5.39

NA, Data are not available.
*"Trade" only includes freight exchange via national railways.
Source: Calculated by the author based on China Association of Communications and Transportation and the National Development and Reform Commission of the PRC (2001 and 2011).

Adjacency

"Interprovincial adjacency" denotes whether or not the provinces share a common land boundary. The data on "interprovincial adjacency" are set as 1 if the provinces share a common land boundary and as 0 otherwise. All data are correct as of 2012.

The data of the above variables are provided in Annex 4.2 at the end of this chapter.

Interprovincial panel data

The major task of this chapter is to quantitatively investigate the sources for changes in China's spatial economic integration over time. Thus, the use of the cross-sectional data from China' s provincial economies in different years enables that the estimated results are not artifact of any particular time period and to allow for changes in coefficients. Generally, a decade-long period is appropriate for this kind of research because analysis for a shorter period would not reflect relevant social and economic changes, but significant changes in transportation and communication technologies would have to be accounted for if a longer one is used. Of course, a longer period is still more helpful if three or more sets of cross-sectional data are available. However, this would increase inevitably the costs in data collection. In this chapter, after taking into account data availability, we only focus on two years, 2000 and 2010.

The largest numbers of observations (i.e., interprovincial samples) for both 2000 and 2010 are 465, which are counted as the following:

$C_{31}^{2} = \frac{31!}{2!(31-2)!} = \frac{31 \times 30}{2} = 465$, where 31 is the number of China's provinces.

However, because the data on interprovincial trade are unavailable for the two provinces of Hainan and Tibet (including 59 province pairs) from 2000 as well as for 13 province pairs (i.e., Beijing–Hainan, Guizhou–Tibet, Hainan–Heilongjiang, Hainan–Jilin, Hainan–Liaoning, Hainan–Ningxia, Hainan–Shanghai, Hainan–Tianjin, Hainan–Tibet, Hainan–Xinjiang, Jilin–Tibet, Ningxia–Tibet, and Tibet–Yunnan) from 2010, the total numbers of observations that can be actually used for our regressions are reduced to 406 (i.e., $465 - 59 = 406$) for 2000 and 452 (i.e., $465 - 13 = 452$) for 2010 accordingly.

A brief statistical description of selected variables included in Equations 4.1 to 4.3 is given in Table 4.2a (for 2000) and 4.2b (for 2010).

Statistical estimation

Using the gravity models constructed in the Analytical Framework section and the data described in the Interprovincial Variables and Data section, the determinants of China's interprovincial trade can be estimated by using the SPSS statistics software. More details about the whole regressions as well as technical notes to the estimated results can be found in Annex 4.3 at the end of this chapter.

Table 4.2a **Descriptive statistics for the panel data on selected variables, 2000**

Variable	Observations (n)	Minimum	Maximum	Mean	SD
$\ln TRADE_{ij}$	406	2.99573	11.59910	6.84499	1.36932
$\ln(GDP_i GDP_j)$	465	5.73532	13.62832	10.70744	1.43231
$\ln(GDPPC_i GDPPC_j)$	465	16.19674	20.00507	17.70224	0.69716
$\ln(Distance_{ij})$	465	4.91998	8.75037	7.47203	0.64053
$Ethnic56_{ij}$	465	0.06160	0.99930	0.75563	0.24827
$k=1$. Bai	465	0.00001	0.00532	0.00004	0.00028
$k=2$. Blang	465	0.00000	0.00001	0.00000	0.00000
$k=3$. Buyi	465	0.00001	0.00129	0.00005	0.00008
$k=4$. Dai	465	0.00000	0.00008	0.00000	0.00001
$k=5$. Daur	465	0.00000	0.00120	0.00001	0.00006
$k=6$. Dong	465	0.00001	0.01331	0.00011	0.00077
$k=7$. Dongxiang	465	0.00000	0.00303	0.00001	0.00015
$k=8$. Gelao	465	0.00000	0.00009	0.00001	0.00001
$k=9$. Han	465	0.06061	0.99682	0.74690	0.25065
$k=10$. Hani	465	0.00000	0.00003	0.00001	0.00001
$k=11$. Hui	465	0.00025	0.15621	0.00371	0.00904
$k=12$. Jingpo	465	0.00000	0.00001	0.00000	0.00000
$k=13$. Kazak	465	0.00000	0.00012	0.00000	0.00001
$k=14$. Kirgiz	465	0.00000	0.00004	0.00000	0.00000
$k=15$. Korean	465	0.00002	0.01072	0.00013	0.00064
$k=16$. Lahu	465	0.00000	0.00002	0.00000	0.00000
$k=17$. Li	465	0.00000	0.00159	0.00001	0.00007
$k=18$. Lisu	465	0.00000	0.00023	0.00000	0.00001
$k=19$. Manchu	465	0.00006	0.03705	0.00118	0.00443
$k=20$. Maonan	465	0.00000	0.00089	0.00000	0.00004
$k=21$. Miao	465	0.00004	0.03037	0.00069	0.00280
$k=22$. Mongol	465	0.00008	0.01789	0.00064	0.00164
$k=23$. Mulao	465	0.00000	0.00081	0.00000	0.00004
$k=24$. Naxi	465	0.00000	0.00047	0.00000	0.00002
$k=25$. Qiang	465	0.00000	0.00004	0.00000	0.00000
$k=26$. Salar	465	0.00000	0.00047	0.00000	0.00003
$k=27$. She	465	0.00000	0.00372	0.00004	0.00024
$k=28$. Shui	465	0.00000	0.00035	0.00001	0.00003
$k=29$. Tibetan	465	0.00002	0.22530	0.00074	0.01057
$k=30$. Tu	465	0.00000	0.00121	0.00002	0.00006
$k=31$. Tujia	465	0.00003	0.04172	0.00066	0.00438
$k=32$. Uyghur	465	0.00002	0.00027	0.00004	0.00002
$k=33$. Va	465	0.00000	0.00005	0.00000	0.00000
$k=34$. Xibe	465	0.00000	0.00187	0.00001	0.00009
$k=35$. Yao	465	0.00000	0.01114	0.00009	0.00064
$k=36$. Yi	465	0.00002	0.02577	0.00022	0.00196
$k=37$. Zhuang	465	0.00005	0.02701	0.00025	0.00142

SD, Standard deviation.

Table 4.2b Descriptive statistics for the panel data on selected variables, 2010

Variable	Observations (n)	Minimum	Maximum	Mean	SD
$\ln TRADE_{ij}$	452	2.30259	12.62984	6.95446	1.76181
$\ln(GDP_i GDP_j)$	465	8.83243	16.76316	13.75672	1.38476
$\ln(GDPPC_i GDPPC_j)$	465	19.15152	22.40275	20.60043	0.62203
$\ln(DISTANCE_{ij})$	465	4.91998	8.75037	7.47203	0.64053
$Ethnic56_{ij}$	465	0.08280	0.99870	0.75979	0.24414
$k=1$. Bai	465	0.00000	0.00526	0.00005	0.00027
$k=2$. Blang	465	0.00000	0.00016	0.00000	0.00001
$k=3$. Buyi	465	0.00001	0.00231	0.00007	0.00016
$k=4$. Dai	465	0.00000	0.00011	0.00001	0.00002
$k=5$. Daur	465	0.00000	0.00105	0.00001	0.00005
$k=6$. Dong	465	0.00001	0.01301	0.00013	0.00076
$k=7$. Dongxiang	465	0.00000	0.00282	0.00002	0.00015
$k=8$. Gelao	465	0.00000	0.00033	0.00001	0.00003
$k=9$. Han	465	0.08176	0.99660	0.75070	0.24660
$k=10$. Hani	465	0.00000	0.00014	0.00001	0.00001
$k=11$. Hui	465	0.00020	0.14827	0.00356	0.00865
$k=12$. Jingpo	465	0.00000	0.00002	0.00000	0.00000
$k=13$. Kazak	465	0.00000	0.00071	0.00002	0.00004
$k=14$. Kirgiz	465	0.00000	0.00089	0.00000	0.00004
$k=15$. Korean	465	0.00001	0.00856	0.00013	0.00058
$k=16$. Lahu	465	0.00000	0.00003	0.00000	0.00000
$k=17$. Li	465	0.00001	0.00396	0.00003	0.00018
$k=18$. Lisu	465	0.00000	0.00026	0.00001	0.00001
$k=19$. Manchu	465	0.00011	0.03156	0.00111	0.00378
$k=20$. Maonan	465	0.00000	0.00080	0.00000	0.00004
$k=21$. Miao	465	0.00005	0.03136	0.00088	0.00296
$k=22$. Mongol	465	0.00005	0.01774	0.00056	0.00157
$k=23$. Mulao	465	0.00000	0.00073	0.00001	0.00003
$k=24$. Naxi	465	0.00000	0.00038	0.00000	0.00002
$k=25$. Qiang	465	0.00000	0.00005	0.00001	0.00001
$k=26$. Salar	465	0.00000	0.00053	0.00001	0.00003
$k=27$. She	465	0.00000	0.00306	0.00004	0.00021
$k=28$. Shui	465	0.00000	0.00029	0.00001	0.00003
$k=29$. Tibetan	465	0.00002	0.24438	0.00080	0.01149
$k=30$. Tu	465	0.00000	0.00120	0.00003	0.00007
$k=31$. Tujia	465	0.00006	0.04210	0.00079	0.00438
$k=32$. Uyghur	465	0.00001	0.00036	0.00004	0.00003
$k=33$. Va	465	0.00000	0.00006	0.00001	0.00001
$k=34$. Xibe	465	0.00000	0.00158	0.00001	0.00008
$k=35$. Yao	465	0.00001	0.01086	0.00011	0.00064
$k=36$. Yi	465	0.00002	0.03288	0.00027	0.00220
$k=37$. Zhuang	465	0.00005	0.02644	0.00031	0.00141

SD, Standard deviation.

Basic results

Table 4.3 shows the estimated results of Equation 4.1. The economic determinants of trade seem controversial in existing studies. For example, according to the Heckscher-Ohlin theorem (Heckscher, 1919; Ohlin, 1933), trading partners with dissimilar levels of per capita income will trade more than the others with similar levels. However, Helpman (1987) and Krugman (1995) predict that the sum of the logs of per capita GNPs of two countries will have a positive effect on the log form of trade between the two countries. With regard to the case of China's interprovincial trade, the estimated coefficients on the product of per capita GDPs are negative and statistically significant in both 2000 (see Table 4.3a) and 2010 (see Table 4.3b). The negative coefficients on per capita GDPs may stem from the fact that China's interprovincial trade mainly includes homogeneous products that are more agricultural.[10]

Early comparative studies, using the international panel data of China and East Asia, show that geographical influence on international trade was reduced from the 1980s to 1990s (Guo, 2007b, 2013b, p. 210). One of the major driving forces contributing to this tendency might be technological advance in transportation and communications. Intuitively, wide application of e-commerce and the declining of distance-related transactions costs have increasingly contributed to the growth of international trade. However, in this chapter, the negative effect of "distance" on interprovincial trade is found to rise from 2000 to 2010. Obviously, this does not reflect China's improvement of transport infrastructures, and it does not conform to

Table 4.3a Regression for interprovincial trade: 56 ethnic groups as a single variable, 2000*

Explanatory variable	Coefficient	SE	VIF
Constant	13.027	1.424†	
$\ln(GDP_i GDP_j)$	0.657	0.047†	1.837
$\ln(GDPPC_i GDPPC_j)$	−0.178	0.070†	1.449
$\ln(DISTANCE_{ij})$	−1.239	0.098†	2.146
$ADJACENT_{ij}$	0.515	0.151†	1.705
$ETHNIC56_{ij}$	−1.447	0.327†	2.034
Coefficient of correlation (R^2)	0.633		
SE of regression	0.834		
F-statistic	138.195		
Sig. of regression	0.000		
Number of observations	405		

SE, Standard error; *VIF*, variance inflation factor.
*The regression is done by the ordinary least squares method. The dependent variable is the natural log of interprovincial trade in 2000.
†Statistically significant at greater than the 1% level.

[10] Based on Professor James E. Rauch's (University of California at Santiago) e-mail sent to the author.

the general pattern of international trade. It simply reveals that the distance-related transactions costs have been *increased* in China during the past decade. The main cause of China's interprovincial trade barriers may be the market-segmenting behavior that the Chinese provinces carry on to maintain social stability and maximize fiscal incomes (Poncet, 2005). Undoubtedly, our finding shows a sign of China's spatial economic disintegration during the first decade of the 21st century.

The estimated coefficients on "ADJACENT," which are statistically significant, slightly increase from 2000 to 2010, indicating that adjacent provinces tend to trade more easily over time than distant provinces. However, this variable may, at least to some extent, be correlated with some specific ethnic variables.[11] Consequently, compared with those that will be reported in Tables 4.4 and 4.6 (in which the individual ethnic variables are included), the estimated coefficients on "ADJACENT" might be artificially enlarged in Table 4.3 (in which the individual ethnic variables are not included).

The estimated coefficients on "ETHNIC56" are statistically significant for 2000 and 2010. However, they are negative, suggesting that the interprovincial links of 56 ethnic groups as a whole have only but impeded China's interprovincial economic activities. Obviously, this provides no evidence that supports the widely recognizable view that ethnic linkage index tends to encourage trade between

Table 4.3b Regression for interprovincial trade: 56 ethnic groups as a single variable, 2010*

Explanatory variable	Coefficient	SE	VIF
Constant	25.977	2.351†	
$\ln(GDP_i GDP_j)$	0.807	0.063†	2.336
$\ln(GDPPC_i GDPPC_j)$	− 0.923	0.105†	1.423
$\ln(DISTANCE_{ij})$	− 1.377	0.129†	2.222
$ADJACENT_{ij}$	0.597	0.199†	1.618
$ETHNIC56_{ij}$	− 1.302	0.372†	2.595
Coefficient of correlation (R^2)		0.571	
SE of regression		1.160	
F-statistic		118.960	
Sig. of regression		0.000	
Number of observations		451	

SE, Standard error; *VIF*, variance inflation factor.
*The regression is done by the ordinary least squares method. The dependent variable is the natural log of interprovincial trade in 2010.
†Statistically significant at greater than the 1% level.

[11] For example, because some ethnic minorities are usually found in China's transprovincial border areas (here ADJACENT = 1), it is natural to believe that interprovincial ethnic linkage scores are large when ADJACENT = 1 and small when ADJACENT = 0. However, because the Pearson correlation coefficients of "ADJACENT" and all the ethnic variables are less than 0.30 (detailed information is not reported here), they do not suggest potential multicollinearity causing imprecise regression results.

provinces that are multi-ethnically linked. In fact, because the partial correlation between the natural log of TRADE and the ETHNIC56 scores yields an inverted U–shaped curve for 2010 (Figure 4.1), the above-estimated coefficients on ETHNIC56 may be misleading (at least for 2010).

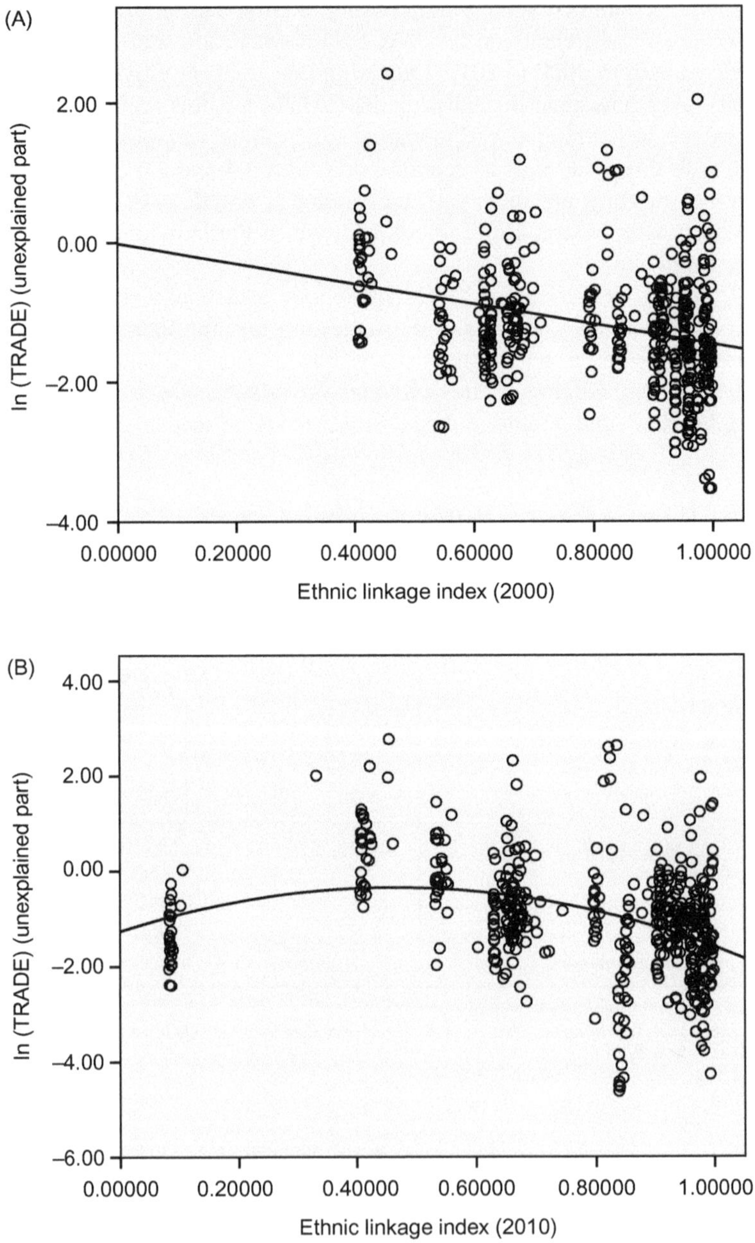

Figure 4.1 Partial correlations between trade and ethnic linkage, 2000 (**A**) and 2010 (**B**).

Ethnic influences

To have a better clarification of the complicated relationships between ethnic links and trade, we need to examine if (or how) China's ethnic groups have played different roles in the promotion of interprovincial trade. To go further, we run Equation 4.2 and obtain the estimated coefficients on a group of ethnic variables. The estimated results shown in Tables 4.4a (for 2000) and 4.4b (for 2010) are derived by excluding the variables whose VIFs (variance inflation factors) exceed 10 (a value that is often regarded as indicating multicollinearity). These results, compared with those shown in Tables 4.3a (for 2000) and 4.3b (for 2010), can help us to better explain the diverse ethnic influences on interprovincial trade:

- As for 2000, the estimated coefficients on 14 ethnic variables (Bai, Blang, Dai, Daur, Dongxiang, Gelao, Han, Hani, Hui, Jingpo, Li, Manchu, Miao, and Tujia) are statistically significant (see Table 4.4a). Specifically, whereas seven ethnic groups (Daur, Dongxiang, Gelao, Hui, Jingpo, Manchu, and Miao) have positive effects, seven others (Bai, Blang, Dai, Han, Hani, Li, and Tujia) have negative effects on interprovincial trade.

Table 4.4a Regression for interprovincial trade: ethnicity as individual variables, 2000*

Explanatory variable	Coefficient	SE	VIF
Constant	12.026	1.388†	
$\ln(GDP_iGDP_j)$	0.751	0.053†	3.178
$\ln(GDPPC_iGDPPC_j)$	− 0.204	0.075†	2.162
$\ln(DISTANCE_{ij})$	− 1.207	0.093†	2.576
$ADJACENT_{ij}$	0.258	0.151§	2.253
Bai	− 1111.725	311.344†	6.594
Blang	− 143382.289	82687.366§	2.648
Dai	− 25322.387	15047.769§	6.929
Daur	1459.585	653.472‡	1.324
Dong	89.568	65.501	2.241
Dongxiang	1283.312	485.477†	4.523
Gelao	17661.905	8009.100‡	5.595
Han	− 1.298	0.317†	2.617
Hani	− 26808.936	11710.097‡	3.891
Hui	9.726	4.739‡	1.605
Jingpo	359133.304	85213.774†	3.611
Kazak	− 8361.329	11470.119	7.672
Kirgiz	− 15958.902	19559.097	1.284
Korean	− 51.497	69.669	1.767
Lahu	7943.778	34481.342	4.622
Li	− 22444.486	8884.008†	3.903
Lisu	6391.919	6291.013	4.079
Manchu	51.197	11.158†	2.143
Miao	74.991	32.200‡	6.594
Mongol	28.096	25.884	1.582
Qiang	− 8033.854	16369.829	2.315

(Continued)

Table 4.4a **(Continued)**

Explanatory variable	Coefficient	SE	VIF
She	− 4.971	150.345	1.119
Shui	205.540	2401.597	3.323
Tibetan	47.256	35.007	1.867
Tu	− 616.774	1044.623	3.182
Tujia	− 23.329	11.271‡	2.145
Uyghur	1093.855	2390.064	1.673
Va	6985.266	13451.429	3.397
Xibe	− 6.959	408.855	1.191
Yao	− 46.837	77.176	2.091
Yi	43.219	37.176	4.702
Zhuang	14.840	38.157	2.258
Coefficient of correlation (R^2)	0.745		
SE of regression	0.725		
F-statistic	29.910		
Sig. of regression	0.000		
Number of observations	405		

SE, Standard error; *VIF,* variance inflation factor.
*The regression is done by the ordinary least squares method. Dependent variable is the natural log of interprovincial trade in 2000. The "Buyi," "Maonan," "Mulao," "Naxi" and "Salar" variables with VIFs above 10 are omitted from the regression.
†Statistically significant at greater than the 1% level.
‡Statistically significant at greater than the 5% level.
§Statistically significant at greater than the 10% level.

- As for 2010, the estimated coefficients on 17 ethnic variables (Dai, Daur, Dong, Dongxiang, Han, Hui, Jingpo, Kazak, Kirgiz, Lahu, Manchu, Mongol, Qiang, She, Tibetan, Va, and Zhuang) are statistically significant (see Table 4.4b). Specifically, whereas 13 ethnic groups (Daur, Dong, Dongxiang, Hui, Jingpo, Kirgiz, Lahu, Manchu, Mongol, Qiang, She, Tibetan and Zhuang) have positive effects, four others (Dai, Han, Kazak, and Va) have negative effects on interprovincial trade.

It is noteworthy that the fact that there are fewer ethnic groups with negative influences on interprovincial trade than those with positive influences does not contradict the negative coefficients on ETHNIC56 shown in Tables 4.3a (for 2000) and 4.3b (for 2010). This may stem from the fact that the Han majority whose estimated coefficients are negative for both 2000 (see Table 4.4a) and 2010 (see Table 4.4b) has a much larger weight than any other ethnic minorities.

Using the estimated coefficients reported in Tables 4.4a (for 2000) and 4.4b (for 2010), we may calculate each ethnic group's contributions to interprovincial trade (the results are reported in Table 4.5). Let us take the Hui ethnic group as an example. Because the estimated coefficient on the Hui is 12.977 (statistically significant at greater than the 5 percent level) in Table 4.4b and the interprovincial linkage indexes of the Hui are 0.00020 (minimum value), 0.14827 (maximum value), and

Table 4.4b Regression for interprovincial trade: ethnicity as individual variables, 2010*

Explanatory variable	Coefficient	SE	VIF
Constant	31.400	2.696†	
$\ln(GDP_i GDP_j)$	0.982	0.067†	3.487
$\ln(GDPPC_i GDPPC_j)$	−1.258	0.124†	2.639
$\ln(DISTANCE_{ij})$	−1.471	0.126†	2.829
$ADJACENT_{ij}$	0.087	0.201	2.176
Bai	−265.726	342.161	3.902
Buyi	632.081	734.375	6.337
Dai	−16370.263	5133.512†	3.085
Daur	2591.335	968.310†	1.168
Dong	157.650	87.212§	2.002
Dongxiang	1188.605	402.562†	1.707
Gelao	−3560.112	4361.579	5.925
Han	−1.462	0.363†	3.351
Hani	−1333.259	8917.799	5.583
Hui	12.977	6.610‡	1.492
Jingpo	58569.747	33647.494§	2.048
Kazak	−7360.507	3106.760‡	6.439
Kirgiz	4312.912	2560.362§	5.138
Korean	−104.386	105.163	1.697
Lahu	62076.007	27479.538‡	5.361
Li	−230.772	267.051	1.101
Lisu	4720.585	7208.820	4.082
Manchu	53.390	17.787†	2.063
Miao	−8.304	34.847	4.848
Mongol	112.320	36.450†	1.491
Naxi	−3290.571	8397.319	2.406
Qiang	28800.598	11888.284‡	2.449
She	493.943	247.431‡	1.267
Shui	−1416.603	2558.354	2.698
Tibetan	13.845	4.513†	1.227
Tu	−881.422	929.877	1.683
Tujia	−16.134	14.245	1.778
Uyghur	2626.353	1984.043	1.522
Va	−44560.824	11534.513†	4.851
Xibe	−62.065	669.836	1.191
Yao	62.694	102.244	1.946
Yi	9.777	40.396	3.615
Zhuang	84.596	43.125‡	1.687
Coefficient of correlation (R^2)		0.699	
SE of regression		1.008	
F-statistic		26.039	
Sig. of regression		0.000	
Number of observations		451	

SE, Standard error; *VIF*, variance inflation factor.

*The regression is done by the ordinary least squares method. The dependent variable is the natural log of interprovincial trade in 2010. The "Blang," "Maonan," "Mulao," and "Salar" variables with VIFs above 10 are omitted from the regression.

†Statistically significant at greater than the 1% level.

‡Statistically significant at greater than the 5% level.

§Statistically significant at greater than the 10% level.

Table 4.5 **Ethnic influences on interprovincial trade by ethnic group***

Ethnic group	Minimum (%)		Maximum (%)		Mean (%)	
	2000	2010	2000	2010	2000	2010
Bai	−0.431†	−0.103	−99.711†	−75.275	−5.650†	−1.381
Blang	0.000§	NA	−100.000§	NA	−9.882§	NA
Buyi	NA	0.662	NA	331.313	NA	4.364
Dai	−4.899§	−3.195†	−93.793§	−83.418†	−27.036§	−18.435†
Daur	0.087‡	0.154†	363.840‡	1424.279†	1.192‡	2.126†
Dong	0.048	0.084§	220.771	677.967§	1.156	2.043§
Dongxiang	0.047†	0.044†	3653.127†	2772.134†	2.254†	2.086†
Gelao	4.236‡	−0.833	32029.822‡	−68.762	29.987‡	−5.149
Han	−10.066†	−11.263†	−72.561†	−76.697†	−62.248†	−66.619†
Hani	−6.863‡	−0.353	−97.551‡	−16.846	−24.644‡	−1.397
Hui	0.194‡	0.260‡	322.947‡	584.975‡	3.528‡	4.734‡
Jingpo	0.000†	0.000§	40969.594†	166.827§	86.661†	10.715§
Kazak	−3.537	−3.120‡	−99.745	−99.479‡	−18.791	−16.742‡
Kirgiz	−0.093	0.025§	−100.000	4600.213§	−4.747	1.323§
Korean	−0.045	−0.090	−35.635	−59.062	−0.682	−1.377
Lahu	0.228	1.798‡	27.439	565.102‡	2.889	24.929‡
Li	−17.678†	−0.200	–	−59.901	−53.571†	−0.786
Lisu	0.549	0.406	434.249	244.712	3.875	2.847
Manchu	0.569†	0.594†	403.131†	439.185†	5.832†	6.090†
Maonan	NA	NA	NA	NA	NA	NA
Miao	0.345‡	−0.038	950.438‡	−22.927	6.858‡	−0.732
Mongol	0.133	0.532†	64.612	633.387†	1.582	6.475†
Mulao	NA	NA	NA	NA	NA	NA
Naxi	NA	−0.168	NA	−71.143	NA	−1.429
Qiang	−0.710	2.589‡	−31.459	287.346‡	−5.510	22.531‡
Salar	NA	NA	NA	NA	NA	NA

She	−0.001	0.105‡	−1.507	352.347‡	−0.018	1.835‡
Shui	0.017	−0.119	6.243	−34.121	0.231	−1.577
Tibetan	0.073	0.021†	–	2847.607†	3.858	1.115†
Tu	−0.162	−0.232	−52.399	−65.384	−1.730	−2.463
Tujia	−0.129‡	−0.089	−62.546‡	−49.297	−1.825‡	−1.265
Uyghur	1.314	3.184	47.554	154.481	3.956	9.763
Va	1.174	−7.173†	50.770	−92.714†	8.012	−38.840†
Xibe	−0.001	−0.011	−1.091	−9.325	−0.009	−0.082
Yao	−0.038	0.051	−39.856	97.497	−0.522	0.702
Yi	0.081	0.018	314.109	37.910	1.158	0.261
Zhuang	0.080	0.458‡	48.050	836.251‡	0.454	2.614‡

–, figures cannot be derived because the data reported in Table 4.2a are excluded from the regression reported in Table 4.4a; NA = not available for ethnic variables that are omitted from the regressions in Table 4.4.

*Figures in each row are calculated based on Tables 4.2a and 4.4a (for 2000) and on Tables 4.2b and 4.4b (for 2010) (detailed calculation process is defined in the text). They represent percentages by which provinces that are linked by the left-side ethnic group would increase (or decrease if the figures are negative) bilateral trade as opposed to those that are not linked by the same ethnic group.

†Statistically significant at greater than the 1% level.

‡Statistically significant at greater than the 5% level.

§Statistically significant at greater than the 10% level.

0.00356 (mean value) in Table 4.2b, Hui's contributions to interprovincial trade would range

from 0.260 percent (i.e., $\exp(12.977 \times 0.00020)/\exp(12.977 \times 0.00000) - 1$)
to 584.975 percent (i.e., $\exp(12.977 \times 0.14827)/\exp(12.977 \times 0.00000) - 1$),
with the mean of 4.734 percent (i.e., $\exp(12.977 \times 0.00356)/\exp(12.977 \times 0.00000) - 1$).

In other words, compared with those that are not linked by the Hui group, provinces with Hui links would increase their bilateral trade by 4.734 percent (mean level) in 2010. Using the mean values reported in Table 4.5, we observe that, from 2000 to 2010:[12]

- Three ethnic groups (Daur, Han, and Hui) have *increased* their influences—either positive or negative—on interprovincial trade.
- Three ethnic groups (Dai, Dongxiang, and Jingpo) have *reduced* their influences—either positive or negative—on interprovincial trade.
- Ten ethnic groups (Dong, Kazak, Kirgiz, Lahu, Mongol, Qiang, She, Tibetan, Va, and Zhuang) have *increased* their statistical significance.
- Six ethnic groups (Bai, Gelao, Hani, Li, Miao, and Tujia) have *reduced* their statistical significance.

Focusing Uyghurs

It must be noted that the estimated coefficients on Mongol, Tibetan, and Uyghur—three important ethnic minorities in China—are statistically insignificant in Table 4.4a. This result may indicate that the three ethnic minorities did not exert any significant influences on China's interprovincial trade in 2000. Yet, there may be other reasons. For example, in China's Fifth National Population Census conducted in November 2000, because "floating" populations were not counted according to their current residences, this could affect the final estimated coefficients. (Remember that the "floating" populations may sometimes play more important roles in interprovincial marketing and trade than permanent residents.) Because the ultimate reason(s) leading to the statistically insignificantly estimated coefficients on Mongol, Tibetan, and Uyghur is (are) still unclear, one must be very careful when intending to analyze the changes of ethnic influences on interprovincial trade from 2000 to 2010.

In the Analytical Framework section, Equations 4.1 and 4.2 each only provide partial information about ethnic influences on trade. To provide a complete picture for relationship between ethnic linkages and interprovincial trade, let us run Equation 4.3. The estimated results are reported in Tables 4.6a (for 2000) and 4.6b (for 2000). As for 2000, only 13 ethnic groups (Bai, Blang, Dai, Daur, Dongxiang,

[12] Note that because their maximum values are not available, the mean values of the Li and Tibetan groups should be slightly smaller than those reported in Table 4.5. However, this will not affect the analytical results below. In addition, because we have excluded, for purpose of overcoming the problems with multicollinearity, six ethnic groups (Blang, Buyi, Maonan, Mulao, Naxi, and Salar) from the regressions (shown in Table 4.4), we are not able to identify how these ethnic groups have changed their influences on interprovincial trade during the period from 2000 to 2010.

Gelao, Hani, Hui, Jingpo, Li, Manchu, Miao, and Tujia) are statistically significantly estimated in Table 4.6a compared with 14 ethnic groups in Table 4.4a. It is noteworthy that the estimated coefficients on Mongol, Tibetan, and Uyghur—three important ethnic minorities in China—are statistically insignificant in both Tables 4.4a and 4.6a.

However, our 2010 estimated results shown Table 4.6b seem to be more ideal than those shown in Table 4.4b. The main reason may be twofold: First, 19 ethnic variables and the ADJACENT variable are statistically significantly estimated in Table 4.6b, but only 17 ethnic variables are statistically significantly estimated, and that the ADJACENT variable is statistically insignificantly estimated in Table 4.4b. Second, given that the two regressions have very similar model significances, the regression shown in Table 4.6b includes more statistical information about ethnic variables than the one shown in Table 4.4b.

Using the statistically significantly estimated coefficients shown in Table 4.6b, we observe that in 2010:

- For seven ethnic groups (Bai, Blang, Dai, Gelao, Shui, Uyghur, and Va), the negative effects of ethnic linkages on interprovincial trade tend to increase with respect to the increase of per capita GDPs of the provinces concerned.
- For 12 ethnic groups (Buyi, Daur, Dongxiang, Hui, Jingpo, Manchu, Maonan, Miao, Mongol, Tibetan, Yi, and Zhuang), the positive effects of ethnic linkages on interprovincial trade tend to decrease with respect to the increase of per capita GDPs of the provinces concerned.

As for the first case, because the negative effects on interprovincial trade follow an increasing marginal law (with respect to the provincial economic development), the Uyghur and six other ethnic groups will increasingly contribute to the making of China's spatial economic disintegration. As for the second case, since all the threshold values (represented by $-\beta_k/\alpha_4$ in Equation 4.4, where $k = 3, 5, 7, 11, 12, 19, 20, 21, 22, 29, 36$, and 37) are much greater than the maximum value of ln ($GDPPC_i GDPPC_j$) (i.e., 22.40275, which is shown in Table 4.2b), it is unlikely that all the Tibetan and 11 other ethnic groups would exert negative influences on interprovincial trade.[13] In other words, even though their positive effects on interprovincial trade follow a diminishing marginal law, these ethnic groups will, ceteris paribus, continue to contribute to the making of China's spatial economic integration in the future.

Analytical implications

Although there has been a growing concern about the role of culture in international economic analyses, few quantitative studies have been conducted for intranational cases. The Chinese economy is far too huge, spatially complicated, and culturally

[13] For example, the threshold value for the Tibetan group is $\ln(GDPPC_i GDPPC_j)^* = -\beta_k/\alpha_4 = -13.694/(-0.115) = 119.078$, indicating that the positive effect of the Tibetan linkage on interprovincial trade will not reverse until the geometric mean of per capita GDP of two trading provinces reaches 7.20304×10^{25} yuan!

Table 4.6a Regression for interprovincial trade: ethnicity as nonlinear variables, 2000*

Explanatory variable	Coefficient	SE	VIF
Constant	9.096	0.896†	
$\ln(GDP_iGDP_j)$	0.724	0.049†	2.703
$\ln(DISTANCE_{ij})$	− 1.220	0.093†	2.597
$ADJACENT_{ij}$	0.285	0.149‡	2.183
$\ln(GDPPC_iGDPPC_j)ETHNIC56_{ij}$	− 0.087	0.017†	2.747
Bai	− 1043.873	377.405†	9.681
Blang	− 156376.962	82334.270‡	2.624
Buyi	− 479.532	1232.347	8.338
Dai	− 29622.302	15015.583‡	6.894
Daur	1461.096	653.743‡	1.324
Dong	61.092	69.215	2.500
Dongxiang	1327.445	485.050†	4.511
Gelao	17938.606	10024.476§	8.759
Hani	− 25805.959	11811.008‡	3.955
Hui	10.300	4.707‡	1.582
Jingpo	381356.119	83737.313†	3.484
Kazak	− 8706.316	11471.360	7.667
Kirgiz	− 20077.795	19489.611	1.274
Korean	− 55.645	69.639	1.764
Lahu	13928.307	34171.524	4.536
Li	− 24338.588	8912.331†	3.925
Lisu	6938.655	6270.095	4.048
Manchu	51.314	11.137†	2.133
Maonan	1300.350	1140.108	1.936
Miao	76.241	34.190‡	7.428
Mongol	27.886	25.852	1.577
Qiang	− 9344.785	16336.634	2.304
She	10.181	151.928	1.142
Tibetan	51.286	34.997	1.865
Tu	− 603.635	1044.716	3.179
Tujia	− 19.055	11.507§	2.234
Uyghur	− 542.286	2241.309	1.470
Va	8460.306	13444.415	3.390
Xibe	− 67.759	408.801	1.190
Yao	− 31.027	77.674	2.116
Yi	53.539	37.494	4.779
Zhuang	27.264	34.207	1.813
Coefficient of correlation (R^2)		0.745	
SE of regression		0.725	
F-statistic		29.877	
Sig. of regression		0.000	
Number of observations		405	

SE, Standard error; *VIF,* variance inflation factor.
*The regression is done by the ordinary least squares method. Dependent variable is the natural log of interprovincial trade in 2000. The "Han," "Mulao," "Naxi," "Salar," and "Shui" variables with VIFs above 10 are omitted from the regression.
†Statistically significant at greater than the 1% level.
‡Statistically significant at greater than the 5% level.
§Statistically significant at greater than the 10% level.

Table 4.6b Regression for interprovincial trade: ethnicity as nonlinear variables, 2010*

Explanatory variable	Coefficient	SE	VIF
Constant	7.893	1.433†	
$\ln(GDP_iGDP_j)$	0.852	0.071†	3.313
$\ln(DISTANCE_{ij})$	−1.391	0.137†	2.830
$ADJACENT_{ij}$	0.361	0.216§	2.133
$\ln(GDPPC_iGDPPC_j)ETHNIC56_{ij}$	−0.115	0.019†	3.408
Bai	−852.609	365.675‡	3.774
Blang	−15049.321	8101.364§	1.484
Buyi	2162.286	812.611†	6.571
Dai	−14120.100	5578.333†	3.085
Daur	1979.042	1049.567§	1.162
Dong	35.859	100.950	2.272
Dongxiang	1453.097	459.453†	1.883
Gelao	−10982.303	4742.520‡	5.932
Hani	6180.082	9703.332	5.597
Hui	16.204	7.192‡	1.496
Jingpo	73328.024	36594.619‡	2.051
Kazak	−4504.447	3257.443	5.995
Kirgiz	1915.167	2715.880	4.895
Korean	−163.609	114.056	1.690
Lahu	45512.270	29790.704	5.335
Li	−224.571	290.145	1.101
Lisu	−7684.539	7695.459	3.940
Manchu	38.324	19.250‡	2.046
Maonan	5071.086	1869.775†	1.876
Miao	59.170	36.985§	4.625
Mongol	68.249	39.168§	1.458
Naxi	4013.692	9075.684	2.380
Qiang	−3440.074	12399.241	2.256
She	420.341	269.303	1.271
Shui	−7021.754	3219.605‡	3.619
Tibetan	13.694	4.796†	1.173
Tujia	−7.173	15.752	1.841
Uyghur	−5678.266	1947.121†	1.242
Va	−52403.342	12530.668†	4.848
Xibe	−287.616	727.727	1.190
Yao	85.332	111.853	1.973
Yi	98.013	42.656‡	3.413
Zhuang	100.583	47.247‡	1.714
Coefficient of correlation (R^2)	0.645		
SE of regression	1.095		
F-statistic	20.337		
Sig. of regression	0.000		
Number of observations	451		

SE, Standard error; *VIF*, variance inflation factor.
*The regression is done by the ordinary least squares method. Dependent variable is the natural log of interprovincial trade in 2010. The "Han," "Mulao," "Salar," and "Tu" variables with VIFs above 9 are omitted from the regression.
†Statistically significant at greater than the 1% level.
‡Statistically significant at greater than the 5% level.
§Statistically significant at greater than the 10% level.

diversified to be misinterpreted. Most of China's 31 provinces are the average size and scale of a European country in population and land area, yet many still are considerable political and cultural systems in their own right. During the past decades, along with the gradual reform in the decentralization of authority i.e., transferring economic management and decision making from the central government to provincial and local governments), China's interprovincial relations have been transformed accordingly. Naturally, the examination of the driving forces to the causes and consequences of interprovincial economic (dis)integration in China is an important taskforce not only to economists but also to policymakers who have concerns about their internal spatial economic efficiencies.

It has been suggested that overseas ethnic Chinese (mainly encompassing the Han ethnic Chinese) networks play an important role in international trade. Rauch and Trindade (2002), for example, find that ethnic Chinese networks have a quantitatively important impact on bilateral trade through the mechanisms of market information and matching and referral services in addition to their effect through community enforcement of sanctions that deter opportunistic behavior. Their estimated results show that for trade between countries with ethnic Chinese population shares at the levels prevailing in Southeast Asia, the smallest estimated average increase in bilateral trade in differentiated products attributable to ethnic Chinese networks is nearly 60 percent.

However, in this chapter, we have not found any evidence that supports that the Han majority has played positive roles in China's interprovincial trade. It is impossible for us to provide more detailed evidence here. But we believe that our negative coefficients on the Han (see Table 4.4) stem from the very fact that the Han majority accounts for more than 90 percent of China's total population (more than 1.3 billion). A large population per se also implies a great degree of diversity or dissimilarity of its members among the provinces concerned. As a result, a common standard cannot be fully realized among different provinces' Han people. In addition, because the estimated coefficients on the ETHNIC56 variable are negative (see Table 4.3), we can only but conclude that all the 56 ethnic groups as a whole have a negative effect on China's interprovincial trade (although this kind of effect has slightly been reduced from 2000 to 2010). Nevertheless, from Tables 4.4 and 4.5, one may find both negative and positive effects for the ethnic influences on China's interprovincial economic cooperation or integration.

It is quite difficult for us to judge which one of 2000's estimated results reported in Tables 4.4a and 6a is better in statistics. However, as for the year 2010, our estimated coefficients shown in Table 4.6b seem to be more ideal than those shown in Table 4.4b (reasons have been discussed under Statistical Estimation). If the results shown in Table 4.6b are correct, we may conclude that seven ethnic groups (Bai, Blang, Dai, Gelao, Shui, Uyghur, and Va) tend to play growing roles in the possible making of China's interprovincial economic disintegration and that 12 ethnic groups (Buyi, Daur, Dongxiang, Hui, Jingpo, Manchu, Maonan, Miao, Mongol, Tibetan, Yi, and Zhuang) tend to play positive roles in the making of China's spatial economic integration, even though the effects follow a diminishing marginal law.

Among the above-mentioned ethnic minorities, the Uyghur (a true ethnic majority in Xinjiang) and Tibetan (a true ethnic majority in Tibet) groups are noteworthy. During the past decades, these two ethnic groups have been labeled as being "problematic" in China. Furthermore, there have been Uyghur and Tibetan exiles seeking the separations of Xinjiang and Tibet from China, respectively. However, the Uyghurs (with a negative coefficient) and the Tibetans (with a positive coefficient) are found to play different roles in China's interprovincial economic integration. More detailed analyses of these issues are presented in Chapter 5.

Even though we have constructed 56 ethnic groups into an explanatory variable in this chapter, we have only estimated China's 37 ethnic groups (each with a population of more than 100,000) as individual ethnic variables. Therefore, we cannot clarify if or how the other small ethnic minorities have influenced China's interprovincial economic activities. For purpose of overcoming the problems with multicollinearity, we have also excluded a few of other ethnic groups from some regressions in this chapter. Consequently, we are not able to identify the roles that these ethnic groups have played in interprovincial trade. But we will continue to pursue this research by either exploring new analytical techniques or incorporating more explanatory variables.

Annex 4.1. A list of China's 56 ethnic groups[14]

1. Achang (395,550 persons)
   Five major host provinces: Yunnan, Guangdong, Henan, Shandong, and Jiangsu
   Language(s): Achang; Religion(s): Buddhism
2. Bai (1,933,510 persons)
   Five major host provinces: Yunnan, Guizhou, Hunan, Guangdong, and Zhejiang
   Language(s): Bai, most also speak Chinese; Religion(s): Animism
3. Baonan (20,070 persons)
   Five major host provinces: Gansu, Qinghai, Xinjiang, Inner Mongolia, and Yunnan
   Language(s): Baonan, Chinese (spoken and written); *Religion(s)*: Islam
4. Blang (119,640 persons)
   Five major host provinces: Yunnan, Guangdong, Shandong, Zhejiang, and Chongqing
   Language(s): Blang, Dai; Religion(s): Buddhism
5. Buyi (2,870,030 persons)
   Five major host provinces: Guizhou, Zhejiang, Guangdong, Yunnan, and Fujian
   Language(s): Dai; Religion(s): Buddhism
6. Dai (1,261,310 persons)
   Five major host provinces: Yunnan, Sichuan, Guangdong, Zhejiang, and Shandong
   Language(s): Dai, most also speak Chinese; Religion(s): Buddhism
7. Daur (131,990 persons)
   Five major host provinces: Inner Mongolia, Heilongjiang, Xinjiang, Beijing, and Liaoning

[14] Source: The Sixth (2010) National Population Census of the PRC for the population of each ethnic group and author for the other indicators.

Language(s): Daur (spoken), Chinese (written); Religion(s): Lamaism

8. Deang (20,560 persons)
   Five major host provinces: Yunnan, Guangdong, Shandong, Zhejiang, and Sichuan
   Language(s): Deang; Religion(s): Buddhism
9. Derung (6,930 persons)
   Five major host provinces: Yunnan, Guizhou, Henan, Guangdong, and Sichuan
   Language(s): Derung; Religion(s): NA
10. Dong (2,879,970 persons)
   Five major host provinces: Guizhou, Hunan, Guangxi, Zhejiang, and Guangdong
   Language(s): Dong, Chinese; Religion(s): animism
11. Dongxiang (621,500 persons)
   Five major host provinces: Gansu, Xinjiang, Qinghai, Ningxia, and Guizhou
   Language(s): Dongxiang, most also speak Chinese; Religion(s): Islam
12. Ewenki (30,880 persons)
   Five major host provinces: Inner Mongolia, Heilongjiang, Liaoning, Beijing, and Shandong
   Language(s): Ewenki (spoken), Mongolian (written), Chinese (written); Religion(s): shamanism
13. Gaoshan (4,010 persons)
   Five major host provinces: Henan, Fujian, Guangxi, Liaoning, and Hebei
   Language(s): Gaoshan (spoken), Chinese; Religion(s): NA
14. Gelao (550,750 persons)
   Five major host provinces: Guizhou, Zhejiang, Guangdong, Guangxi, and Yunnan
   Language(s): Gelao, Chinese; Religion(s): Islam
15. Han (1,220,844,520 persons)
   Five major host provinces: Guangdong, Shandong, Henan, Jiangsu, and Sichuan
   Language(s): Mandarin; Religion(s): individual choice
16. Hani (1,660,930 persons)
   Five major host provinces: Yunnan, Guangdong, Zhejiang, Shanghai, and Shandong
   Language(s): Hani; Religion(s): animism
17. Hezhe (5,350 persons)
   Five major host provinces: Heilongjiang, Guangdong, Jilin, Beijing, and Liaoning
   Language(s): Hezhe (spoken), Chinese; Religion(s): NA
18. Hui (10,586,090 persons)
   Five major host provinces: Ningxia, Gansu, Xinjiang, Henan, and Qinghai
   Language(s): Chinese; Religion(s): Islam
19. Jing (28,200 persons)
   Five major host provinces: Guangxi, Guizhou, Yunnan, Guangdong, and Jiangxi
   Language(s): Jing, Chinese (spoken and written); Religion(s): NA
20. Jingpo (147,830 persons)
   Five major host provinces: Yunnan, Guangdong, Shandong, Guizhou, and Jilin
   Language(s): Jingpo; Religion(s): animism
21. Jino (23,140 persons)
   Five major host provinces: Yunnan, Sichuan, Chongqing, Guangdong, and Jiangsu
   Language(s): Jino; Religion(s): NA
22. Kazak (1,462,590 persons)
   Five major host provinces: Xinjiang, Henan, Guangdong, Gansu, and Hunan
   Language(s): Kazaki; Religion(s): Islam

23. Kirgiz (186,710 persons)
Five major host provinces: Xinjiang, Tibet, Heilongjiang, Guangdong, and Zhejiang
Language(s): Kirgiz, Uygur (written), Kazaki (written); Religion(s): Islam, Lamaism

24. Korean (1,830,930 persons)
Five major host provinces: Jilin, Heilongjiang, Liaoning, Shandong, and Beijing
Language(s): Korean, Chinese; Religion(s): individual choice

25. Lahu (485,970 persons)
Five major host provinces: Yunnan, Shandong, Zhejiang, Guangdong, and Jiangsu
Language(s): Lahu; Religion(s): animism

26. Lhoba (3,680 persons)
Five major host provinces: Tibet, Guizhou, Fujian, Beijing, and Liaoning
Language(s): Lhoba (spoken); Religion(s): Lamaism

27. Li (1,463,060 persons)
Five major host provinces: Hainan, Guizhou, Guangdong, Zhejiang, and Guangxi
Language(s): Li, some also speak Chinese; *Religion(s)*: animism

28. Lisu (702,840 persons)
Five major host provinces: Yunnan, Sichuan, Hebei, Shandong, and Guangdong
Language(s): Lisu; Religion(s): NA

29. Manchu (10,387,960 persons)
Five major host provinces: Liaoning, Hebei, Jilin, Heilongjiang, and Inner Mongolia
Language(s): most speak Chinese; a small portion speak Manchu; Religion(s): individual choice

30. Maonan (101,190 persons)
Five major host provinces: Guangxi, Guizhou, Guangdong, Zhejiang, and Fujian
Language(s): Maonan, Zhuang, Chinese (written); Religion(s): Islam

31. Miao (9,426,010 persons)
Five major host provinces: Guizhou, Hunan, Yunnan, Chongqing, and Guangxi
Language(s): Miao; the majority also assimilated into Chinese language; Religion(s): animism

32. Monba (10,560 persons)
Five major host provinces: Tibet, Jiangsu, Gansu, Jiangxi, and Guangxi
Language(s): Monba, Tibetan; Religion(s): Lamaism

33. Mongol (5,981,840 persons)
Five major host provinces: Inner Mongolia, Liaoning, Hebei, Xinjiang, and Jilin
Language(s): Mongolian, Mandarin; Religion(s): Lamaism

34. Mulao (216,260 persons)
Five major host provinces: Guangxi, Guizhou, Guangdong, Zhejiang, and Hunan
Language(s): Mulam and Zhuang (spoken), Chinese (written); Religion(s): Lamaism

35. Naxi (326,300 persons)
Five major host provinces: Yunnan, Sichuan, Tibet, Zhejiang, and Beijing
Language(s): Naxi, most also speak Chinese; Religion(s): Dongba

36. Nu (37,520 persons)
Five major host provinces: Yunnan, Hainan, Guangdong, Tibet, and Shandong
Language(s): Nu; Religion(s): NA

37. Oroqen (8,660 persons)
Five major host provinces: Heilongjiang, Inner Mongolia, Liaoning, Beijing, and Hebei
Language(s): Oroqen (spoken), Chinese (written); Religion(s): shamanism

38. Pumi (42,860 persons)
Five major host provinces: Yunnan, Sichuan, Guangdong, Shandong, and Chongqing
Language(s): Pumi; Religion(s): NA

39. Qiang (309,580 persons)
Five major host provinces: Sichuan, Guangdong, Guizhou, Zhejiang, and Jiangsu
Language(s): Qiang (spoken); Religion(s): Lamaism

40. Russian (15,390 persons)
Five major host provinces: Xinjiang, Inner Mongolia, Beijing, Heilongjiang, and Shanghai
Language(s): Russian; Religion(s): Eastern Orthodox

41. Salar (130,610 persons)
Five major host provinces: Qinghai, Gansu, Xinjiang, Shanghai, and Guangdong
Language(s): Salar (spoken), Chinese (spoken and written); Religion(s): Islam

42. She (708,650 persons)
Five major host provinces: Fujian, Zhejiang, Jiangxi, Guizhou, and Guangdong
Language(s): Chinese; Religion(s): animism

43. Shui (411,850 persons)
Five major host provinces: Guizhou, Guangxi, Jiangsu, Zhejiang, and Yunnan
Language(s): Shui, most also speak Chinese; Religion(s): animism

44. Tajik (51,070 persons)
Five major host provinces: Xinjiang, Zhejiang, Guangdong, Jiangxi, and Shandong
Language(s): Tajik (spoken), Uygur; Religion(s): Islam

45. Tatar (3,560 persons)
Five major host provinces: Xinjiang, Guangdong, Guangxi, Beijing, and Jiangsu
Language(s): Tatar, Uygur, Kazaki; Religion(s): Islam

46. Tibetan (6,282,190 persons)
Five major host provinces: Tibet, Sichuan, Qinghai, Gansu, and Yunnan
Language(s): Tibetan; Religion(s): Lamaism

47. Tu (289,570 persons)
Five major host provinces: Qinghai, Gansu, Guangdong, Yunnan, and Guizhou
Language(s): Tu, Chinese; Religion(s): Lamaism

48. Tujia (8,353,910 persons)
Five major host provinces: Hunan, Hubei, Guizhou, Chongqing, and Zhejiang
Language(s): Tujia, most also speak Chinese; Religion(s): animism

49. Uyghur (10,069,350 persons)
Five major host provinces: Xinjiang, Beijing, Hunan, Guangdong, and Zhejiang
Language(s): Uygur; Religion(s): Islam

50. Uzbek (5,670 persons)
Five major host provinces: Xinjiang, Zhejiang, Guangdong, Beijing, and Hunan
Language(s): Uzbek, Uygur, Kazaki; Religion(s): Islam

51. Va (429,710 persons)
Five major host provinces: Yunnan, Shandong, Guangdong, Zhejiang, and Henan
Language(s): Va; Religion(s): animism

52. Xibe (190,480 persons)
Five major host provinces: Liaoning, Xinjiang, Heilongjiang, Jilin, and Inner Mongolia
Language(s): Xibe; Religion(s): Islam

53. Yao (2,796,000 persons)
Five major host provinces: Guangxi, Hunan, Guangdong, Yunnan, and Guizhou
Language(s): Yao, most also speak Chinese; Religion(s): animism
54. Yi (8,714,390 persons)
Five major host provinces: Yunnan, Sichuan, Guizhou, Zhejiang, and Guangdong
Language(s): Yi (spoken), males also speak and write Chinese; Religion(s): animism
55. Yugur (14,380 persons)
Five major host provinces: Gansu, Xinjiang, Qinghai, Beijing, and Shandong
Language(s): Yugur, Chinese (spoken and written); Religion(s): Lamaism
56. Zhuang (16,926,380 persons)
Five major host provinces: Guangxi, Yunnan, Guangdong, Zhejiang, and Guizhou
Language(s): Zhuang (spoken), most also speak and write Chinese; Religion(s): animism

Annex 4.2. Data on selected interprovincial variables, 2000 and 2010

Province–Province	Distance (km)	Ethnic Links		Export (1000 tons)		Import (1000 tons)	
		2000	2010	2000	2010	2000	2010
Anhui–Beijing	1,074	0.9636	0.9658	160	220	210	130
Anhui–Chongqing	1,562	0.9366	0.9343	60	210	80	80
Anhui–Fujian	1,196	0.9870	0.9828	1720	1720	380	240
Anhui–Gansu	1,832	0.9190	0.9119	150	380	230	700
Anhui–Guangdong	1,826	0.9864	0.9818	1200	1100	220	70
Anhui–Guangxi	2,098	0.6179	0.6301	170	500	310	510
Anhui–Guizhou	2,076	0.6274	0.6611	70	340	100	200
Anhui–Hainan	2,448	0.8283	0.8380		10		
Anhui–Hebei	914	0.9631	0.9647	320	1050	600	600
Anhui–Heilongjiang	2,227	0.9554	0.9673	160	240	430	1,380
Anhui–Henan	645	0.9940	0.9942	600	1090	3060	5,450
Anhui–Hubei	1,181	0.9585	0.9591	260	3620	560	740
Anhui–Hunan	1,222	0.9012	0.9028	330	2790	150	290
Anhui–Inner Mongolia	1,777	0.7984	0.8018	70	230	400	680
Anhui–Jiangsu	312	0.9960	0.9961	17170	19550	3040	6,360
Anhui–Jiangxi	478	0.9944	0.9945	2150	8060	360	290
Anhui–Jilin	1,985	0.9140	0.9253	190	220	320	790
Anhui–Liaoning	1,650	0.8459	0.8544	320	320	670	460
Anhui–Ningxia	2,002	0.6610	0.6550	10	40	60	140
Anhui–Qinghai	2,048	0.5470	0.5367	30	180	90	350
Anhui–Shaanxi	1,156	0.9979	0.9978	240	360	750	1,700
Anhui–Shandong	613	0.9993	0.9987	980	3430	4290	5,470
Anhui–Shanghai	615	0.9978	0.9926	2040	1790	580	390
Anhui–Shanxi	1,145	0.9960	0.9957	150	350	3890	7,480
Anhui–Sichuan	1,998	0.9523	0.9414	220	900	310	400
Anhui–Tianjin	973	0.9796	0.9810	110	200	140	70
Anhui–Tibet	3,863	0.0649	0.0868		80		20
Anhui–Xinjiang	3,724	0.4125	0.4114	70	180	130	320
Anhui–Yunnan	3,098	0.6725	0.6728	100	570	110	230
Anhui–Zhejiang	451	0.9926	0.9797	5550	8230	450	380

(Continued)

(Continued)

Province–Province	Distance (km)	Ethnic Links		Export (1000 tons)		Import (1000 tons)	
		2000	2010	2000	2010	2000	2010
Beijing–Chongqing	2,087	0.9377	0.9366	100	170	40	50
Beijing–Fujian	2,334	0.9624	0.9668	120	50	170	80
Beijing–Gansu	1,811	0.9320	0.9204	160	80	90	180
Beijing–Guangdong	2,289	0.9601	0.9644	410	140	620	70
Beijing–Guangxi	2,561	0.6192	0.6321	70	90	140	60
Beijing–Guizhou	2,539	0.6309	0.6661	60	160	60	30
Beijing–Hainan	3,088	0.8300	0.8409				
Beijing–Hebei	277	0.9867	0.9869	5180	4750	14720	12,580
Beijing–Heilongjiang	1,288	0.9779	0.9847	330	140	1710	1,200
Beijing–Henan	689	0.9694	0.9711	520	260	550	490
Beijing–Hubei	1,225	0.9598	0.9614	210	230	280	290
Beijing–Hunan	1,583	0.9028	0.9053	220	120	180	190
Beijing–Inner Mongolia	667	0.8237	0.8273	540	810	3760	5,530
Beijing–Jiangsu	1,160	0.9603	0.9638	560	280	350	210
Beijing–Jiangxi	1,449	0.9581	0.9606	160	60	70	120
Beijing–Jilin	1,046	0.9365	0.9482	230	240	1010	630
Beijing–Liaoning	741	0.8691	0.8775	1290	1030	1790	1,300
Beijing–Ningxia	1,343	0.6775	0.6675	70	30	340	240
Beijing–Qinghai	2,092	0.5633	0.5499	40	40	20	180
Beijing–Shaanxi	1,159	0.9618	0.9642	410	310	170	420
Beijing–Shandong	497	0.9638	0.9667	880	850	2270	330
Beijing–Shanghai	1,463	0.9631	0.9696	250	70	410	260
Beijing–Shanxi	514	0.9600	0.9618	820	840	14030	9,200
Beijing–Sichuan	2,042	0.9537	0.9437	300	330	310	330
Beijing–Tianjin	137	0.9838	0.9837	5180	3230	3180	3,500
Beijing–Tibet	4,064	0.0657	0.0877		10		
Beijing–Xinjiang	3,768	0.4294	0.4253	130	200	190	450
Beijing–Yunnan	3,178	0.6839	0.6828	150	110	110	90
Beijing–Zhejiang	1,589	0.9596	0.9646	260	200	160	170
Chongqing–Fujian	2,196	0.9380	0.9394	80	180	200	390
Chongqing–Gansu	1,466	0.9137	0.9070	60	100	520	750
Chongqing–Guangdong	1,670	0.9396	0.9391	800	1090	1390	2,720
Chongqing–Guangxi	1,338	0.6282	0.6404	1220	1610	620	2,270
Chongqing–Guizhou	463	0.6801	0.7152	1200	1490	1260	3,660
Chongqing–Hainan	1,837	0.8361	0.8463		40		30
Chongqing–Hebei	1,810	0.9367	0.9343	100	240	480	1,080
Chongqing–Heilongjiang	3,431	0.9365	0.9339	50	200	220	400
Chongqing–Henan	1,598	0.9365	0.9339	140	320	630	1,410
Chongqing–Hubei	1,220	0.9766	0.9740	390	340	570	690
Chongqing–Hunan	1,094	0.9581	0.9583	130	320	400	1,040
Chongqing–Inner Mongolia	2,081	0.7930	0.7969	20	70	80	430
Chongqing–Jiangsu	1,828	0.9371	0.9357	160	340	260	360
Chongqing–Jiangxi	1,579	0.9365	0.9341	40	120	150	500
Chongqing–Jilin	3,185	0.9096	0.9215	20	50	120	330
Chongqing–Liaoning	2,827	0.8406	0.8495	70	90	230	210
Chongqing–Ningxia	1,596	0.6557	0.6503	20	20	40	170
Chongqing–Qinghai	1,682	0.5418	0.5321	10	30	70	430
Chongqing–Shaanxi	747	0.9363	0.9342	120	130	340	870
Chongqing–Shandong	1,956	0.9366	0.9341	160	290	280	740
Chongqing–Shanghai	2,167	0.9373	0.9376	70	70	150	210

(Continued)

(Continued)

Province–Province	Distance (km)	Ethnic Links		Export (1000 tons)		Import (1000 tons)	
		2000	2010	2000	2010	2000	2010
Chongqing–Shanxi	1,441	0.9365	0.9339	40	70	80	700
Chongqing–Sichuan	338	0.9389	0.9372	3650	6050	2820	6,240
Chongqing–Tianjin	2,091	0.9371	0.9353	40	60	100	290
Chongqing–Tibet	3,654	0.0621	0.0833		20		30
Chongqing–Xinjiang	3,358	0.4082	0.4074	60	180	270	460
Chongqing–Yunnan	1,101	0.6838	0.6849	240	620	540	1,460
Chongqing–Zhejiang	2,312	0.9389	0.9445	150	220	260	400
Fujian–Gansu	3,065	0.9166	0.9099	130	230	200	280
Fujian–Guangdong	1,588	0.9864	0.9872	380	2060	80	820
Fujian–Guangxi	1,860	0.6191	0.6345	60	120	360	360
Fujian–Guizhou	1,838	0.6290	0.6671	150	400	310	820
Fujian–Hainan	2,374	0.8298	0.8423				10
Fujian–Hebei	1,915	0.9610	0.9628	270	180	640	230
Fujian–Heilongjiang	3,451	0.9552	0.9675	270	80	410	340
Fujian–Henan	1,549	0.9869	0.9825	470	460	1810	2,020
Fujian–Hubei	1,013	0.9602	0.9645	570	490	1270	1,170
Fujian–Hunan	984	0.9029	0.9084	1170	730	1440	1,020
Fujian–Inner Mongolia	3,303	0.7959	0.7998	90	70	180	200
Fujian–Jiangsu	1,174	0.9862	0.9831	770	250	1120	570
Fujian–Jiangxi	622	0.9859	0.9819	1070	8500	3430	5500
Fujian–Jilin	3,209	0.9125	0.9244	120	30	210	400
Fujian–Liaoning	2,904	0.8435	0.8524	280	70	170	30
Fujian–Ningxia	3,235	0.6587	0.6532	50	70	60	70
Fujian–Qinghai	3,281	0.5447	0.5351	60	70	70	140
Fujian–Shaanxi	2,389	0.9868	0.9826	300	620	360	120
Fujian–Shandong	1,837	0.9869	0.9827	320	230	1280	670
Fujian–Shanghai	1,173	0.9878	0.9875	470	440	470	200
Fujian–Shanxi	2,521	0.9857	0.9810	140	100	1140	1,020
Fujian–Sichuan	2,805	0.9533	0.9445	390	1120	300	310
Fujian–Tianjin	2,197	0.9778	0.9801	70	20	140	10
Fujian–Tibet	4,887	0.0648	0.0863		20		
Fujian–Xinjiang	4,957	0.4113	0.4105	210	500	200	320
Fujian–Yunnan	2,477	0.6710	0.6750	260	440	280	590
Fujian–Zhejiang	972	0.9896	0.9900	2620	1800	790	1,140
Gansu–Guangdong	2,787	0.9138	0.9073	790	1690	350	470
Gansu–Guangxi	3,059	0.6179	0.6298	100	250	70	270
Gansu–Guizhou	2,139	0.6283	0.6616	130	320	40	990
Gansu–Hainan	3,596	0.8284	0.8384		10		
Gansu–Hebei	1,599	0.9224	0.9151	360	1590	450	470
Gansu–Heilongjiang	3,099	0.9177	0.9097	80	150	190	380
Gansu–Henan	1,187	0.9247	0.9173	1240	3090	930	2,930
Gansu–Hubei	1,723	0.9146	0.9079	490	2490	120	950
Gansu–Hunan	2,081	0.9011	0.9025	320	810	150	180
Gansu–Inner Mongolia	1,144	0.8026	0.8059	330	690	1270	2,280
Gansu–Jiangsu	1,182	0.9151	0.9083	1000	2520	750	1,490
Gansu–Jiangxi	2,088	0.9135	0.9066	90	440	40	80
Gansu–Jilin	2,952	0.9150	0.9115	60	160	70	140
Gansu–Liaoning	2,552	0.8475	0.8552	320	320	300	400
Gansu–Ningxia	468	0.7039	0.6996	670	1210	4440	7,550
Gansu–Qinghai	215	0.6094	0.6031	1570	1510	1570	1,930

(Continued)

(Continued)

Province–Province	Distance (km)	Ethnic Links		Export (1000 tons)		Import (1000 tons)	
		2000	2010	2000	2010	2000	2010
Gansu–Shaanxi	676	0.9174	0.9107	2210	6360	720	2,570
Gansu–Shandong	1,853	0.9191	0.9125	360	2220	440	1,560
Gansu–Shanghai	2,185	0.9176	0.9108	310	1080	150	140
Gansu–Shanxi	1,327	0.9156	0.9083	340	830	540	1,340
Gansu–Sichuan	1,172	0.9303	0.9267	2900	3310	790	720
Gansu–Tianjin	1,948	0.9320	0.9212	500	610	260	1,330
Gansu–Tibet	2,188	0.0827	0.1067		230		20
Gansu–Xinjiang	1,892	0.4570	0.4551	870	1950	9970	20,340
Gansu–Yunnan	2,272	0.6854	0.6857	400	490	520	660
Gansu–Zhejiang	2,311	0.9135	0.9074	380	1660	170	170
Guangdong–Guangxi	1,334	0.6290	0.6449	3630	12560	3880	3,660
Guangdong–Guizhou	1,560	0.6300	0.6657	2550	5710	4500	6,730
Guangdong–Hainan	794	0.8374	0.8469		110		150
Guangdong–Hebei	2,012	0.9582	0.9602	810	260	1940	800
Guangdong–Heilongjiang	2,928	0.9524	0.9655	790	100	750	160
Guangdong–Henan	1,600	0.9863	0.9815	1050	1060	6250	5,480
Guangdong–Hubei	1,064	0.9612	0.9638	1970	1300	4200	4,310
Guangdong–Hunan	706	0.9062	0.9100	7170	15380	13950	10,540
Guangdong–Inner Mongolia	2,962	0.7932	0.7972	160	90	690	400
Guangdong–Jiangsu	1,804	0.9871	0.9837	480	120	1820	590
Guangdong–Jiangxi	1022	0.9866	0.9818	1340	3080	2840	2,480
Guangdong–Jilin	3,341	0.9098	0.9218	310	20	560	110
Guangdong–Liaoning	3,036	0.8408	0.8498	890	10	580	100
Guangdong–Ningxia	2,957	0.6559	0.6505	130	110	150	420
Guangdong–Qinghai	3,003	0.5420	0.5324	90	170	210	410
Guangdong–Shaanxi	2,111	0.9862	0.9817	820	1220	1130	500
Guangdong–Shandong	2,151	0.9864	0.9819	590	140	1720	380
Guangdong–Shanghai	1,803	0.9874	0.9868	390	190	470	190
Guangdong–Shanxi	2,243	0.9864	0.9815	390	290	2170	1,680
Guangdong–Sichuan	2527	0.9532	0.9437	2330	6540	2090	3,270
Guangdong–Tianjin	2,431	0.9752	0.9775	210	20	290	20
Guangdong–Tibet	4,980	0.0622	0.0837		20		
Guangdong–Xinjiang	4,679	0.4086	0.4078	650	970	650	1,150
Guangdong–Yunnan	2,199	0.6780	0.6825	3530	5950	2360	4,210
Guangdong–Zhejiang	1,602	0.9899	0.9878	830	260	610	310
Guangxi–Guizhou	865	0.6408	0.6522	2320	7940	10610	28,410
Guangxi–Hainan	739	0.6340	0.6453		230		170
Guangxi–Hebei	2,262	0.6183	0.6302	490	390	860	650
Guangxi–Heilongjiang	3,855	0.6179	0.6297	100	50	350	350
Guangxi–Henan	1,870	0.6179	0.6298	710	1260	2620	3,160
Guangxi–Hubei	1,336	0.6227	0.6342	690	1430	1410	2,460
Guangxi–Hunan	978	0.6468	0.6581	1750	8570	3050	5,650
Guangxi–Inner Mongolia	3,234	0.6180	0.6301	40	70	190	540
Guangxi–Jiangsu	2,076	0.6185	0.6316	590	530	360	350
Guangxi–Jiangxi	1,294	0.6174	0.6296	420	960	660	1,230
Guangxi–Jilin	6,313	0.6179	0.6297	60	60	160	650
Guangxi–Liaoning	3,411	0.6180	0.6300	280	130	210	120
Guangxi–Ningxia	3,229	0.6180	0.6304	20	50	30	50
Guangxi–Qinghai	3,275	0.5422	0.5324	10	70	80	130
Guangxi–Shaanxi	2,383	0.6178	0.6299	120	450	780	430

(*Continued*)

(Continued)

Province–Province	Distance (km)	Ethnic Links		Export (1000 tons)		Import (1000 tons)	
		2000	2010	2000	2010	2000	2010
Guangxi–Shandong	2,538	0.6179	0.6299	340	430	540	390
Guangxi–Shanghai	2,075	0.6185	0.6331	370	430	200	430
Guangxi–Shanxi	2,515	0.6179	0.6298	120	220	1080	950
Guangxi–Sichuan	1,832	0.6199	0.6323	2030	5640	2110	2,870
Guangxi–Tianjin	2,703	0.6185	0.6310	80	60	100	60
Guangxi–Tibet	4,992	0.0624	0.0837		20		10
Guangxi–Xinjiang	4,951	0.4082	0.4072	40	160	70	190
Guangxi–Yunnan	1,504	0.6610	0.6724	2040	9110	2860	7,950
Guangxi–Zhejiang	1,874	0.6199	0.6397	890	930	310	240
Guizhou–Hainan	1,374	0.6366	0.6731		110		10
Guizhou–Hebei	2,262	0.6293	0.6627	480	490	210	410
Guizhou–Heilongjiang	3,833	0.6275	0.6595	50	330	150	360
Guizhou–Henan	1,850	0.6284	0.6617	330	760	530	1,170
Guizhou–Hubei	1,314	0.6653	0.6976	250	940	730	1,280
Guizhou–Hunan	956	0.7118	0.7445	1480	6710	1040	2,310
Guizhou–Inner Mongolia	3,100	0.6290	0.6627	30	160	70	210
Guizhou–Jiangsu	2,054	0.6251	0.6593	400	710	280	450
Guizhou–Jiangxi	1,272	0.6241	0.6570	340	1890	250	1,430
Guizhou–Jilin	3,591	0.6288	0.6612	30	320	50	370
Guizhou–Liaoning	3,286	0.6290	0.6625	270	280	120	100
Guizhou–Ningxia	2,309	0.6286	0.6567	40	210	20	30
Guizhou–Qinghai	2,355	0.5480	0.5389	10	50	10	40
Guizhou–Shaanxi	1,809	0.6266	0.6595	60	310	180	390
Guizhou–Shandong	2,516	0.6276	0.6612	480	1670	220	490
Guizhou–Shanghai	2,053	0.6275	0.6646	260	200	150	330
Guizhou–Shanxi	2,450	0.6248	0.6572	140	280	80	220
Guizhou–Sichuan	967	0.6504	0.6845	1710	4910	1820	2,620
Guizhou–Tianjin	2,681	0.6296	0.6639	180	80	50	100
Guizhou–Tibet	4,117	0.0656	0.0875				
Guizhou–Xinjiang	3,993	0.4146	0.4143	40	280	140	190
Guizhou–Yunnan	639	0.6862	0.7217	940	4050	1680	1,230
Guizhou–Zhejiang	1,852	0.6277	0.6743	440	730	230	420
Hainan–Hebei	2,811	0.8288	0.8386				10
Hainan–Heilongjiang	4,433	0.8284	0.8381				
Hainan–Henan	2,399	0.8283	0.8382		20		70
Hainan–Hubei	1,883	0.8324	0.8418		10		120
Hainan–Hunan	1,501	0.8381	0.8482		40		90
Hainan–Inner Mongolia	3,747	0.7940	0.7983				10
Hainan–Jiangsu	2,597	0.8289	0.8397				10
Hainan–Jiangxi	1,750	0.8274	0.8370		50		40
Hainan–Jilin	4,187	0.8284	0.8382				
Hainan–Liaoning	3,925	0.8285	0.8384				
Hainan–Ningxia	3,716	0.6567	0.6517				
Hainan–Qinghai	3,802	0.5428	0.5336				10
Hainan–Shaanxi	2,887	0.8281	0.8381				10
Hainan–Shandong	2,795	0.8283	0.8382				10
Hainan–Shanghai	2,574	0.8293	0.8416				
Hainan–Shanxi	2,976	0.8284	0.8378				20
Hainan–Sichuan	2,829	0.8305	0.8408		60		140
Hainan–Tianjin	3,198	0.8293	0.8398				

(Continued)

(Continued)

Province–Province	Distance (km)	Ethnic Links		Export (1000 tons)		Import (1000 tons)	
		2000	2010	2000	2010	2000	2010
Hainan–Tibet	5,774	0.0629	0.0845				
Hainan–Xinjiang	5,478	0.4090	0.4087				
Hainan–Yunnan	1,567	0.6839	0.6841		40		50
Hainan–Zhejiang	2,407	0.8296	0.8457				10
Hebei–Heilongjiang	1,673	0.9863	0.9835	2860	1290	4340	3,040
Hebei–Henan	412	0.9666	0.9679	2770	3300	960	1,640
Hebei–Hubei	948	0.9587	0.9592	1450	2680	1150	1,190
Hebei–Hunan	1,306	0.9015	0.9027	1180	1370	410	330
Hebei–Inner Mongolia	871	0.8245	0.8250	2600	1900	10640	10,9520
Hebei–Jiangsu	964	0.9594	0.9613	3300	2930	700	4,160
Hebei–Jiangxi	1,293	0.9576	0.9595	600	860	160	200
Hebei–Jilin	1,431	0.9481	0.9579	1980	1170	2440	1,030
Hebei–Liaoning	1,126	0.8807	0.8872	5430	4860	5090	6,290
Hebei–Ningxia	1,547	0.6680	0.6622	160	210	530	14,540
Hebei–Qinghai	1,815	0.5534	0.5429	150	60	100	1,240
Hebei–Shaanxi	923	0.9614	0.9632	550	1230	740	3,100
Hebei–Shandong	301	0.9632	0.9652	3990	12040	4760	20,740
Hebei–Shanghai	1,267	0.9618	0.9643	1470	1430	280	210
Hebei–Shanxi	231	0.9596	0.9609	3910	4680	105090	300,860
Hebei–Sichuan	1,765	0.9527	0.9417	770	2570	670	880
Hebei–Tianjin	419	0.9725	0.9753	14030	30070	4280	1,8120
Hebei–Tibet	3,787	0.0650	0.0869		70		
Hebei–Xinjiang	3,491	0.4184	0.4170	360	750	900	940
Hebei–Yunnan	2,901	0.6758	0.6757	290	540	500	760
Hebei–Zhejiang	1,393	0.9580	0.9603	1340	1600	320	180
Heilongjiang–Henan	2,085	0.9565	0.9683	1060	1250	440	480
Heilongjiang–Hubei	2,519	0.9533	0.9588	410	720	320	590
Heilongjiang–Hunan	2,877	0.9011	0.9022	440	880	280	110
Heilongjiang–Inner Mongolia	1,955	0.8234	0.8221	2330	3840	9170	39,590
Heilongjiang–Jiangsu	2,277	0.9538	0.9666	1610	1060	610	560
Heilongjiang–Jiangxi	2,689	0.9522	0.9648	260	690	80	70
Heilongjiang–Jilin	242	0.9557	0.9548	18330	17240	4710	12,580
Heilongjiang–Liaoning	547	0.8818	0.8797	26210	40960	7040	11,960
Heilongjiang–Ningxia	2,631	0.6633	0.6566	130	110	60	60
Heilongjiang–Qinghai	3,386	0.5499	0.5380	50	140	30	100
Heilongjiang–Shaanxi	2,453	0.9555	0.9678	490	560	180	160
Heilongjiang–Shandong	1,614	0.9558	0.9684	3990	2030	2590	2,150
Heilongjiang–Shanghai	2,577	0.9563	0.9697	590	580	300	140
Heilongjiang–Shanxi	1,802	0.9542	0.9666	720	630	550	530
Heilongjiang–Sichuan	3,336	0.9525	0.9413	850	1920	230	210
Heilongjiang–Tianjin	1,354	0.9631	0.9766	2120	680	570	470
Heilongjiang–Tibet	5,409	0.0648	0.0851		50		
Heilongjiang–Xinjiang	5,062	0.4153	0.4125	150	240	80	110
Heilongjiang–Yunnan	4,472	0.6706	0.6699	210	650	80	310
Heilongjiang–Zhejiang	2,706	0.9522	0.9656	680	1230	410	130
Henan–Hubei	536	0.9585	0.9589	22970	24780	2210	2,490
Henan–Hunan	894	0.9011	0.9024	5480	10120	600	710
Henan–Inner Mongolia	1,362	0.8028	0.8060	450	380	920	2,110
Henan–Jiangsu	695	0.9901	0.9905	9210	8470	3320	12,620

(Continued)

(Continued)

Province–Province	Distance (km)	Ethnic Links		Export (1000 tons)		Import (1000 tons)	
		2000	2010	2000	2010	2000	2010
Henan–Jiangxi	927	0.9885	0.9889	3250	5070	160	330
Henan–Jilin	1,843	0.9152	0.9263	400	320	490	630
Henan–Liaoning	1,538	0.8477	0.8554	820	2360	1250	2,130
Henan–Ningxia	1,357	0.6669	0.6603	160	70	170	430
Henan–Qinghai	1,403	0.5528	0.5421	410	1200	400	1,310
Henan–Shaanxi	511	0.9924	0.9928	2120	960	1930	4,770
Henan–Shandong	666	0.9941	0.9947	4650	5160	3420	17,410
Henan–Shanghai	998	0.9924	0.9930	1270	1180	470	470
Henan–Shanxi	577	0.9905	0.9906	1710	1280	7170	25,400
Henan–Sichuan	1,353	0.9525	0.9414	1760	5000	960	1,030
Henan–Tianjin	831	0.9854	0.9863	410	200	540	1,090
Henan–Tibet	3,375	0.0648	0.0867		250		30
Henan–Xinjiang	3,079	0.4182	0.4167	340	970	2740	4,250
Henan–Yunnan	2,489	0.6776	0.6775	360	1250	650	770
Henan–Zhejiang	1,124	0.9885	0.9793	2650	2350	190	230
Hubei–Hunan	358	0.9422	0.9431	2630	4690	1570	1,350
Hubei–Inner Mongolia	1,898	0.7940	0.7977	100	350	420	950
Hubei–Jiangsu	1,231	0.9591	0.9604	560	1070	560	750
Hubei–Jiangxi	391	0.9575	0.9582	1530	2040	490	1,460
Hubei–Jilin	2,277	0.9106	0.9224	180	430	170	540
Hubei–Liaoning	1,972	0.8416	0.8504	340	480	410	610
Hubei–Ningxia	1,893	0.6567	0.6511	40	90	240	330
Hubei–Qinghai	1,939	0.5428	0.5329	40	180	100	1,430
Hubei–Shaanxi	1,047	0.9584	0.9591	570	1690	3020	10,380
Hubei–Shandong	1,202	0.9585	0.9590	1690	2710	1220	3,910
Hubei–Shanghai	1,230	0.9593	0.9625	220	180	270	250
Hubei–Shanxi	1,179	0.9586	0.9589	610	620	7950	20,010
Hubei–Sichuan	1,737	0.9543	0.9439	1680	4160	2430	3,950
Hubei–Tianjin	1,367	0.9591	0.9601	290	230	180	230
Hubei–Tibet	3,911	0.0628	0.0841		70		
Hubei–Xinjiang	3,615	0.4092	0.4083	130	680	850	950
Hubei–Yunnan	1,953	0.6718	0.6718	640	1000	150	410
Hubei–Zhejiang	1,029	0.9602	0.9669	660	980	220	210
Hunan-Inner Mongolia	2,256	0.7943	0.7977	70	70	430	1,360
Hunan–Jiangsu	1,200	0.9017	0.9040	470	550	530	1,030
Hunan–Jiangxi	418	0.8999	0.9017	2020	3650	1580	5,830
Hunan–Jilin	2,635	0.9011	0.9023	160	50	170	1,180
Hunan–Liaoning	2,330	0.8419	0.8504	360	160	370	520
Hunan–Ningxia	2,251	0.6570	0.6512	50	50	70	240
Hunan–Qinghai	2,297	0.5431	0.5330	30	30	190	600
Hunan–Shaanxi	1,405	0.9009	0.9025	200	400	870	2,680
Hunan–Shandong	1,560	0.9011	0.9024	320	940	840	1,700
Hunan–Shanghai	1,189	0.9021	0.9064	730	530	400	540
Hunan–Shanxi	1,537	0.9011	0.9023	180	280	2320	8,490
Hunan–Sichuan	1,923	0.9032	0.9052	540	1950	820	1,670
Hunan–Tianjin	1,725	0.9020	0.9039	160	100	130	160
Hunan–Tibet	4,273	0.0635	0.0843		10		20
Hunan–Xinjiang	3,973	0.4097	0.4084	120	230	120	580
Hunan–Yunnan	1,595	0.6997	0.7016	530	680	390	1,220

(Continued)

(Continued)

Province–Province	Distance (km)	Ethnic Links		Export (1000 tons)		Import (1000 tons)	
		2000	2010	2000	2010	2000	2010
Hunan–Zhejiang	9,98	0.9029	0.9141	1470	1940	1160	310
Inner Mongolia–Jiangsu	1,827	0.7945	0.7983	1490	1810	220	280
Inner Mongolia–Jiangxi	2,674	0.7928	0.7964	200	670	20	30
Inner Mongolia–Jilin	1,713	0.8258	0.8246	5280	29560	1480	1,830
Inner Mongolia–Liaoning	1,408	0.8371	0.8359	10740	70060	4790	4,850
Inner Mongolia–Ningxia	676	0.6690	0.6634	1120	1480	720	890
Inner Mongolia–Qinghai	1,360	0.5696	0.5593	220	280	160	1,790
Inner Mongolia–Shaanxi	1,291	0.7967	0.8004	530	1190	50	220
Inner Mongolia–Shandong	1,164	0.7986	0.8028	3560	4360	820	1,740
Inner Mongolia–Shanghai	2,130	0.7971	0.8021	710	1330	100	180
Inner Mongolia–Shanxi	640	0.7949	0.7980	1610	1360	2390	2,670
Inner Mongolia–Sichuan	2,133	0.7944	0.7982	560	1770	140	190
Inner Mongolia–Tianjin	801	0.8092	0.8141	8520	10270	700	4,620
Inner Mongolia–Tibet	3,332	0.0650	0.0871		20		
Inner Mongolia–Xinjiang	3,035	0.4253	0.4233	160	530	400	720
Inner Mongolia–Yunnan	3,233	0.6764	0.6768	60	150	100	260
Inner Mongolia–Zhejiang	2,256	0.7929	0.7974	800	1640	120	80
Jiangsu–Jiangxi	838	0.9976	0.9965	670	2630	620	310
Jiangsu–Jilin	2,035	0.9111	0.9229	460	310	650	520
Jiangsu–Liaoning	1,730	0.8421	0.8509	760	370	1420	480
Jiangsu–Ningxia	2,052	0.6572	0.6517	90	320	200	350
Jiangsu–Qinghai	2,095	0.5433	0.5335	400	2000	400	1,760
Jiangsu–Shaanxi	1,205	0.9975	0.9976	580	3100	3140	6,740
Jiangsu–Shandong	663	0.9957	0.9952	1360	2510	10380	6,070
Jiangsu–Shanghai	303	0.9971	0.9928	2360	710	360	170
Jiangsu–Shanxi	1,195	0.9992	0.9976	360	6560	18500	27,880
Jiangsu–Sichuan	2,048	0.9528	0.9427	1020	2030	1220	950
Jiangsu–Tianjin	1,023	0.9760	0.9784	320	130	380	90
Jiangsu–Tibet	4,072	0.0635	0.0847		50		
Jiangsu–Xinjiang	3,774	0.4090	0.4086	470	1760	800	2,500
Jiangsu–Yunnan	2,693	0.6691	0.6704	500	810	440	800
Jiangsu–Zhejiang	429	0.9933	0.9817	2680	1560	250	300
Jiangxi–Jilin	2,456	0.9095	0.9212	60	60	210	1,690
Jiangxi–Liaoning	2,151	0.8404	0.8491	170	200	260	160
Jiangxi–Ningxia	2,258	0.6555	0.6497	10	30	50	40
Jiangxi–Qinghai	2,304	0.5414	0.5315	10	20	20	250
Jiangxi–Shaanxi	1,412	0.9959	0.9958	60	80	560	3,500
Jiangxi–Shandong	1,137	0.9940	0.9933	250	440	1400	2,600
Jiangxi–Shanghai	837	0.9949	0.9895	970	820	660	490
Jiangxi–Shanxi	1,944	0.9979	0.9974	40	100	1870	4,550
Jiangxi–Sichuan	2,239	0.9511	0.9402	340	800	220	460
Jiangxi–Tianjin	1,444	0.9741	0.9758	30	70	180	60
Jiangxi–Tibet	4,101	0.0616	0.0828		10		10
Jiangxi–Xinjiang	4,391	0.4069	0.4061	50	150	80	290
Jiangxi–Yunnan	1,911	0.6669	0.6675	120	350	540	860
Jiangxi–Zhejiang	636	0.9943	0.9812	4120	4900	2370	7,210
Jilin–Liaoning	305	0.8939	0.8953	16250	23800	8540	15,550
Jilin–Ningxia	2,389	0.6645	0.6583	10	50	30	140
Jilin–Qinghai	3,144	0.5536	0.5418	30	70	10	100
Jilin–Shaanxi	2,211	0.9134	0.9251	130	270	50	90

(Continued)

(Continued)

Province–Province	Distance (km)	Ethnic Links		Export (1000 tons)		Import (1000 tons)	
		2000	2010	2000	2010	2000	2010
Jilin–Shandong	1,373	0.9145	0.9264	1590	930	1620	1,540
Jilin–Shanghai	2,335	0.9137	0.9268	510	250	300	240
Jilin–Shanxi	1,560	0.9115	0.9229	280	300	830	1,440
Jilin–Sichuan	3,094	0.9110	0.9227	650	1650	150	160
Jilin–Tianjin	1,012	0.9217	0.9346	780	410	380	410
Jilin–Tibet	5,163	0.0649	0.0867				
Jilin–Xinjiang	4,820	0.4186	0.4159	130	120	50	110
Jilin–Yunnan	4,230	0.6719	0.6717	170	690	90	340
Jilin–Zhejiang	2,464	0.9095	0.9219	740	1400	220	100
Liaoning–Ningxia	2,084	0.6663	0.6598	110	150	940	1,460
Liaoning–Qinghai	2,839	0.5650	0.5530	180	130	90	150
Liaoning–Shaanxi	1,906	0.8443	0.8531	390	890	230	160
Liaoning–Shandong	1,067	0.8462	0.8555	2320	2110	2350	2,260
Liaoning–Shanghai	2,033	0.8447	0.8548	540	190	410	130
Liaoning–Shanxi	1,255	0.8425	0.8507	830	1080	11620	17,070
Liaoning–Sichuan	2,789	0.8419	0.8507	850	810	410	350
Liaoning–Tianjin	707	0.8543	0.8639	3080	2720	610	530
Liaoning–Tibet	4,901	0.0649	0.0869		10		
Liaoning–Xinjiang	4,515	0.4238	0.4208	200	330	260	400
Liaoning–Yunnan	3,925	0.6736	0.6732	170	240	190	250
Liaoning–Zhejiang	2,159	0.8405	0.8499	690	310	400	170
Ningxia–Qinghai	684	0.7002	0.6824	410	550	50	240
Ningxia–Shaanxi	846	0.6594	0.6535	1430	640	80	530
Ningxia–Shandong	1,840	0.6610	0.6553	120	630	190	800
Ningxia–Shanghai	2,355	0.6596	0.6548	300	370	50	70
Ningxia–Shanxi	1,316	0.6575	0.6511	80	240	190	280
Ningxia–Sichuan	1,342	0.6570	0.6515	740	5450	220	240
Ningxia–Tianjin	1,480	0.6776	0.6685	1450	1130	240	1,010
Ningxia–Tibet	2,656	0.0650	0.0874				
Ningxia–Xinjiang	2,088	0.4544	0.4533	230	1450	240	1,210
Ningxia–Yunnan	2,442	0.6712	0.6655	50	70	50	290
Ningxia–Zhejiang	2,481	0.6556	0.6507	70	480	50	20
Qinghai–Shaanxi	892	0.5453	0.5353	390	740	230	380
Qinghai–Shandong	2,068	0.5470	0.5371	220	1190	160	1,230
Qinghai–Shanghai	2,401	0.5458	0.5366	80	430	30	70
Qinghai–Shanxi	1,543	0.5435	0.5328	210	970	350	730
Qinghai–Sichuan	1,388	0.5585	0.5518	360	1120	270	210
Qinghai–Tianjin	2,235	0.5616	0.5483	150	210	130	140
Qinghai–Tibet	1,972	0.2906	0.3323		1010		50
Qinghai–Xinjiang	2,108	0.4626	0.4610	60	90	420	1,010
Qinghai–Yunnan	2,488	0.5603	0.5504	30	190	30	350
Qinghai–Zhejiang	2,527	0.5417	0.5326	80	550	50	60
Shaanxi–Shandong	1,177	0.9978	0.9972	890	9480	670	3,320
Shaanxi–Shanghai	1,509	0.9982	0.9927	470	520	450	420
Shaanxi–Shanxi	651	0.9979	0.9975	510	1500	1390	2,510
Shaanxi–Sichuan	842	0.9521	0.9414	2650	6540	1600	950
Shaanxi–Tianjin	1,301	0.9779	0.9794	340	220	310	460
Shaanxi–Tibet	2,964	0.0647	0.0865		70		10
Shaanxi–Xinjiang	2,468	0.4107	0.4099	260	460	1100	2,310
Shaanxi–Yunnan	1,942	0.6706	0.6710	430	1060	620	750

(Continued)

(Continued)

Province–Province	Distance (km)	Ethnic Links		Export (1000 tons)		Import (1000 tons)	
		2000	2010	2000	2010	2000	2010
Shaanxi–Zhejiang	1,635	0.9923	0.9795	570	1480	190	150
Shandong–Shanghai	966	0.9979	0.9934	1980	670	390	290
Shandong–Shanxi	532	0.9960	0.9950	2850	27790	36030	92,070
Shandong–Sichuan	2,019	0.9523	0.9412	800	2240	820	1,260
Shandong–Tianjin	360	0.9798	0.9819	970	780	680	780
Shandong–Tibet	3,925	0.0648	0.0868		60		
Shandong–Xinjiang	3,745	0.4124	0.4117	420	1840	770	2,770
Shandong–Yunnan	3,119	0.6724	0.6729	320	830	500	1,400
Shandong–Zhejiang	1,092	0.9925	0.9797	6500	4880	390	140
Shanghai–Shanxi	1,498	0.9968	0.9907	140	140	2120	2,010
Shanghai–Sichuan	2,351	0.9530	0.9442	630	1250	430	760
Shanghai–Tianjin	1,326	0.9789	0.9827	220	280	230	30
Shanghai–Tibet	4,373	0.0652	0.0867		10		
Shanghai–Xinjiang	4,077	0.4116	0.4120	350	550	220	580
Shanghai–Yunnan	3,069	0.6711	0.6743	270	410	280	660
Shanghai–Zhejiang	201	0.9934	0.9847	780	510	1320	930
Shanxi–Sichuan	1,493	0.9523	0.9411	830	2930	350	300
Shanxi–Tianjin	650	0.9761	0.9770	34980	27400	1200	3,870
Shanxi–Tibet	3,515	0.0633	0.0842		30		
Shanxi–Xinjiang	3,219	0.4089	0.4075	170	1140	530	720
Shanxi–Yunnan	2,593	0.6688	0.6687	70	210	410	310
Shanxi–Zhejiang	1,624	0.9925	0.9794	4370	3280	120	140
Sichuan–Tianjin	2,185	0.9531	0.9426	420	450	350	760
Sichuan–Tibet	3,360	0.0786	0.1030		190		100
Sichuan–Xinjiang	3,026	0.4094	0.4088	470	570	1660	2,960
Sichuan–Yunnan	1,100	0.6993	0.7074	2730	5410	2700	7,660
Sichuan–Zhejiang	2,552	0.9529	0.9445	700	1030	440	800
Tianjin–Tibet	4,174	0.0652	0.0874		30		
Tianjin–Xinjiang	3,911	0.4270	0.4230	690	900	1020	1,370
Tianjin–Yunnan	3,320	0.6831	0.6824	110	250	190	130
Tianjin–Zhejiang	1,452	0.9749	0.9777	210	40	110	60
Tibet–Xinjiang	4,080	0.0659	0.0896				30
Tibet–Yunnan	4,460	0.0691	0.0910				
Tibet–Zhejiang	4,308	0.0620	0.0839				40
Xinjiang–Yunnan	4,126	0.4235	0.4225	410	1060	190	550
Xinjiang–Zhejiang	4,065	0.4083	0.4081	430	1880	320	760
Yunnan–Zhejiang	2,868	0.6691	0.6780	590	830	350	570

Note: Blank space indicates that data are not available.

Annex 4.3. Notes to the regressions

Equations 4.2 to 4.3 can be estimated by using standard statistical techniques. If the equations include variables that may be strongly correlated with each other, then additional regressions should be pursued by excluding the variables that are found to have the potential impacts of multicollinearity. Because this chapter uses cross-sectional data, it is also necessary to conduct tests for heteroscedasticity even though taking logs of the dependent and explanatory variables can be quite effective at reducing heteroscedasticity and usually does not have adverse affects on interpretation or specification. More specifically, ordinary least squares (OLS)–estimated coefficients are biased, so weighed least squares (WLS) estimation should be used to provide more efficient results in terms of smaller coefficient standard errors (Greene, 2002, p. 499). After each OLS run, heteroscedasticity tests are performed for each individual regression model. If heteroscedasticity is significant, WLS estimation should be performed to correct this problem.

To overcome the problems with multicollinearity, we have omitted a number of ethnic groups from our regressions. These include the Buyi, Maonan, Mulao, Naxi, and Salar in Table 4.4a; the Blang, Maonan, Mulao, and Salar in Table 4.4b; the Han, Mulao, Naxi, Salar, and Shui in Table 4.6a; and the Han, Mulao, Salar, and Tu in Table 4.6b. The general rule of thumb is that whereas VIF (variance inflation factor) values exceeding 4 warrant further investigation, VIFs exceeding 10 are signs of serious multicollinearity requiring correction (Simon, 2004).

In weaker models, especially in those that are not supported by large sets of data, VIFs above 2.5 may also merit further investigation (Berry and Feldman, 1985, p. 49; Arceneaux and Huber, 2007). In this chapter, we have rerun all the regressions by omitting the explanatory variables with VIFs exceeding 4 (the estimated results are not reported here). But we have found that the estimated results are quite stable after the variables with VIFs exceeding 10 (for Tables 4.4a, 4.4b, and 4.6a) or 9 (for Table 4.6b) are omitted from the regressions. Thus, even though the variables with VIFs exceeding 4 are included, the estimated coefficients reported in this chapter are not affected by multicollinearity.

In the Sixth National Population Census, conducted on November 1, 2010, China adopted a different method form than that used in the Fifth National Population Census in 2000. For example, "floating" populations were not counted in 2000 (they had to be counted in their original, permanent residences); in 2010, however, these populations were counted if they had already resided in the current residences for more than 6 months. Because these "floating" populations may sometimes play more important roles in interprovincial marketing and trade than permanent residents, 2000's estimated results would be less convincing than 2010's.

The data on interprovincial trade (which is the sum of export and import) are only represented by those of the freight exchange via national railways. Note that China has both national and local and privately owned railways. It should also be noted that interprovincial freight exchange via national railways only accounts for a portion of the whole interprovincial freight exchange, especially in China's nearby provinces, where railway is a less economical means of transportation than highway. In addition, the 2000 data on interprovincial trade do not include those of Hainan and Tibet, China's two provincial economies that are homes to the Tibetan and the Li ethnic groups, respectively. Accordingly, this could affect the quality of estimated coefficients on these two ethnic groups.

Going back to Xinjiang: Analytic narrative

5

A bird's-eye view of Xinjiang

International connections

Compared with other frontier Chinese provinces, Xinjiang has much more complicated boundary and external conditions. Specifically, Xinjiang shares land borders with Afghanistan, Tajikistan, Pakistan, and India on the southwest; Kyrgyzstan on the west; Kazakhstan on the northwest; Russia on the north; and Mongolia on the northeast. Most of these land boundaries are set along the water-parting of high-elevation mountains (including the Altai, Tianshan, Pamirs, Karakoram range, and Himalayas) and at uninhabited places that are not suitable for cross-border communication and transportation.

In May 1985, the construction of the 500-km long Northern Xinjiang Railway was announced. This Railway connects the West Urumqi Station with the Alashankou (i.e., the Ala Pass) Station on the China–Kazakhstan boundary (Figure 5.1). And it was completed 5 years later in September 1990. This frontier rail line not only makes it easier for Xinjiang to conduct cross-border trade with central Asian economies but it also connects the Trans-Eurasian Continental Railway, which extends from Rotterdam (The Netherlands) on the North Sea to Lianyungang (Jiangsu province, China) on the East China Sea. The second frontier railway opened in 2009 to supplement rail transport capacity on the Northern Xinjiang Railway between Urumqi and Jinghe. From Jinghe, the Jinghe-Yining-Horgos Railway heads southwest into the Ili River Valley to Yining, Huocheng, and Horgos, a second rail border crossing with Kazakhstan.

China and Pakistan have discussed several times the establishment of a joint taskforce to evaluate the feasibility of the Gwadar-Khunjerab-Kashgar rail line, which starts at Gwadar, Pakistan and ends at Kashgar in southern Xinjiang. The project will route Chinese goods destined for the Middle East and other global destinations through the Gwadar port. It will save the Chinese half of their current voyage time and secure their oil supplies and commercial routes. The distance from Dubai to Shanghai via the Indian Ocean is about 15,000 km; however, the distance from Dubai to Kashgar via the Gwadar port is less than a half of that via the Indian Ocean. The implementation of the Gwadar-Khunjerab-Kashgar rail network will help China secure oil supply and commercial routes on the Indian Ocean, furthering its plans to secure yet another strategic energy and trade corridor. The project is

Figure 5.1 The railway systems of western China.
Source: Author.

expected to provide a major boost to the Sino–Pakistani economic ties.[1] The actual cost for this project is yet to be determined, but the 2005 estimates showed it at more than US$10 billion (Rana, 2013, p. 1). The successful implementation of this transnational rail line does not depend on China's resolve to finance it; the social stability in Xinjiang matters the most.

There have been worries in India that the cross-border rail connectivity will make Nepal and Bangladesh—India's traditional partners—come closer to China. In addition, India also fears that China now has the capability to deploy and sustain more than half a million troops for more than a month on the Line of Actual Control (LAC) in case of a high threat scenario with India (Gupta, May 11, 2011). The China–Indian relations have been shadowed by the territorial disputes in Jammu and Kashmir. India lays claim to vast territories of land that is in the possession of China. For a long time, the demarcation of China's land boundaries with

[1] At present, there is only one highway connecting China and Pakistan, which, because of the harsh climate, only opens for 6 months (i.e., from April 15 to October 15) each year, with the annual capacities of 50,000 tons of goods and of 50,000 person-times of passengers (Xia, 2010, p. 1).

India has been the subject of political argument. The whole disputed area includes Aksai Chin (which is currently under the administration of Xinjiang Uygur autonomous region) and some small pieces of land (which is currently under the administration of Tibet autonomous region). India, however, claims the area as part of Ladakh district of the Indian state of Jammu and Kashmir. In 1962, there was a short border war between China and India. The war lasted from October 20 to November 22. It ended with a Chinese victory and the birth of the LAC that India never accepts (Guo, 2012, p. 65).

In brief, Xinjiang has the longest international land boundaries than any other provincial administrations in China. And the external influences of the international adjacencies on Xinjiang have been more obvious than those on any other frontier regions in China. (See Table 5.1 for a brief comparison of international and boundary conditions between Xinjiang and Tibet.) For example, during the past decades, even though many other domestic issues have played some roles in Xinjiang's social unrest (as shown in Chapter 3), it seems that the fact that Xinjiang's geographical proximity to Afghanistan and Pakistan is also a critical factor. The most illustrating case is the East Turkestan Islamic Movement (ETIM). The ETIM, which

Table 5.1 Boundary and external conditions: Xinjiang and Tibet

Geopolitical indicator	Xinjiang	Tibet
Land area (sq km)	1,660,000	1,228,400
Length of international land borders (km)	6,012	3,800
Per capita GDP in PPP	8,300*	5,600**
Adjacent countries (per capita GDP in PPP)	Afghanistan (1,079), Kazakhstan (15,701), Kyrgyzstan (2,626), India (4,148), Mongolia (4,889), Pakistan (2,559), Russia (17,553), and Tajikistan (2,561)	Bhutan (5,449), India (4,148), Myanmar (1,300), and Nepal (1,396)
Adjacent Chinese provinces	Gansu, Qinghai, and Tibet	Qinghai, Sichuan, Xinjiang and Yunnan
Political status:		
(1) Pre-PRC era	Province	Independent kingdom[†]
(2) PRC era	Autonomous region	Autonomous region
Political goal(s) of elite-in-exile	Independent from China	Full political autonomy[†]; independent from China[‡]

*Estimated by author. *GDP*, Gross domestic product; *PPP*, purchasing power parity; *PRC*, People's Republic of China.
**Tibet was unilaterally proclaimed as an independent state from 1913 to 1951, but this was not recognized by Beijing or a portion of the Tibetans.
[†]It is claimed by the Dalai Lama (1996, pp. 47–51).
[‡]It is claimed by the Tibetan Youth Congress (2009).
Sources: Guo (2013b, p. 200) for the data on the length of international land borders and Heston et al. (2012) for the data on per capita GDP in PPP (except for those that are cited otherwise).

was found in 1997, is believed to organize various terrorist attacks in southern Xinjiang near the border with Afghanistan and Pakistan.[2] On September 11, 2002, the ETIM was at the United Nations Security Council list of entities associated with Al-Qaeda and the Taliban.

In terms of religion, Xinjiang and its neighboring countries are not homogeneous. Except a few Mongols and Tibetans, who are Buddhists, most of the other non-Han ethnic groups (e.g., Uyghur, Kazakh, Hui-Chinese, and Kirgiz) in Xinjiang are Muslims. Furthermore, Xinjiang's neighboring countries have followed at least three different—and sometimes incompatible—religious beliefs:

- Buddhism (adopted in northern India and Mongolia)
- Islam (adopted in Afghanistan, part of Kazakhstan, part of Kyrgyzstan, Pakistan, and Tajikistan)
- Eastern Orthodox (adopted in part of Kazakhstan, part of Kyrgyzstan, and Russia)

When different religions meet together, it does not always indicate a conflict. However, conflict and disagreement do occur more frequently in religious heterogeneous places (e.g., Xinjiang) than in religious homogeneous places (e.g., Tibet). This is discussed in more detail later in this chapter.

Interprovincial linkages

The interprovincial boundaries of Xinjiang are much simpler than their international boundaries. Xinjiang Uyghur autonomous region shares borders with three Chinese provincial administrations (Gansu, Qinghai, and Tibet). Without good reason, interprovincial boundaries are usually more geographically accessible and less politically sensitive than international boundaries. As a result, there are always, *ceteris paribus*, strong interprovincial vis-à-vis international socioeconomic links in the contemporary world. Xinjiang has no exceptions.

Xinjiang is linked to the rest of China by a single railway, the Lanzhou-Xinjiang (or Lanxin in Chinese for short) Railway, which runs from Urumqi to Lanzhou through the Hexi Corridor in Gansu province. First constructed in 1952, and as the only railway system connecting Xinjiang with inland Chinese provinces, the Lanzhou-Xinjiang Railway is near 2,000 km long, running from Lanzhou city in the east to Urumqi city in the west. The double-tracking railway system was constructed by the early 1990s, and the electrification of the whole line was completed by the end of 2012. All of this has enabled the transport capacity of the railway to increase from 12 million tons in 1992 up to 150 million tons (Jia, January 1, 2013).

On November 4, 2009, the construction work of the Lanzhou-Urumqi High-Speed Railway (also known as the Lanzhou-Xinjiang Passenger Railway or the Second Lanxin Railway) began. Unlike the existing Lanxin railway, which runs entirely in Gansu and Xinjiang, the new high-speed (350 km/hr) rail will be routed from Lanzhou to Xining (Qinghai province) before heading northwest across the Qilian Mountains into the Hexi Corridor (see Figure 5.1). The rail tracks in the

[2] See Chapter 3 for details.

section near Qilianshan Tunnel is at 3,858 m above sea level, making it the highest high-speed rail track in the world.[3] After its completion on December 26, 2014 an overnight sleeper train has connected Beijing to Urumqi in less than 12 hours.

On September 7, 2004, the Dunhuang Railway was announced and went into operation on August 5, 2006. This 170-km long railway starts at the Liugou Station of the Lanzhou-Xinjiang Railway and ends at the city of Dunhuang, Gansu province. On October 20, 2012, the construction of the 500-km Golmud-Dunhuang Railway line was announced. This single-track electrified rail line will run from Dunhuang (in Gansu province) to the Yinmaxia Station on the Qinghai–Tibet Railway north of Golmud. The project is expected to take 5 years and, after completion, will allow a fairly direct connection between Tibet and other Chinese provinces (especially Gansu and Xinjiang). In the fall of 2011, the Golmud-Korla Railway was announced. This railway is 1,182 km long and runs across the northwest Qinghai and via Ruoqiang and Weili counties of Bayingolin Mongol autonomous prefecture of Xinjiang. After its completion in 2016, the railway will open a second rail line linking Xinjiang the inland China (see Figure 5.1).

Since the 1980s, China has implemented a more flexible policy to ease interprovincial migration. As a result, interprovincial labor flows have been increased. It is noteworthy that these flows have also been conducted by people coming from the inland, ethnic-minority areas and moving into the coastal, Han-majority areas. Consequently, China's interprovincial ethnic networks have been enhanced. Using the data released by China's Fifth and Sixth National Population Censuses (which were conducted on November 1, 2000 and 2010, respectively), the interprovincial flows of Uyghurs (the ethnic majority of Xinjiang) are worthy of attention.

The Uyghurs have been found in all of China's 31 provinces, and they have stronger interprovincial links in 2010 and than 2000. Specifically, Xinjiang Uyghur autonomous region has the largest Uyghur links with the following provincial administrations (represented by the share of Uyghur population):

(i) Beijing (0.04 percent in 2010, up from 0.02 percent in 2000)
(ii) Shanghai (0.02 percent in 2010, up from 0.01 percent in 2000)
(iii) Tianjin (0.02 percent in 2010, up from 0.01 percent in 2000)
(iv) Hunan (0.01 percent in both 2010 and 2000)
(v) Zhejiang (0.01 percent in 2010, up from 0.00 percent in 2000)
(vi) Ningxia (0.01 percent in both 2010 and 2000)
(vii) Gansu (0.01 percent in both 2010 and 2000)
(viii) Tibet (0.01 percent in 2010, up from 0.00 percent in 2000)
(ix) Guangdong (0.01 percent in 2010, up from 0.00 percent in 2000)
(x) Jiangsu (0.01 percent in 2010, up from 0.00 percent in 2000)[4]

[3] Source: http://www.chinadaily.com.cn/dfpd/gansu/2010-10-01/content_954064.html. Accessed on May 5, 2012.

[4] Calculated by author based on the Fifth (2000) and the Sixth (2010) National Population Censuses of the PRC.

Internal economic performance

General situation[5]

More than 40 percent of Xinjiang's total area is considered suitable for agriculture, forestry, and animal husbandry. Of this, there are some 48 million ha of natural grassland for grazing, 9 million ha available for reclamation, more than 4 million ha under cultivation, and 666,700 ha of human-made pastures. The region is one of the country's five major grazing areas. In addition, there are some 4.8 million ha of land available for forestry, including 1.5 million ha in production with reserves of some 250 million cubic meters of timber.

Among the 122 minerals that have been discovered in Xinjiang, several are the largest reserves nationwide. These include beryllium, muscovite, natron saltpeter, pottery clay, and serpentine. Known reserves of iron ore are put at 730 million tons, and those for salt are 318 million tons, mirabilite 170 million tons, and natron saltpeter more than 2 million tons. With its deposits of more than 70 nonmetallic minerals, the region is well known for its muscovite, gemstones, asbestos, and Hotan (Hetian) jade. In addition, estimates put its coal reserves at more than one third of the national total. Petroleum and natural gas reserves are estimated at 30 billion tons and account for more than 25 percent of the national total. Xinjiang is noted for producing salt, soda, borax, gold, jade, and coal. It is also known for its fruits and produce, including grapes, melons, pears, cotton, wheat, silk, walnuts, and sheep.

Thanks to its abundant reserves of coal, crude oil, and natural gas on the one hand and China's Western Development Policy introduced by the State Council on the other, Xinjiang has achieved rapid economic development during the past decade. Its gross regional product (GRP) doubled between 2004 and 2010. The oil and gas extraction industry in Aksu and Karamay is booming, with the West–East Gas Pipeline connecting to Shanghai. The oil and petrochemical sector accounts for 60 percent of the local economy.

The region has recently become one of the most important energy producers in China. Although the discovery of natural resources has certainly been a boost for the province, these remain scattered about an uninhabited and undeveloped landscape. Development in the areas of production and transportation will be necessary to maximize the region's economic growth. In 2009, Xinjiang produced more natural gas than any other province, the fourth most crude oil in China, and a large amount of coal. It also has a thriving agriculture sector.

As of 2010, compared with other provinces, Xinjiang has relatively advantages in such sectors as "agriculture, forestry, animal husbandry and fishery," "mining" and "public management and social organization," but is relatively weak in "manufacturing," "services to households and other services," and "information transmission, computer service and software."[6] Xinjiang's well-developed industrial

[5] This subsection is an excerpt of Guo (2013a, pp. 320–324).
[6] Note that all the sectors defined here are according to China's official categories.

infrastructure focuses on a variety of industries, such as raw and refined oil, iron and steel, metallurgy, machinery, chemicals, and power generation. The region's natural resources include coal, oil, iron, manganese, chromium, lead, molybdenum, zinc, beryllium, lithium, niobium, tantalum, cesium, white mica, asbestos, and crystal. Oil and petrochemicals, food and beverages, textiles, metallurgy, building materials, and electric power are the region's pillar industries of Xinjiang.

Because of Xinjiang's sparse population and underdeveloped transport network, foreign direct investment (FDI) remains relatively low. However, in recent years, Xinjiang's FDI has increased dramatically. The top three sectors that use the most foreign capital are manufacturing, mining, and quarrying and the production and distribution of electricity, gas, and water. Denmark has injected the most FDI into the region. Other key sources are Australia, Hong Kong, and Singapore.

Comparing Xinjiang with Tibet

Located at the westernmost end of China, both Xinjiang and Tibet have large, sparsely populated areas. In terms of the United Nations Development Program's Human Development Index, Tibet is ranked the lowest among China's 31 provinces (United Nations Development Program, 2010). Tibet has had a much higher illiterate rate of population than any other Chinese provinces. For example, the proportion of ethnic Tibetans older than age 15 years in the Tibetan autonomous region recorded as illiterate or semiliterate in the 1990 census was as high as 72.8 percent compared with China's national average of 22.8 percent (Ma, 1996, p. 51). In 2000, its illiterate rate of population age 15 years or older was 32.5 percent, which is much higher than that of Xinjiang (5.56 percent); in 2010, the ratio has reduced to 24.42 percent, but it is still higher than that of Xinjiang (2.36 percent) (Table 5.2).

Ever since the initiation of China's opening up and reform drive in 1979, Xinjiang's economy has been changed dramatically. As of 2010, industry leads with a contribution of 47.70 percent to the GRP. The service sector also makes a substantial contribution at 32.50 percent; agriculture contributes the remaining 19.80 percent (see Table 2.3 in Chapter 2). In Tibet, industry is playing an increasingly important role in the economy, although the service sector has still been the major economic player over the past few decades (see Table 3.1 in Chapter 3). Industrial products such as minerals, medicine, Qingke barley wine, carpets, and building materials are renowned globally. Traditional Tibetan medicine, in particular, boasts a long history in Tibet. Although Tibet could be a large producer of natural resources and raw materials, there have been few advances in these areas. The focus is on expanding secondary industries, in particular energy, mining, and new building materials. Because of limited arable land, the primary occupation of the Tibetan Plateau is raising livestock, such as sheep, cattle, goats, camels, yaks, dzo, and horses. The main crops grown are barley, wheat, buckwheat, rye, potatoes, and assorted fruits and vegetables.

From 2000 to 2010, Tibet's net income level of rural residents has increased at a much faster rate than its income level of urban residents. For example, in 2000, the urban-to-rural income ratio of Tibet was as high as 5.58, which was much higher than

Table 5.2 **Socioeconomic performances: Xinjiang versus Tibet***

Indicator	Year	(1) Xinjiang	(2) XPCC	(3) Xinjiang excl. XPCC	(4) Tibet	(5) = (3) ÷ (4)
Population (million persons)	2000	19.25	2.43	16.82	2.62	6.42
	2010	21.85	2.57	19.28	3.01	6.41
Ratio of urban population (%)	2000	33.8	41.9	31.09	18.9	1.75
	2010	42.2	47.1	41.55	28.2	1.47
Population density (persons/sq km)	2000	11.59	35.2	10.48	2.13	4.92
	2010	13.16	37.2	12.03	2.45	4.91
Illiterate rate of population (%)	2000	5.56	2	6.07	32.5	0.19
	2010	2.36	1.08	2.53	24.42	0.10
Per capita GRP (yuan)	2000	7,372	4,076	7,848	4,484	1.75
	2010	25,057	23,416	25,276	16,861	1.50
Per capita income of urban residents (yuan)	2000	5,645			7,426	
	2010	13,644	14,391	13,531	14,980	0.90
Per capita income of rural residents (yuan)	2000	1,618			1,330	
	2010	4,643	9,169	4,097	4,138	0.99
Urban/rural income ratio	2000	3.49			5.58	
	2010	2.94	1.57	3.30	3.62	0.91
Per capita GRP ratio of top to bottom prefecture	2000	25.62			3.76	
	2010	23.43			1.63	

GRP, Gross regional product; *XPCC*, Xinjiang Production and Construction Corps.
*All monetary values are measured at current prices.
Source: Calculated by author based on Xinjiang Bureau of Statistics (2001 and 2011), Tibet Bureau of Statistics (2001 and 2011), and XPCC (2001 and 2011).

that of Xinjiang (3.49). 10 ten years, in 2010, Tibet had dramatically reduced its urban-to-rural income ratio to 3.62, which is much close to that of Xinjiang (see Table 5.2). A simple comparison of the income levels between Xinjiang and Tibet also reveals that the people's living conditions in Tibet have been improved more significantly than those in Xinjiang during the period from 2000 to 2010, especially in urban areas. For example, Xinjiang's per capita GRP was 1.75 and 1.50 times that of Tibet in 2000 and 2010, respectively. However, in 2010, its per capita incomes of urban and rural residents have been only 90 and 99 percent those of Tibet, respectively (see Table 5.2).

When referring to Xinjiang's regional (especially its rural area) economic development, one must pay attention to the Xinjiang Production and Construction Crops (XPCC) (see Chapter 2). In general, the XPCC, equipped with the well-educated staff and with strong support from the Chinese central government, has much higher economic growth rate than the rest of Xinjiang (Shao, April 3, 2012). However, after excluding the XPCC, the rest of Xinjiang has made less social and economic progress than Xinjiang as a whole. For example, because the rural residents of the

XPCC have a much higher income level than the other rural residents of Xinjiang, the inclusion of the XPCC's agricultural areas into Xinjiang's rural areas has automatically increased the net income of rural residents and therefore reduced the urban-to-rural income ratio in Xinjiang.

Last but not least, Xinjiang and Tibet are different from each other in terms of spatial economic disparity. Tibet's economy is a rather convergent among its regions. And its interregional gap of per capita GRP, represented by the ratio of the richest region's per capita GRP to the poorest one, has reduced from 3.76 to 1.63 from 2000 to 2010. Given China's great spatial economic disparities,[7] Tibet can be treated as an exception. By way of contrast, Xinjiang has much greater spatial economic disparities than Tibet and any other inland Chinese provinces as well. In 2000, the per capita GRP of the richest region (i.e., Karamay Municipality) was 25.62 times that of the poorest region (i.e., Ili prefecture). In 2010, this ratio was slightly reduced to 23.43 times but still much higher than another other places in China.

External economic performance

An export–import puzzle

China's border development has mainly benefited from its "open-door" policy and rapprochement with the neighboring countries since the mid-1980s. In 1984, the Chinese government promulgated the "Provisional Regulations for the Management of 'Small-volume' Border Trade" and opened up hundreds of frontier cities and towns. Inspired by Deng Xiaoping's Southern Speech in early 1992, China has embarked on a deeper outward-looking policy in an attempt to promote development in the frontier regions. As for Xinjiang, favorable and flexible measures have been granted to international and cross-border trade and economic cooperation. They include "Notification of Promoting Trade and Economic Cooperation with Neighboring and Eastern European Countries," which was issued by the State Council of the People's Republic of China (PRC) on February 9, 1992.[8]

In 2010, Xinjiang's exports amounted to US$12.9 billion (which is 38.68 times that in 1990), but its imports turned out to be only US$4.2 billion (which is 55.48 times that in 1990) (Xinjiang Bureau of Statistics, 2011). Major imports in the region include rolled steel, medical equipment, crude oil, oil products, and fertilizers; major exports are clothing and other daily consumers' goods.

Xinjiang has far poorer foreign trade performances than their coastal counterparts. This is simply because in China, frontier provinces have always disadvantageous locations in conducting trade and economic cooperation with the world's major market economies. However, compared with other inland Chinese provinces,

[7] For example, as of 2010, the per capita GDP ratio of China's top five to bottom five provinces was 3.98 (if Beijing, Shanghai, and Tianjin are included) or 3.16 (if Beijing, Shanghai, and Tianjin are excluded) (cited from Guo, 2013b, p. 157).

[8] For the full text of this document, see Bulletins of the State Council of the People's Republic of China, 1992.

Xinjiang still has locational advantages in cross-border trade and economic cooperation with its respective adjacent nations.

By cross-border trade (or border trade for short), it generally refers to the flow of goods and services across the international borders between jurisdictions. In this sense, it is a part of normal trade that flows through standard export/import frameworks of nations. In China, border trade is defined the one that is conducted by people living on the frontier areas within 15 km (sometimes 20 km) away from an international boundary (Cihai, 1999, p. 1250). Subject to government approval, border trade may enjoy tariff exemption for a certain amount of goods (in monetary value) and may be able to receive a reduced tariff rate for remaining goods.

Generally, cross-border economic cooperation and trade are facilitated by both geographical factor and the fact that people on both sides of the border either belong to the same ethnic group or share similar cultural characteristics. Although both have international geographical adjacencies, Xinjiang has cross-border trade advantages over Tibet. For example, China's first border free trade zone (i.e., the Horgos Free Trade Zone) is located at the Xinjiang–Kazakhstan border city of Horgos. Horgos is the largest "land port" in China's far western region, and it has easy access to the Central Asian market. In March 2006, Xinjiang opened its second border trade market—called the Jeminay Border Trade Zone—near its border with Kazakhstan.

Xinjiang's cross-border trade was very small before 1990; since then, it has grown steadily. This is because Alashankou (the Ala Pass), which is located on the China–Kazakhstan boundary and has been the only railway station connecting Xinjiang and its neighboring nations (i.e., Afghanistan, India, Kazakhstan, Kyrgyzstan, Mongolia, Pakistan, Russia, and Tajikistan), was constructed in the 1980s and went into operation in September 1990. As a result, most of Xinjiang's cross-border trade has been directed to and from Kazakhstan. In 2010, for example, Xinjiang's exports to and imports from Kazakhstan account for 60.82 percent and 87.65 percent of its total exports to and imports from all the neighboring nations, respectively (Xinjiang Bureau of Statistics, 2011). Xinjiang's cross-border trade has followed a nonlinear pattern of growth during the period from 2000 to 2010 (shown in Figure 5.2). Specifically, the sharp declining of exports in 2009 and 2010 may have stemmed from (i) the 2008 U.S. financial crisis, which resulted in world-wide trade stagnation, (ii) a series of violent riots that occurred in Urumqi in 2009 and damaged the business environment in Xinjiang.[9]

Until now, there is still one puzzling issue. Xinjiang currently has a much more developed cross-border railway network than Tibet. However, its foreign trade growth has been much slower than the latter during the past decade. Even worse, regardless of the fact that Tibet's cross-border exports had increased by 110.20 percent from 2008 to 2010, Xinjiang's cross-border exports had declined by 51.33

[9] Note that because most of Xinjiang's cross-border trade has been conducted with Kazakhstan in northern Xinjiang where the Han Chinese account for the majority of population, it is reasonable to say that the Han Chinese have been major player of cross-border trade in Xinjiang.

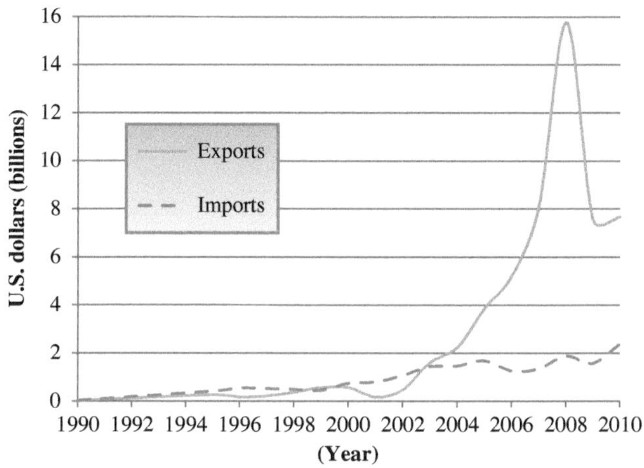

Figure 5.2 Xinjiang's cross-border trade (1990–2010).
Source: Author based on Xinjiang Bureau of Statistics (2011).

percent during the same period.[10] If the U.S. financial crisis, which had resulted in the globe-wide trade stagnation, had affected Xinjiang's foreign trade from 2008 to 2010, why did Tibet not experience a declining of foreign trade for that period of time? If the Han-Uyghur unrest from 2007 to 2010 (see Chapter 3 for details) had been responsible for Xinjiang's foreign trade stagnation from 2008 to 2010, why did Tibet (where there was also serious social unrest in 2008) not experience a declining of foreign trade for that period of time?

In addition, as shown in Figure 5.3, Tibet's remarkable growth in foreign trade for the period from 2000 to 2010 has only happened since the mid-2000s when the Qinghai–Tibet Railway went into operation. Because we cannot find any other key events or factors contributing to this remarkable foreign trade growth of Tibet, we must presume that it was the Qinghai–Tibet Railway that helped Tibet to serve as an entrepot by which China's inland provinces conduct exports to or imports from the South Asian nations. For example, with the operation of the Qinghai–Tibet railway, the cost of transportation of both passengers and goods should be greatly reduced, allowing for an increase in volume—the cost per ton-kilometer will be reduced from 0.38 to 0.12 yuan (Cnradio, November 10, 2006). As a result, more commodities will be carried to and from Tibet by the railway.

If Tibet's robust cross-border exports have benefited from the Qinghai–Tibet Railway that was completed in 2006, why did its cross-border imports decrease by 36.96 percent from 2006 to 2010 (see Figure 5.3)? Nevertheless, the above presumption seems to be reasonable because Tibet's exports have been much larger than its imports.[11] Tibet has natural and economic conditions similar to, and has no

[10] Calculated by author based on Tibet Bureau of Statistics (TBS) (2011) and Xinjiang Bureau of Statistics (XBS) (2011).

[11] For example, in 2010 the export-to-import ratio of Tibet was as high as 171 times (TBS, 2011), and that of Xinjiang was about 3.2 times (XBS, 2011).

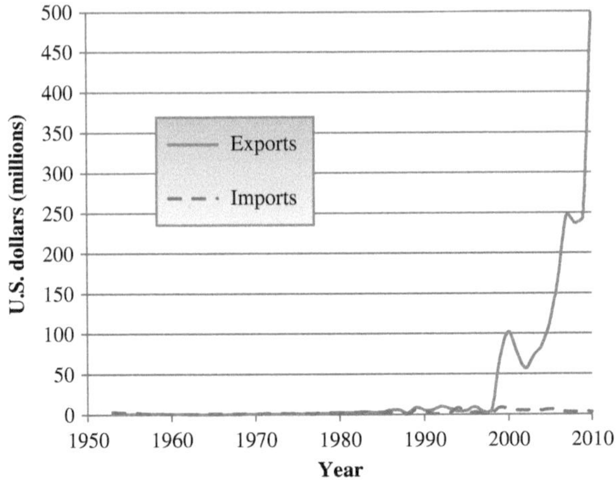

Figure 5.3 Tibet's cross-border trade (1953–2010).
Source: Author based on Tibet Bureau of Statistics (2011).

obvious industrial advantages over, its neighboring nations. Obviously, without the participation by inland provinces, Tibet could not have sustained such large amount of cross-border trade surplus.

Compared with Tibet's stagnation in cross-border import from 2006 to 2010, Xinjiang's cross-border import has enjoyed an 87.26 percent growth during the same period. How can we explain the Xinjiang–Tibet differences in both exports and imports? We must mention the fact that Xinjiang has a much more developed railway networks than Tibet. However, the railway system is, although still important, not a sufficient factor by which to explain the Xinjiang-Tibet puzzle. To have a concrete account of Tibet's (vis-à-vis Xinjiang's) remarkable foreign trade (export in particular) growth, we must pay some attention to its social and economic ties with China's inland provinces.

Explaining the puzzle

What have the above interprovincial ethnic links implied to the trade puzzle of Xinjiang? To have a concrete understanding of this issue, let us first look at the estimated results reported in Chapter 4. Because the estimated coefficients on Uyghur and Tibetan ethnic groups are statistically insignificant for 2000 (see Table 4.6a), we may simply assume that, the interprovincial Uyghur and Tibetan links—no matter how large they are—do not have any significant influences on the interprovincial trade of Xinjiang and Tibet, respectively. However, because the estimated coefficients are statistically significant for 2010, the interprovincial Uyghur and Tibetan and links will tend to have influenced interprovincial trade in 2010.

To go further, let us use the estimated coefficients reported in Tables 4.6b to calculate each ethnic group's contributions to interprovincial trade in 2010 (the results are reported in Table 5.3). The figures reported in the third and fifth columns of this table denote percentages by which provinces that are linked by an ethnic group—Uyghur or Tibetan—would increase (or decrease if the figures are negative) bilateral trade as opposed to those that are not linked by the same ethnic group. From Table 5.3, one may observe that ethnic links exerted different influences on interprovincial trade performances in Xinjiang and Tibet in 2010. For example, although the presence of the Tibetans only slightly increased Tibet's trade with most inland Chinese provinces by percentages of less than 0.5 percent, it increased Tibet's trade with the four neighbors of Qinghai, Gansu, Sichuan, and Yunnan—where certain amounts of Tibetans reside—by as high as 2740.4746 percent, 29.8863 percent, 29.0254 percent, and 4.3294 percent, respectively.

However, ethnic links have not always promoted interprovincial trade in China. In fact, the Uyghur ethnic group has already been proved to retard interprovincial trade in 2010 (as stated in Table 4.6b). This is a quite unusual phenomenon. After further calculations (see Table 5.3), one may observe that Xinjiang's interprovincial trade has been reduced by its Uyghur presence at the inland Chinese provinces, with the reductions ranging from 6.5999 percent (with Hebei) to as high as 86.7273 percent (with Beijing).

How can we explain the negative correlation between Uyghur links and interprovincial trade in Xinjiang? It seems that our 2010 estimated results on Xinjiang and the Uyghur ethnic group in particular might have closely stemmed from the various incidents of Han–Uyghur unrest from 2007 to 2010.[12] Among the many other incidents that could have affected Xinjiang's interprovincial trade in 2010, the Shaoguan incident and the Urumqi riots (both in 2009) and the Aksu bombing (in 2010) are worth mentioning. However, we should be cautious of any arbitrary conclusions before more concrete theoretical and empirical findings are discovered. In addition to the above-mentioned factor, other factors—especially the differing natural resources, geographical and cultural features, and regional development policies—may also have some influences on the differing trade performances of Xinjiang and Tibet.

Next, let us explain how Tibet's large foreign trade surplus has been determined by China's interprovincial trade. After replacing the dependent variable "ln($TRADE_{ij}$)" in Equation 4.3 with ln($EXPORT_{ij}$) and ln($IMPORT_{ij}$), we may quantitatively test the determinants of China's interprovincial export and import, respectively (see Annex 5.1 at the end of this chapter for the estimated results). Note that sometimes the terms "export" and "import" may be interchangeable. For example, Xinjiang's export to Anhui is also Anhui's import from Xinjiang. Because all province pairs are arranged in alphabetic order, the bilateral export and import between Xinjiang and Anhui are only reported in the "Anhui–Xinjiang" entry. As a result, in most circumstances, the export and import concepts used in this section can also

[12] See Chapter 3 for a more detailed account of the Han–Uyghur unrest during the past decades.

Table 5.3 How the Uyghurs and Tibetans influence interprovincial trade, 2010*

Province	Xinjiang		Tibet	
	Uyghur link	Trade effect (%)	Tibetan link	Trade effect (%)
Anhui	1.1933E-5	− 6.5513	2.1496E-5	0.0294
Beijing	3.5565E-4	− 86.7273	2.8426E-4	0.3900
Chongqing	4.0283E-5	− 20.4463	1.0698E-4	0.1466
Fujian	3.1417E-5	− 16.3385	4.7138E-5	0.0646
Gansu	7.5738E-5	− 34.9530	1.9095E-2	29.8863
Guangdong	6.1715E-5	− 29.5618	5.3720E-5	0.0736
Guangxi	3.9002E-5	− 19.8654	1.7708E-5	0.0243
Guizhou	1.6054E-5	− 8.7125	3.7527E-5	0.0514
Hainan	4.5321E-5	− 22.6900	2.8600E-5	0.0392
Hebei	1.2024E-5	− 6.5999	2.6930E-5	0.0369
Heilongjiang	2.3073E-5	− 12.2793	1.5373E-5	0.0211
Henan	3.2277E-5	− 16.7463	1.9260E-5	0.0264
Hubei	4.5023E-5	− 22.5591	3.8000E-5	0.0521
Hunan	1.0222E-4	− 44.0350	2.4688E-5	0.0338
Inner Mongolia	2.6633E-5	− 14.0349	1.3191E-4	0.1808
Jiangsu	5.5518E-5	− 27.0392	4.2691E-5	0.0585
Jiangxi	1.9117E-5	− 10.2869	2.5804E-5	0.0353
Jilin	4.1052E-5	− 20.7930	2.3750E-5	0.0325
Liaoning	4.3821E-5	− 22.0285	4.2998E-5	0.0589
Ningxia	9.7281E-5	− 42.4427	1.0411E-4	0.1427
Qinghai	3.7144E-5	− 19.0158	2.4438E-1	2740.4746
Shaanxi	4.2060E-5	− 21.2451	1.6998E-4	0.2330
Shandong	4.8386E-5	− 24.0236	2.2403E-5	0.0307
Shanghai	2.2825E-4	− 72.6394	1.0452E-4	0.1432
Shanxi	1.8761E-5	− 10.1053	2.9318E-5	0.0402
Sichuan	2.4186E-5	− 12.8323	1.8610E-2	29.0254
Tianjin	1.6772E-4	− 61.4160	1.3719E-4	0.1880
Tibet	6.8337E-5	− 32.1611	9.0551E-1	NA
Xinjiang	4.5854E-1	NA	3.8128E-4	0.5235
Yunnan	2.7892E-5	− 14.6473	3.0950E-3	4.3294
Zhejiang	9.8810E-5	− 42.9403	5.2373E-5	0.0717

NA, No interprovincial trade.

*Interprovincial Uyghur and Tibetan links are measured using Equation 4.5 in Chapter 4. Trade effects denote percentages by which provinces that are linked by an ethnic group—either Uyghur or Tibetan—would increase (or decrease if the figures are negative) bilateral trade as opposed to those that are not linked by the same ethnic group. The calculation is based on the following formula: $\exp(xy)$-1, where x denotes interprovincial Uyghur and Tibetan links (see the second and fourth columns of this table) and y denotes the estimated coefficients on the Uyghur group (−52403.342) and Tibetan group (13.694) shown in Table 4.6b.

be known as inland Chinese provinces' export from and import to Xinjiang or Tibet, respectively.[13]

The marginal effects of the ethnic links on interprovincial exports and imports can be obtained by deriving the first-order differential of the dependent variable—$\ln(\text{EXPORT}_{ij})$ and $\ln(\text{IMPORT}_{ij})$—with respect to Ethnic_{ijk}, respectively. From Table 5.4, we may observe that the marginal effect of the Tibetan ethnic links on interprovincial exports in 2010 (denoted by $17.124-0.119x$) follows a decreasing law with respect to x (denoted by the natural log of per capita GDPs of two trading provinces). However, this marginal effect is always positive because x is much less than $17.124/0.119 = 143.90$. In the meantime, the Tibetan ethnic links are not found to exert any influences on interprovincial imports. Obviously, this indicates that the Tibetan ethnic links tend to promote interprovincial exports vis-à-vis imports. Because the negative marginal effect of the Han ethnic links on interprovincial imports are always larger than that on interprovincial exports, it can be judged that interprovincial imports are more seriously retarded by the Han ethnic links than interprovincial exports.

The above results suggest that most of the inland Chinese provinces' exportation to Tibet is more robust than their importation from Tibet. In the meantime, we can also conclude that China's inland provinces fostered Tibet's exportation to its neighboring nations in 2010. Unfortunately, because Tibet's interprovincial trade data are not available for the year 2000, we are not able to clarify the differences of ethnic influences on trade between 2000 and 2010.

How can we explain Xinjiang's robust cross-border importation (vis-à-vis exportation) from 2006 to 2010? Different from Tibet, which is mainly dominated by a single ethnic group (Tibetan), Xinjiang is ethnically diverse (see the Focusing Uyghurs section for details). To clarify how these ethnic groups have exerted different influences on Xinjiang's interprovincial exports and imports, let us use the estimated coefficients on seven major ethnic groups (i.e., Dongxiang, Han, Hui, Kazak, Manchu, Mongol, and Uyghur) to calculate their marginal effects on interprovincial exports and imports (see Table 5.4). Specifically, these ethnic groups' influences on trade have different patterns:

- Dongxiang: Its marginal effect on imports is always larger than that on exports in 2010. And its marginal effect on imports in 2010 is always larger than that in 2000.
- Han: Its marginal effects on exports and imports in 2010 are always smaller than those in 2000. And for both years, its marginal effects on imports are always smaller than those on exports.
- Hui: Its marginal effect on exports in 2010 is smaller than that in 2000; by contrast, its marginal effect on imports in 2010 is larger than that in 2000.
- Kazak: Its marginal effects on exports in both 2000 and 2010 cannot be determined. However, its marginal effect on imports in 2010 is always smaller than that in 2000.
- Manchu: Its marginal effects on exports and imports in 2010 are always smaller than those in 2000. However, its marginal effects on imports are always larger than those on exports in both years.
- Mongol: Its marginal effects on imports in both 2000 and 2010 cannot be determined. However, its marginal effect on exports in 2010 is always smaller than that in 2000.

[13] This is because both Xinjiang and Tibet are located behind most of the Chinese provinces (Yunnan and Zhejiang are the only exceptions) in all the 465 province pairs shown in Annex 4.2.

Table 5.4 The marginal effects of interprovincial ethnic links on trade (2000 and 2010)*

Ethnic group	Year	(I) Exports	(II) Imports	(III) = (II)−(I)
Dongxiang	(A) 2000	–	$1615.179-0.110x>0$	>0
	(B) 2010	–	$1708.348-0.149x>0$	>0
	(C) = (B)−(A)		>0	
Han	(A) 2000	$-0.089x<0$	$-0.110x<0$	<0
	(B) 2010	$-0.119x<0$	$-0.149x<0$	<0
	(C) = (B)−(A)	<0	<0	
Hui	(A) 2000	$20.287-0.089x>0$	–	<0
	(B) 2010	19.307−0.119x) > 0	$14.504-0.149x>0$	<0
	(C) = (B)−(A)	<0	>0	
Kazak	(A) 2000	–	–	
	(B) 2010	–	$-7433.313-0.149x<0$	<0
	(C) = (B)−(A)		<0	
Manchu	(A) 2000	$39.180-0.089x>0$	$68.726-0.110x>0$	>0
	(B) 2010	–	$54.840-0.149x>0$	>0
	(C) = (B)−(A)	<0	<0	
Mongol	(A) 2000	$65.428-0.089x>0$	–	<0
	(B) 2010	$55.066-0.119x>0$	–	<0
	(C) = (B)−(A)	<0		
Tibetan	(A) 2000	NA	NA	
	(B) 2010	$17.124-0.119x>0$	–	<0
	(C) = (B)−(A)	>0		
Uyghur	(A) 2000	–	–	
	(B) 2010	$-4722.224-0.119x<0$	$-4489.638-0.149x<0$	>0
	(C) = (B)−(A)	<0	<0	

–, No statistically significant effect exists. *NA*, not available for Tibet because the latter had no interprovincial trade via railway in 2000.

*The explanatory variable $\ln(GDPPCiGDPPC_j)Ethnic56_{ij}$ as included in Annex 1 can be re-written as $\ln(GDPPC_iGDPPC_j)$ $(Ethnic_{ij1} + Ethnic_{ij2} + \ldots + Ethnic_{ij56})$. $x = \ln(GDPPCiGDPPC_j)$. Because GDPPC (per capita GDP) ranges between from 2,662 yuan and 13,119 yuan (for Guizhou in 2000 and 2010, respectively) to 34,547 yuan and 76,074 yuan (for Shanghai in 2000 and 2010, respectively) for all provinces, x ranges from 15.773 and 20.900 in 2000 and from 18.964 and 22.479 in 2010.

Source: See Annex 5.1.

- Uyghur: Its marginal effects on exports and imports in 2010 are always smaller than those in 2000. However, its marginal effect on imports is always larger than that on exports in 2010.

After taking into account of all these ethnic groups, we may conclude that the ethnic determinants of inland Chinese provinces' importation from and exportation to Xinjiang are quite complicated. Specifically, the Dongxiang and the Manchu ethnic groups have fostered China's inland provinces' importation from Xinjiang as well as from its neighboring nations for which Xinjiang has served as an entrepot. In the meantime, the Uyghur ethnic group has retarded China's inland provinces' exportation to Xinjiang as well as to its neighboring nations for which Xinjiang has served as an entrepot. All of these have made Xinjiang different from Tibet in terms of cross-border trade.

Probing the Xinjiang problem

What have been related—both endogenously and exogenously—to the existing social and economic problems in Xinjiang? How do they affect Xinjiang's economic development and social stability? This section analyzes this issue via both cultural and economic perspectives. We will treat the cultural conditions as endogenous factors and the economic development policies as exogenous factors.

Xinjiang is culturally diverse

Ethnic diversity is another key factor by which to distinguish Tibet and Xinjiang. Unlike Tibet, which is ethnically homogeneous, with 90 percent of its population being Tibetan, Xinjiang is a much more ethnically heterogeneous place.

After 1949, the Han Chinese began to return to Xinjiang. And until 1964, they comprised 33 percent of the population (with the Uyghurs being 54 percent), a share similar to that of the Qing times. A decade later, at the beginning of the Chinese economic reform in 1978, the demographic balance was 46 percent of the Uyghurs and 40 percent of the Han Chinese (Toops, 2004). Military personnel are not counted, and national minorities are undercounted in the Chinese population census, as in most censuses (Starr, 2004, p. 242). In addition to the Uyghurs, the Han Chinese, Kazakhs, and Hui Chinese, other ethnic groups in the region include the Uzbeks, Kyrgyz, Tatars, Mongols, Daurs, Dongxiang, Russians, Xibes, and Manchus.

Using the method and the data shown in Annex 5.2 at the end of this chapter, we can calculate the ethnic diversity scores for Xinjiang and Tibet:

- Xinjiang: 0.6242 (for 2000); 0.6194 (for 2010), with a slight reduction of 0.77 percent from 2000 to 2010
- Tibet: 0.1357 (for 2000); 0.1733 (for 2010), with an increase of 27.71 percent from 2000 to 2010

Note that the increase of ethnic diversity score in Tibet mainly results from the faster growth of the Han-Chinese minority (with a rate of 54.67 percent) from 2000 to 2010; during the same period, however, the total amount of the Tibetan majority only increased by 11.92 percent (see Annex 5.2 at the end of this chapter for details). It should be noted that many of the Chinese population in Tibet were cadres and government workers sent to Tibet to participate in economic development and to further the PRC's political control there. Since the early 1990s, there has been another upsurge of Han immigration. There are still Han military, who are not counted in the census, and various other Han government employees. However, since the 1990s, the balance of Han immigrants has shifted to entrepreneurs and others keen to take advantage of the economic opportunities that derived from the newly invigorated policies of economic development (Iredale et al., 2001, pp. 157–8).[14]

Xinjiang is much more ethnically diverse than Tibet. Moreover, the spatial distribution of ethnic groups is quite uneven in Xinjiang. For example, the Uyghurs are the majority in southwestern Xinjiang, including the prefectures of Kashgar, Hotan, Kizilsu, and Aksu (about 80 percent of Xinjiang's Uyghurs live in those four prefectures), as well as Turpan prefecture in eastern Xinjiang. The Han Chinese are the majority in eastern and northern Xinjiang (Zungar), including the cities of Urumqi, Karamay, and Shihezi and the prefectures of Changji, Bortala, Bayingolin, Ili (especially the city of Kuitun), and Kumul. The Kazakhs are mostly concentrated in northern Xinjiang, especially in Altay prefecture in the northernmost part of Xinjiang (Table 5.5).

There have been two divergent views on the development of multiculturally based economies. On the one hand, some global-scale cities, such as New York and Los Angeles, are among the most troubled in terms of racial relations; at the same time, they are constant producers of innovation in the arts and business. As a matter of fact, the United States itself is an economically successful melting pot, but many of its social problems are related to racial and ethnic cleavages (Alesina and Ferrara, 2005). On the other hand, the "tragedy of Africa" is, according to Easterly and Levine (1997), largely a result of ethnic conflict, which is indeed pervasive in many parts of the developing world.

It has been found that (i) religious diversity tends to retard growth in high-inequality nations and to encourage growth in low-inequality places, and (ii) income inequality tends to encourage growth in religious homogeneous (but not in heterogeneous) nations (Guo, 2009, pp. 120–129). The above finding supports the presumption that lower inequality economies will not only be less sensitive to the measures of religious diversity than higher inequality places in which religious diversity leads to barriers to intranational trade or, more significantly, to violence. A brief comparison of the interethnic unrest cases of Xinjiang and Tibet (see Chapter 3 and Guo (forthcoming), respectively) can further support—at least in part—that Tibet's relatively lower frequency of social unrest has stemmed from its lower ethnic diversity or lower income inequality and that Xinjiang's relatively higher frequency of social unrest has stemmed from its higher ethnic diversity *and* higher income inequality.[15]

[14] One of the implications of this is that "many Han immigrants, possibly even most, do not stay in Tibet long. They may even stay too short a period to be counted in the census figures. That means that there are probably far more Han than the census shows" (Mackerras, 2005, p. 21).

[15] Even though there have not been precise calculations of Xinjiang and Tibet's income inequalities (which are represented by the Gini coefficients), it has been generally admitted that Xinjiang has had a much higher Gini coefficient than Tibet (see, e.g., Lu and Xu, 2004 and Liu et al., 2009). Clearly, this conforms to the fact that the spatial economic disparities in Xinjiang are larger than those in Tibet (shown in Table 5.2).

Table 5.5 Population shares of major ethnic groups in Xinjiang by region, 2010*

Region	Uyghur (%)	Han (%)	Kazakh (%)	Others (%)
Aksu P (including Aral SPM)	**71.9**	26.6	0.1	1.4
Altay P	1.8	40.9	**51.4**	5.9
Bayingolin Mongol AP	32.7	**57.5**	0.1	9.7
Bortala Mongol AP	12.5	**67.2**	9.1	11.1
Changji Hui AP (including Wujiaqu SPM)	3.9	**75.1**	8.0	13.0
Hotan P	**96.4**	3.3	0.1	0.2
Ili Kazakh AP	16.1	**44.4**	25.6	13.9
Karamay PM	13.8	**78.1**	3.7	4.5
Kashgar P (including Tumushuke SPM)	**89.3**	9.2	0.0	1.5
Kizilsu Kirgiz AP	**64.0**	6.4	0.0	29.6
Kuitun M	0.5	**94.6**	1.8	3.1
Kuitun SPM	0.5	**94.6**	1.8	3.1
Kumul P	18.4	**68.9**	8.8	3.9
Shihezi M	1.2	**94.5**	0.6	3.7
Shihezi SPM	1.2	**94.5**	0.6	3.7
Tacheng P	4.1	**58.6**	24.2	13.1
Turpan P	**70.0**	23.3	0.1	6.6
Urumqi PM	12.8	**75.3**	2.3	9.6
Total	**45.9**	40.5	6.5	7.1

AP, autonomous prefecture; *M*, municipality; *P*, prefecture; *PM*, prefecture-level municipality; *SPM*, subprefectural level municipality (administered by the Xinjiang Production and Construction Corps).
*Members of the People's Liberation Army in active service are not included.
Source: The Sixth National Population Census, 2010.

Focusing Uyghurs

The differences between two ethnic groups can be identified according to various criteria. Obviously, linguistic difference is an important indicator. Although it is not the only tool for building trusting relationships, doors usually open more quickly when knocked on by someone who speaks a familiar language. Sharing a common language, however, does not necessarily mean effective communication in technical terms. More important, religion can have a deep impact not only on attitudes toward economic matters but also on values that influence them. Specifically, religious attitudes and values help to determine what one thinks is right or appropriate, what is important, what is desirable, and so on (Guo, 2007b).

The Tibetans and the Han Chinese belong to the Mongoloid group. This group, including most peoples of East Asia and the American Indians, has been described as having skin of saffron to yellow or reddish brown. The hair is dark and straight.

The eyes are from black to dark brown. In addition, Chinese and Tibetan—two major languages adopted by the Han and Tibetans, respectively—encompass the most important part of the Sino–Tibetan family of language. The Tibetan language is spoken in numerous regional dialects that generally cannot be understood by the speakers of the different oral forms. Although spoken Tibetan varies according to the region, the written language, based on Classical Tibetan, is consistent throughout. This is probably because of the long-standing influence of the Tibetan empire, whose rule embraced (and extended at times far beyond) the present Tibetan linguistic area, which runs from northern Pakistan in the west to Yunnan and Sichuan in the east and from north of Lake Qinghai to south as far as Bhutan.

Unlike the Tibetans and the Han Chinese, the Uyghurs—the ethnic majority of Xinjiang—belong to the Caucasoid. The Caucasoid group, found in Europe, North Africa, and from the Middle East to North India, is characterized as having skin of pale reddish white to olive brown. The hair is light blond to dark brown. The color of the eyes varies from light blue to dark brown. In addition, Uyghur—one of the Turkic languages—belongs to the Ural-Altaic Phylum. The other Turkic languages adopted in Xinjiang include Kazakh, Uzbek, Kirgiz, and so on.

Religion is extremely important to the Tibetans and has a strong influence over all aspects of their lives. Tibetan Buddhism, a distinctive form of Mahayana and Vajrayana, was introduced into Tibet from the Sanskrit Buddhist tradition of northern India. Tibetan Buddhism is practiced not only in Tibet but also in Mongolia, parts of northern India, and some other parts of China. Although Buddhism has been adopted by both the Tibetans and the Han Chinese in most parts of China, the Uyghurs and many other ethnic groups in Xinjiang are Muslims. In the mid-7th century, Muslim Arab and Persian merchants came overland through Central Asia to today's Xinjiang, bringing with them the Islamic faith. Now, Muslim peoples in Xinjiang include not only the Uyghurs but also several other ethnic groups such as the Uzbeks, Kyrgyz, Tatars, Kazakhs, and Hui Chinese.

In short, the Uyghurs—not the Tibetans—are different from the Han Chinese. And because the Uyghurs, Tibetans, and Han Chinese represent the ethnic majorities of Xinjiang, Tibet, and the other Chinese provinces as a whole, respectively, this may have largely contributed to the differing interprovincial trade patterns of Xinjiang and Tibet (see Table 5.3).

Development policies

Historically and culturally, Xinjiang had been quite far away from China proper. It has only become China's provincial administration since the 1880s. Since the PRC was founded in 1949, the Chinese central government has made various efforts to stabilize Xinjiang and to fully assimilate it into China proper. At present, Xinjiang has also received huge amount of fiscal subsidies from the central government.

The establishment of the XPCC, which has been organized as more than a dozen of quasimilitaristic development zones, is not new in Chinese history. Similar organs had been established in the Qing dynasty (AD 1644–1911), especially during the period from AD 1760 to 1830 when "state farms" were opened and the Chinese in Xinjiang grew rapidly. At the start of the 19th century, there approximately 155,000 Han and Hui Chinese in northern Xinjiang and somewhat more than twice that number of Uyghurs in southern Xinjiang (Millward, 2007, p. 306). However, as described in Chapter 2, the XPCC is much larger in size than Qing's state farms. With a population of more than 2.5 million , the XPCC is now in fact a quasi-subprovincial level administration in Xinjiang and in China as well.

The XPCC has played a critical role in China's effective rule of Xinjiang during the most years of the PRC era. In the meantime, it has also contributed positively to Xinjiang's local economic development (Shao, April 3, 2012). But it also has negative effects on the Uyghurs and the Han Chinese living in Xinjiang as well as on the Han-Uyghur relations.[16] If it was a necessary measure that the Chinese established the XPCC as quasimilitaristic development zones in politically instable areas such as Xinjiang during the early stage of the PRC, now it is time for Chinese policymakers to reevaluate the legality of the XPCC. Along with China's calling for a harmonious society, it is not a good policy for the Chinese government to keep so many quasimilitaristic administrative zones in Xinjiang. (This issue is discussed in detail in Chapter 6.)

In general, large construction projects have different functions from the above-mentioned aid programs. A large construction project, as its name suggests, will bring about huge amount of capital flows. It will also promote local economic development by stimulating the developments of both the upper and lower chains of small and medium enterprises and by offering a large number of jobs to local residents. Restricted by its natural and geographical conditions, Tibet has hosted a far smaller number of China's large construction projects. The Qinghai–Tibet Railway is the only largest one that China has ever constructed in Tibet during recent history. In 2006, the construction of the 1,956-km Qinghai–Tibet Railway was completed. This stretches from Xining—capital of Qinghai province—to Lhasa and across the Kunlun Mountains and the Tanggulashan Pass. As the world's highest railway, it makes Tibet more accessible (see Chapter 2 of Guo (2014)) for a detailed description). In Xinjiang, China has constructed far more large construction projects (see Chapter 2 for a detailed description).

As the driving force for the fast economic development of a region as a whole, the construction of large construction projects also has several unwanted effects. First of all, as in many other authoritative places throughout the world, the construction of large state-owned industrial projects in China is always accompanied by corruption and rent-seeking activities (Rodrik, 2007; Qian, 2012). Second, the

[16] See Becquelin (2000, pp. 65–90), McMillen (1981, pp. 65–96), O'Neill (April 13, 2008), Rossabi (2005), and Seymour (2000, pp. 171–193) for more detailed accounts.

construction of a large project in a single place—instead of several smaller ones in different places—will, *ceteris paribus*, inevitably result in interregional economic disparities and unequal income distribution.[17] Last but not least, the construction of large construction projects also implies the large consumption of nonrenewable natural resources as well as damage to the environment.

Although the local communities and residents in Xinjiang may have not been the major beneficiaries of the large construction projects that China built, they may easily become the major victims whenever disasters and environmental accidents occur there. In Tibet, however, there is a different story. Compared with the large industrial projects constructed in Xinjiang, such as the West-East Gas Pipeline (see Chapter 2), the Qinghai–Tibet Railway—the only largest infrastructure project built in Tibet until the present—can benefit more local Tibetan residents. Even though the construction and operation of the railway may also bring about some impacts on Tibet's fragile environment and natural ecology, these negative impacts are far less serious than those of the large industrial projects in Xinjiang.

During the past decades, the PRC has undertaken a massive, benevolent, and patriotic policy by which to encourage the wealthier eastern coast to help the western parts of China, including Tibet, catch up in prosperity and living standards. As a result, Tibet has achieved more social and economic progress than what was usually predicted by the outside sources during the past decades. In a paper written for the United Nations High Commissioner for Refugees (UNHCR), Mackerras (2005, p. 20) points out:

> *"[S]ince the early 1960s, the Tibetan population has been increasing, probably for the first time for centuries. What seems to follow from this is that the TGIE's [Tibetan Government in Exile] allegations of population reduction due to Chinese rule probably have some validity for the 1950s but are greatly exaggerated. However, since the 1960s, Chinese rule has had the effect of increasing the population of the Tibetans, not decreasing it, largely due to a modernization process that has improved the standard of living and lowered infant, maternity and other mortality rates."*

After more than 30 years of practice in China, the pairing-aid program has been recognized an effective management measure, especially when dealing with disaster relief and recovery work. For example, within 2 years after the Wenchuan Earthquake happened in May 2008, about 90 percent of the affected infrastructure and residential areas were reconstructed (Qian et al., 2012, pp. 67–74). After comparing the discussion in Chapter 2 and Annex 2.1 (for the Xinjiang case) with Guo (2014) (for the Tibet case), we may find that China's pairing-aid programs have

[17] As shown in the last row of Table 5.2, Xinjiang's interregional economic gap has been much larger than Tibet's.

had different effects on the regional developments of Xinjiang and Tibet. Specifically, the pairing-aid Tibet programs have entirely benefited the Tibetan-based areas, but the pairing-aid Xinjiang programs have only partially benefited the Uyghur- and other non−Han-based areas (Table 5.6).

Table 5.6 Availability of interprovincial pairing-aid programs, Tibet and Xinjiang*

Province	Tibet[†]	Xinjiang	Notes on Xinjiang
Anhui	X	X	
Beijing	X	X	Partly for XPCC-14
Chongqing	X	NA	
Fujian	X	X	Mainly for Han and Hui Chinese
Gansu	X	NA	
Guangdong	X	X	Partly for XPCC-3
Guangxi	X	NA	
Guizhou	X	NA	
Hainan	X	NA	
Hebei	X	X	Entirely for XPCC-2
Heilongjiang	X	X	Mainly for Kazakhs and XPCC-10
Henan	X	X	Entirely for XPCC-13
Hubei	X	X	Mainly for Mongols and XPCC-5
Hunan,	X	X	
Inner Mongolia	X	NA	
Jiangsu	X	X	Mainly for Kirgizs, Kazakhs and XPCC-4(66)
Jiangxi	X	X	Mainly for Kirgizs
Jilin	X	X	Mainly for Kazakhs
Liaoning	X	X	
Ningxia	NA	NA	
Qinghai	X	X	
Shaanxi	X	NA	
Shandong	X	X	
Shanghai	X	X	
Shanxi	X	X	Mainly for Hui Chinese and XPCC-6
Sichuan	X	NA	
Tianjin	X	X	
Tibet	NA	NA	
Xinjiang	X	NA	
Yunnan	X	NA	
Zhejiang	X	X	Partly for XPCC-1

NA, Not available; *XPCC*, Xinjiang Production and Construction Crops; *XPCC*-m*(n)* denotes the *m*th Agricultural Division (the *n*th Regiment) of the XPCC.
*The pairing-aid programs undertaken by China's central ministries and departments and the large state-owned enterprises are not included in this table.
[†]Also includes the "aid-Tibet cadres" and the "inland middle schools and classes for Tibetans" programs and other government-driven investment projects.
Source: Author based on Annex of Chapter 2 (for Xinjiang) and Guo (2014) (for Tibet).

In addition, China's pairing-aid Tibet programs have also been combined with two other similar aid programs (i.e., "aid-Tibet cadres" and the "inland middle schools and classes").[18] All of these programs have had significant effects on the social and economic developments of Tibet, especially in its poor, rural areas. By way of contrast, the pairing-aid Xinjiang programs seem to be limited to certain geographical areas and industrial sectors, not the entire Uyghur community.

What are the differences between the "inland middle school classes for Xinjiang" program and the "inland middle schools and classes for Tibet" program? As their names suggest, as for Xinjiang, there are only inland middle school classes; as for Tibet, however, there are both inland middle schools and the inland middle school classes. For example, as of 2014, there are five inland middle schools that are solely established for Tibetan students, which are Beijing City Tibetan Middle School (Beijing municipality), Kunming Army Seminary Affiliated Tibetan Middle School (Yunnan province), Shaoxing Tibetan Middle School (Zhejiang province), Changzhou City Tibetan Ethnic Middle School (Jiangsu province), Ji'nan Tibetan Middle School (Shandong province), and Chengdu City Tibetan Middle School (Sichuan province). However, there is still no inland middle school that is solely established for either the Uyghur or any other ethnic-minority students coming from Xinjiang.

As shown in Table 5.7, with the exception of the Han students, in which case the College Entrance Leading Group for the Tibet and Xinjiang Students in Inland Provinces, the Ministry of Education, has set higher college entrance scores for Tibet than for Xinjiang, the minority (mainly the Tibetan) students from Tibet have received more preferential treatments than the minority (mainly the Uyghur, Hui, Kazak, and so on) students from Xinjiang.[19]

In addition, after quantitatively comparing the cases of Xinjiang (see Table 2.5) and of Tibet (see Figure 2.1 of Guo, 2014), we may find that:

- **(i)** For Xinjiang, the "inland middle school classes" program was not implemented until 2000. However, for Tibet, the "inland middle schools and classes" program was implemented as early as 1985 (for junior classes) and 1989 (for senior classes).
- **(ii)** After being divided by their respective total populations, the relative number of Tibet's students enrolled in the inland middle schools is much larger than that of Xinjiang's (see Figure 5.4).
- **(iii)** For Xinjiang, students can only enroll in inland provinces' senior middle school classes. However, for Tibet, students can enroll in both junior and senior middle schools and classes in the inland provinces.

What do these findings imply? They only imply that the "inland middle schools and classes" program has had much greater effects in Tibet than in Xinjiang.

[18] See Chapter 2 for a detailed analysis of Tibet's pairing-aid programs.

[19] Of course, the college entrance scores for both Tibet and Xinjiang (as shown in Table 5.7) are still far lower than those for the rest of China (see Table 2.6 for more details).

Table 5.7 A comparison of college entrance criteria between Tibet and Xinjiang*

Type	Scores (liberal arts)		Scores (sciences)	
	Tibet	**Xinjiang**	**Tibet**	**Xinjiang**
Specially planned colleges	490 (H),	415 (H), 330 (MH), 310 (MM)	460 (H),	415 (H), 315 (MH), 300 (MM)
Regular colleges I	320 (M)		280 (M)	
Regular colleges II	345 (H),		325 (H),	
Regular colleges III	278 (M)		242 (M)	
Junior/technical/vocational colleges	320 (H), 240 M)	305 (H), 300 (MH), 284 (MM)	300 (H), 210 (M)	290 (H), 284 (MH), 280 (MM)

H, Han students; *M*, minority students, *MH*, minority students to enter Han-dominated universities, *MM*, minority students to enter minority-dominated universities.

*Data are as of 2012.

Source: The College Entrance Leading Group for the Tibet and Xinjiang Students in Inland Provinces, the Ministry of Education, Beijing, China.

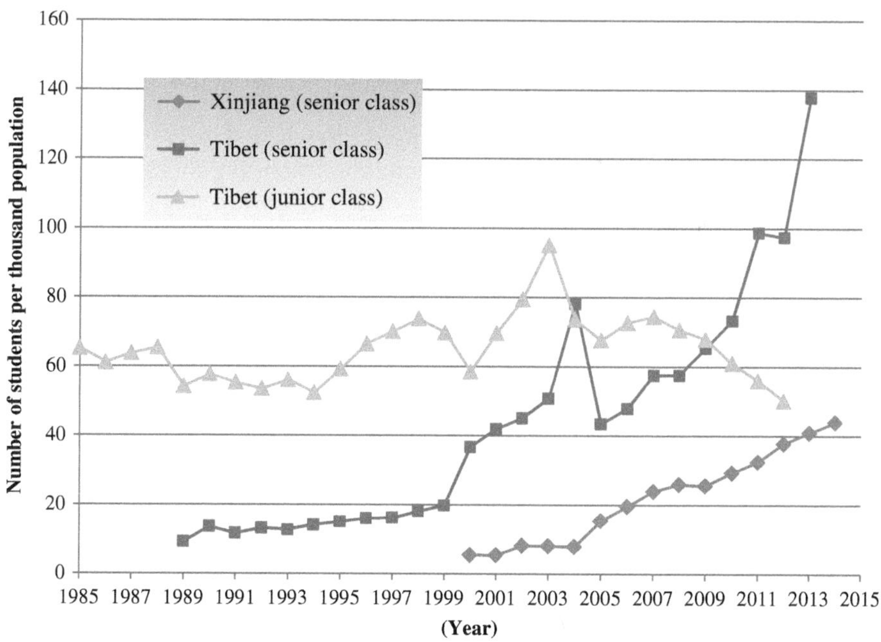

Figure 5.4 How the "inland middle schools and classes" program differs between Xinjiang and Tibet, 1985 to 2014.

Source: Author based on State Ethnic Affairs Commission (various years) and Tibet Bureau of Statistics (various years) for Tibet and Table 2.5 and Xinjiang Bureau of Statistics (various years) for Xinjiang.

Interethnic policy

For a long period of time, especially during the early PRC era, the Chinese government responded to ethnic unrest in Xinjiang and Tibet with a familiar strategy: some suffocating security controls were put in place, significant investment and assistance were promised in development and infrastructure, and more of the Han majority were migrated into both regions. However, it seems that recently China has shifted its policy toward a concept of "interethnic fusion," which is a move away from China's long-standing idea of "separate but equal" ethnicities and toward a more American-style concept of a "melting pot" (Denyer, September 1, 2014).

On August 29, 2014, the government of Qiemo county in the southern area of Xinjiang Uyghur autonomous region announced on its website that it would offer cash rewards and welfare benefits for marriages between ethnic minority groups and the Han people to promote multiethnic unity. Specifically, it would give out an annual 10,000 yuan (US$1,627) of cash reward for 5 years for each interethnic couple after their marriage. The policy offers family members of mixed-marriage couples privileged access to housing, education, employment, and welfare benefits. Ninety percent of these couples' medical expenses after insurance fees will be covered by the local government. The interethnic couples' children will also be exempt from school fees within the county until senior middle school, and an annual 5,000 yuan scholarship will be given to those who reach university. And their parents will also be eligible for housing and medical benefits if their marriages last longer than 3 years.[20]

The new move, mirroring similar incentives offered in Tibet,[21] is believed to be a measure to ease interethnic conflicts amid the increasing incidence of terrorist attacks in the region of Xinjiang. However, the policy might not have its intended impact. Dilxat Raxit, a Munich-based spokesman for the World Uyghur Congress condemned the move. "They are using marriage as a means to achieve Beijing's political ends," he told Radio Free Asia, adding that such marriages are rare and unlikely to succeed. "The Turkic culture of the Uyghurs and Han culture is different in almost every way, and Uyghurs basically don't marry Han Chinese."[22]

Even within Chinese academic circle, this Han–Uyghur intermarriage policy has still attracted skepticism, arguing that marriage is a personal matter in which government policy should not intervene. Li Xiaoxia, a professor with the Xinjiang Academy of Social Sciences (XASS), believes that such mixed marriages are rare in Xinjiang and are not likely to spread. Pan Zhiping, a research fellow with the XASS, said to the Global Times that "marriage is a personal freedom and cannot be encouraged using money. We should not stop mixed

[20] Data source: Wong (September 3, 2014).

[21] For a detailed analysis of the case of Tibet, see the Interethnic Policy section of this chapter.

[22] Cited from Denyer (September 1, 2014).

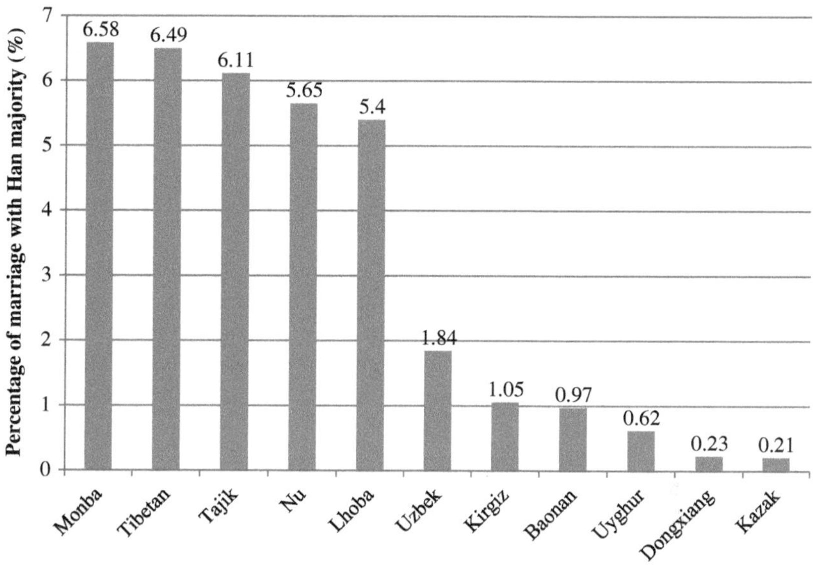

Figure 5.5 The ethnic minorities with the lowest percentages of interethnic marriages with the Han majority.
Source: Author based on the Fifth National Population Census, 2001.

marriages, but neither should we encourage them through policy" (Wong, September 3, 2014).

According to the Fifth National Population Census, the percentage of Uyghur's intermarriages with the Han majority is only 0.62 percent, which is among the lowest of all ethnic minorities in China (Figure 5.5). If taking into account the Uyghur's mixed intermarriages with all the ethnic groups, its interethnic marriage rate is 1.05 percent (Li and Hu, 2010). However, this is still much lower than that of Tibet. At present, it is too early to tell if this interethnic policy will become successful. Nevertheless, it seems that this policy has been less successful in Xinjiang than in Tibet.

Policy implications

When different peoples meet together, it does not always indicate a conflict. However, conflict and disagreement do occur more often in heterogeneous places than in homogeneous places, especially in China's far western regions. Uyghur independence activists claim that the Han population will dilute the Uyghur character of the region. But the Han and the Hui Chinese—who mostly live in northern Xinjiang (also called Zungar) and are separated from areas of historical Uyghur dominance south of the Tian Shan mountains (southwestern Xinjiang)—may insist that their ancestors arrived in the eastern portions of the Tarim basin about 3,000 years ago.

During the past decades, the Uyghur ethnic group has been labeled as "problematic" in China and has had cliques seeking the separations of Xinjiang from China. In this chapter, the Uyghurs (with a negatively estimated coefficient in Table 4.6b) are found to play a negative role in China's interprovincial economic integration. It must be noted that the above results do not imply that most people in Xinjiang want an independent state for themselves.[23]

The findings presented at this chapter would be useful for policymakers to reappraise which of China's ethnic groups are playing the most (least) important roles in and to introduce the optimal informal institutions into the promotion of interprovincial economic cooperation in China. Because there are so many differences in Xinjiang, this chapter calls for different strategies toward these two non-Han ethnic autonomous regions. To this end, differentiated policies will not only help them to enhance the spatial economic efficiencies of their own, but they will also eventually benefit China as a whole. Specifically, given that Xinjiang's ethnic (and religious) diversity is already very high, Xinjiang's income inequality would be harmful to its social stability and economic development. In this case, substantial measures must be taken to reduce the chance of interethnic clash in Xinjiang.

Furthermore, the alternative measures may include:

- Given that Xinjiang's high ethnic (and religious) diversity cannot be reduced, new spatial development and income (re)distribution policies must be implemented so that the income inequality can be reduced in Xinjiang.
- Given that Xinjiang's high level of income inequality cannot be reduced, Xinjiang's current administrative division must be reconstructed so that the ethnic (and religious) diversity can be reduced in each newly established administrative area in Xinjiang.

As for the second measure, the Chinese central government could divide Xinjiang into two carefully designed provincial-level administrative divisions in the southern and northern parts of Xinjiang. As a result, the ethnic (and religious) diversity will be considerably reduced in each smaller provincial division. This is further discussed in Chapter 6.

Annex 5.1. Regressions for interprovincial export and import, 2000 and 2010

The following four tables report the estimated results using the data shown in Annex 4.2.

[23] For example, in an interview with a correspondent of the *Huanqiu Times*, a Beijing-based newspaper, Stephen Frederick Starr (founder and Chairman of the Central Asia-Caucasus Institute of Johns Hopkins University) concluded that most Xinjiangers do not want to separate from China (Starr, July 22, 2013).

Table 5.A.1.1 **Regression for interprovincial export, 2000***

Explanatory variable	Coefficient	SE	VIF
Constant	6.595	1.060†	
$\ln(GDP_iGDP_j)$	0.819	0.058†	2.703
$\ln(Distance_{ij})$	−1.150	0.110†	2.597
$Adjacent_{ij}$	0.351	0.176‡	2.183
$\ln(GDPPC_iGDPPC_j)Ethnic56_{ij}$	−0.089	0.020†	2.747
Bai	−760.910	446.189§	9.681
Blang	−182781.261	97340.146§	2.624
Buyi	155.540	1456.949	8.338
Dai	−18185.339	17752.257	6.894
Daur	660.850	772.891	1.324
Dong	74.658	81.830	2.500
Dongxiang	762.334	573.453	4.511
Gelao	19470.916	11851.492§	8.759
Hani	−13571.259	13963.630	3.955
Hui	20.287	5.564†	1.582
Jingpo	140353.281	98998.902	3.484
Kazak	−13467.204	13562.079	7.667
Kirgiz	−1684.449	23041.700	1.274
Korean	58.256	82.331	1.764
Lahu	−11570.940	40399.474	4.536
Li	−21719.708	10536.653‡	3.925
Lisu	4129.284	7412.855	4.048
Manchu	39.810	13.167†	2.133
Maonan	83.656	1347.899	1.936
Miao	71.785	40.421§	7.428
Mongol	65.428	30.564‡	1.577
Qiang	−17980.181	19314.076	2.304
She	98.786	179.618	1.142
Tibetan	92.398	41.375‡	1.865
Tu	−446.159	1235.122	3.179
Tujia	−22.363	13.605§	2.234
Uyghur	635.522	2649.800	1.470
Va	11635.832	15894.735	3.390
Xibe	−234.930	483.307	1.190
Yao	−16.717	91.830	2.116
Yi	56.901	44.327	4.779
Zhuang	25.434	40.441	1.813
Coefficient of correlation (R^2)	0.692		
SE of regression	0.857		
F-statistic	23.020		
Sig. of regression	0.000		
Number of observations	405		

*The regression is done by the ordinary least squares method. The dependent variable is the natural log of interprovincial export in 2000. The "Han," "Mulao," "Naxi," "Salar," and "Shui" variables with VIFs above 10 are omitted from the regression.
†Statistically significant at greater than the 1% level.
‡Statistically significant at greater than the 5% level.
§Statistically significant at greater than the 10% level.

Table 5.A.1.2 **Regression for interprovincial import, 2000***

Explanatory variable	Coefficient	SE	VIF
Constant	8.003	1.094†	
$\ln(GDP_iGDP_j)$	0.699	0.060†	2.703
$\ln(DISTANCE_{ij})$	−1.118	0.114†	2.597
$ADJACENT_{ij}$	0.219	0.182	2.183
$\ln(GDPPC_iGDPPC_j)ETHNIC56_{ij}$	−0.100	0.021†	2.747
Bai	−949.340	460.489‡	9.681
Blang	−81385.096	100459.722	2.624
Buyi	−1794.339	1503.641	8.338
Dai	−29597.036	18321.184§	6.894
Daur	1977.710	797.661†	1.324
Dong	38.569	84.453	2.500
Dongxiang	1615.179	591.832†	4.511
Gelao	22890.425	12231.311§	8.759
Hani	−34531.277	14411.139‡	3.955
Hui	2.849	5.743	1.582
Jingpo	495810.433	102171.638†	3.484
Kazak	−8014.516	13996.719	7.667
Kirgiz	−38077.094	23780.145§	1.274
Korean	−166.955	84.969‡	1.764
Lahu	10679.459	41694.204	4.536
Li	−25836.816	10874.333‡	3.925
Lisu	5889.771	7650.423	4.048
Manchu	68.726	13.589†	2.133
Maonan	2313.609	1391.097§	1.936
Miao	60.626	41.717	7.428
Mongol	4.097	31.543	1.577
Qiang	−7207.410	19933.057	2.304
She	3.652	185.374	1.142
Tibetan	27.170	42.701	1.865
Tu	−64.798	1274.705	3.179
Tujia	−6.111	14.041	2.234
Uyghur	341.386	2734.722	1.470
Va	10685.150	16404.132	3.390
Xibe	−2.107	498.796	1.190
Yao	5.552	94.773	2.116
Yi	68.282	45.748	4.779
Zhuang	32.165	41.738	1.813
Coefficient of correlation (R^2)	0.638		
SE of regression	0.885		
F-statistic	18.058		
Sig. of regression	0.000		
Number of observations	405		

SE, Standard error; *VIF*, variance inflation factor.

*The regression is done by the ordinary least squares method. The dependent variable is the natural log of interprovincial import in 2000. The "Han," "Mulao," "Naxi," "Salar," and "Shui" variables with VIFs above 10 are omitted from the regression.

†Statistically significant at greater than the 1% level.

‡Statistically significant at greater than the 5% level.

§Statistically significant at greater than the 10% level.

Table 5.A.1.3 Regression for interprovincial export, 2010*

Explanatory variable	Coefficient	SE	VIF
Constant	4.885	1.515†	
$\ln(GDP_iGDP_j)$	0.868	0.078†	3.389
$\ln(DISTANCE_{ij})$	−1.148	0.147†	2.871
$ADJACENT_{ij}$	0.507	0.229‡	2.108
$\ln(GDPPC_iGDPPC_j)ETHNIC56_{ij}$	−0.119	0.021†	3.554
Bai	−613.510	387.083	3.793
Blang	−8718.239	8560.834	1.486
Buyi	2323.611	860.947†	6.579
Dai	−4637.048	6539.570	3.423
Daur	1208.476	1138.550	1.226
Dong	98.081	106.625	2.273
Dongxiang	610.299	489.701	1.909
Gelao	−13505.988	5030.687†	5.937
Hani	8167.987	10370.989	5.706
Hui	19.307	7.616†	1.502
Jingpo	9909.153	38883.464	2.068
Kazak	−3332.796	3667.967	1.907
Kirgiz	−27068.949	21962.448	1.203
Korean	71.405	120.672	1.697
Lahu	1924.840	31583.749	5.350
Li	−49.698	306.809	1.103
Lisu	−7509.658	8224.292	4.031
Manchu	22.090	20.327	2.046
Maonan	3273.855	1974.582§	1.877
Miao	48.015	39.163	4.620
Mongol	55.066	41.385	1.459
Naxi	644.792	9602.879	2.386
Qiang	3243.565	13475.109	2.309
She	445.364	285.042	1.277
Shui	−5595.609	3402.173§	3.622
Tibetan	17.124	5.098†	1.190
Tujia	−8.788	16.643	1.843
Uyghur	−4722.224	2105.352‡	1.291
Va	−30004.668	13393.614‡	4.922
Xibe	−68.108	769.974	1.195
Yao	70.182	118.142	1.974
Yi	87.951	45.220‡	3.442
Zhuang	96.058	49.926‡	1.715
Coefficient of correlation (R^2)	0.556		
SE of regression	1.156		
F-statistic	14.196		
Sig. of regression	0.000		
Number of observations	451		

SE, Standard error; *VIF*, variance inflation factor.

*The regression is done by the ordinary least squares method. The dependent variable is the natural log of interprovincial export in 2010. The "Han," "Mulao," "Salar," and "Tu" variables with VIFs above 9 are omitted from the regression.

†Statistically significant at greater than the 1% level.

‡Statistically significant at greater than the 5% level.

§Statistically significant at greater than the 10% level.

Table 5.A.1.4 Regression for interprovincial import, 2010*

Explanatory variable	Coefficient	SE	VIF
Constant	8.934	1.608†	
$\ln(GDP_iGDP_j)$	0.755	0.080†	3.034
$\ln(DISTANCE_{ij})$	−1.372	0.152†	2.695
$ADJACENT_{ij}$	0.251	0.238	2.130
$\ln(GDPPC_iGDPPC_j)$	−0.149	0.023†	3.056
$ETHNIC56_{ij}$			
Bai	−791.995	405.691‡	3.824
Blang	−13201.843	8930.512	1.485
Buyi	1771.032	897.155‡	6.583
Dai	−9046.386	6193.076	3.123
Daur	2412.806	1157.321‡	1.163
Dong	−39.013	111.363	2.277
Dongxiang	1708.348	518.020‡	1.972
Gelao	−7943.123	5259.897	5.994
Hani	7676.700	10712.254	5.596
Hui	14.502	7.946§	1.503
Jingpo	54498.460	40674.281	2.040
Kazak	−7433.313	4147.905§	7.676
Kirgiz	4123.559	3367.084	6.191
Korean	−218.037	125.806§	1.692
Lahu	33552.767	33373.530	5.448
Li	−758.185	320.527‡	1.106
Lisu	−7250.915	8595.609	4.044
Manchu	54.840	21.219†	2.045
Maonan	6708.817	2060.374†	1.876
Miao	55.448	40.931	4.657
Mongol	30.480	43.378	1.470
Naxi	3012.143	10158.051	2.406
Qiang	−9203.970	14337.173	2.323
She	520.898	296.784§	1.271
Shui	−8706.201	3547.775‡	3.613
Tibetan	1.214	5.354	1.205
Tujia	0.553	17.366	1.843
Uyghur	−4489.638	2164.083‡	1.243
Va	−47127.865	14282.604†	5.148
Xibe	−419.181	802.744	1.193
Yao	125.010	123.302	1.974
Yi	92.856	47.564‡	3.496
Zhuang	84.894	52.078§	1.715
Coefficient of correlation (R^2)	0.536		
SE of regression	1.207		
F-statistic	12.449		
Sig. of regression	0.000		
Number of observations	451		

SE, Standard error; *VIF*, variance inflation factor.
*The regression is done by the ordinary least squares method. The dependent variable is the natural log of interprovincial import in 2010. The "Han," "Mulao," "Salar," and "Tu" variables with VIFs above 9 are omitted from the regression.
†Statistically significant at greater than the 1% level.
‡Statistically significant at greater than the 5% level.
§Statistically significant at greater than the 10% level.

Annex 5.2. Measuring ethnic diversity

Several different methods can be used to measure ethnic diversity (Guo, 2009, pp. 113–118). The simplest method is derived from the number of ethnic groups; thus, the ethnic diversity of a society is positively related to the number of ethnic groups involved. However, this method ignores the influence of population composition among all ethnic groups. For example, given two societies having the same number of ethnic groups but that in which population is equally distributed among all ethnic groups might be more ethnically diverse than one in which population is unevenly distributed among a ethnic *majority* and much smaller ethnic minorities. To demonstrate this point, let us consider an extreme case in which the ethnic majority accounts for almost 100 percent of the total population and each of the minorities retains a tiny share. Such a society can only be defined as a ethnically homogeneous, no matter how many minority groups exist.

The second method defines ethnic diversity in relation to the population ratio of the largest ethnic group. In many cases, the lower the ratio of the largest ethnic group, the greater the ethnic diversity it implies. However, because it only takes account of one (i.e., the largest) ethnic group, this method may miscalculate the ethnic diversity when two or more large ethnic groups exist simultaneously. Although the understanding of ethnic diversity may vary according to the perspective taken, the number of ethnic groups and their populations should be taken into account simultaneously.

In this research, we use the ethnic fractionalization index, which measures the probability that two individuals who meet at random will be from different ethnicgroups (Mauro, 1995; Easterly and Levine, 1997; La Porta et al., 1999; Bluedorn, 2001; Ottaviano and Peri, 2004; Alesina and Ferrara, 2005; and Montalvo and Reynal-Querol, 2005). Specifically, the ethnodiversity measure is defined as follows:

$$\text{Diversity} = 1 - \sum_{i=1}^{N} S_i^2 \qquad (5.1)$$

where s_i is the share of group i over the total of the population. This index represents the probability that two randomly drawn individuals from the population belong to different ethnic groups. This index reaches a theoretical maximum of 1 when every individual belongs to a different group. This measure implies that a country composed of, say, 100 equally sized groups is more fractionalized than a country with two equally sized groups.

Using Equation 5.1 and data shown in Table 5.A.2.1, we may calculate the ethnic diversity scores for Xinjiang and Tibet, which are shown in Table 5.A.2.2 in which the diversity scores of other Chinese provinces are also given.

Table 5.A.2.1 Ethnic populations of Xinjiang and Tibet, 2000 and 2010*

Ethnic group	Xinjiang (in persons)			Tibet (in persons)		
	2000	2010	Change (%)	2000	2010	Change (%)
Achang	2	5	150.00			NA
Bai	409	407	−0.49	722	395	−45.29
Baonan	571	568	−0.53	24	15	−37.50
Blang	9	23	155.56	16	4	−75.00
Buyi	977	797	−18.42	437	81	−81.46
Dai	59	121	105.08	14	35	150.00
Daur	5,541	5,536	−0.09	3	5	66.67
Deang	14	3	−78.57	1		−100.00
Derung	51	11	−78.43	6	37	516.67
Dong	946	753	−20.40	66	179	171.21
Dongxiang	55,841	61,613	10.34	111	757	581.98
Ewenki	72	26	−63.89			NA
Gaoshan	41	44	7.32		2	NA
Gelao	110	260	136.36	32	27	−15.63
Han	7,489,919	8,829,994	17.89	158,570	245,263	54.67
Hani	62	190	206.45	24	23	−4.17
Hezhe	22	33	50.00	1		−100.00
Hui	839,837	983,015	17.05	9,031	12,630	39.85
Jing	12	69	475.00		5	NA
Jingpo	27	33	22.22			NA
Jino		3	NA		1	NA
Kazak	1,245,023	1,418,278	13.92	8	2,143	26687.50
Kirgiz	158,775	180,472	13.67		2,678	NA
Korean	1,463	1,128	−22.90	51	26	−49.02
Lahu	28	73	160.71	19	4	−78.95
Lhoba	33	4	−87.88	2,691	3,489	29.65
Li	115	418	263.48	3	26	766.67
Lisu	34	104	205.88	17	25	47.06
Manchu	19,493	18,707	−4.03	153	718	369.28
Maonan	9	28	211.11		1	NA
Miao	7,006	7,626	8.85	389	416	6.94
Monba	11	4	−63.64	8,481	9,663	13.94
Mongol	149,857	156,280	4.29	690	307	−55.51
Mulao	29	77	165.52	5	2	−60.00
Naxi	73	89	21.92	1,223	1,133	−7.36
Nu	18	58	222.22	408	492	20.59
Oroqen	14	12	−14.29			NA
Pumi	10	12	20.00	15	16	6.67
Qiang	284	317	11.62	20	94	370.00
Russian	8,935	8,489	−4.99	20	3	−85.00
Salar	3,762	3,728	−0.90	228	255	11.84

(Continued)

Table 5.A.2.1 **(Continued)**

Ethnic group	Xinjiang (in persons)			Tibet (in persons)		
	2000	2010	Change (%)	2000	2010	Change (%)
She	166	167	0.60	6	8	33.33
Shui	301	90	−70.10		14	NA
Tajik	39,493	47,261	19.67	4		−100.00
Tatar	4,501	3,242	−27.97			NA
Tibetan	6,153	8,316	35.15	2,427,168	2,716,388	11.92
Tu	2,837	3,455	21.78	335	1,068	218.81
Tujia	15,787	17,850	13.07	303	451	48.84
Uyghur	8,345,622	10,001,302	19.84	701	205	−70.76
Uzbek	12,096	5,444	−54.99	1	2	100.00
Va	68	142	108.82	7	43	514.29
Xibe	34,566	34,399	−0.48		6	NA
Yao	723	942	30.29	26	137	426.92
Yi	1,593	2,954	85.44	287	396	37.98
Yugur	302	391	29.47	3	4	33.33
Zhuang	5,642	5,646	0.07	192	173	−9.90

NA = not available.
*Blanks denote no population is found.
Source: The Fifth and Sixth National Population Census of the People's Republic of China (conducted in 2000 and 2010, respectively).

Table 5.A.2.2 **Ethnic diversity scores by province (2000 and 2010)**

Province	2000	2010	Change (%)
Anhui	0.0134	0.0132	−1.49
Beijing	0.0838	0.0795	−5.13
Chongqing	0.1227	0.1272	3.67
Fujian	0.0338	0.0425	25.74
Gansu	0.1645	0.1764	7.23
Guangdong	0.0295	0.0391	32.54
Guangxi	0.5140	0.5055	−1.65
Guizhou	0.5876	0.5481	−6.72
Hainan	0.2932	0.2804	−4.37
Hebei	0.0841	0.0806	−4.16
Heilongjiang	0.0945	0.0700	−25.93
Henan	0.0248	0.0236	−4.84
Hubei	0.0840	0.0830	−1.19
Hunan	0.1894	0.1866	−1.48
Inner Mongolia	0.3433	0.3377	−1.63
Jiangsu	0.0071	0.0097	36.62
Jiangxi	0.0062	0.0068	9.68

(Continued)

Table 5.A.2.2 (Continued)

Province	2000	2010	Change (%)
Jilin	0.1714	0.1504	−12.25
Liaoning	0.2785	0.2655	−4.67
Ningxia	0.4564	0.4604	0.88
Qinghai	0.6307	0.6351	0.70
Shaanxi	0.0099	0.0101	2.02
Shandong	0.0140	0.0151	7.86
Shanghai	0.0126	0.0238	88.89
Shanxi	0.0063	0.0052	−17.46
Sichuan	0.0966	0.1169	21.01
Tianjin	0.0531	0.0503	−5.27
Tibet	0.1357	0.1733	27.71
Xinjiang	0.6242	0.6194	−0.77
Yunnan	0.5405	0.5402	− 0.06
Zhejiang	0.0171	0.0437	155.56

Spatial efficiency and Xinjiang: Policy options

6

Administrative divisions in China

Historical evolution

During ancient times, the Chinese nation was generally regarded as being divided into nine states (or prefectures). Since the founding of the feudal system, China's provincial administrations have been named as, *inter alia*,

- *jun* in the Qin dynasty (221–206 BC)
- *junguo* in the Western Han dynasty (206 BC–AD 25)
- *zhou* in the Eastern Han (AD 25–220) and the Wei (AD 220–265), the Jin (AD 266–420), and the North and South (AD 420–589) dynasties
- *dao* in the Tang dynasty (AD 618–907)
- *lu* in North and South Song (AD 960–1279) and the Jin (AD 1115–1235) dynasties
- *zhongshu-xingsheng* in the Yuan dynasty (AD 1279–1368)
- *xingsheng* (or *sheng*) in the Ming (AD 1368–1644) and the Qing (AD 1644–1911) dynasties and thereafter

Note that the Chinese character *dao* is still being used as *province* in both North and South Korea. The Chinese character *sheng* originally refers to the term *ministry*, which is still being used in Japan and Korea. *Zhongshu-xingsheng* and *xingsheng* (the latter has evolved to the term *sheng* in contemporary Chinese language) refer to the "ministerial representative agencies of central government to provinces."

At present, China's territorial-administrative hierarchy has three different types of provincial-level units: *sheng* (province), *zizhiqu* (autonomous regions), and *zhixiashi* (municipalities directly under the central government). In the Chinese state, administration *autonomous'* refers to self-government by a large and single (but not necessarily majority) ethnic minority in any given unit within the territorial hierarchy. Autonomous regions are provincial-level units of state administration where the presence of an ethnic minority is officially recognized. Municipalities are large cities, directly subordinate to the Chinese Communist Party Central Committee (CCPCC) and the State Council.

It should be noted that the three kinds of provincial administrations (*sheng, zizhiqu,* and *zhixiashi*) have different functions. More often than not, top *zhixiashi* leaders have been appointed as members of the Politburo of the CCPCC, something which has only happened to a small number of *sheng* and *zizhiqu* leaders.

China's Spatial (Dis)integration.

The autonomous regions (*zizhiqu*) are only established in areas where the ethnic minorities consist of the major portion of population. Compared with other forms of provincial administrations, the *zizhiqu* is, at least in form, the most politically and culturally autonomous of the three kinds of provincial administrations.

In addition, Hong Kong and Macao—which returned to China in 1997 and 1999, respectively—are now China's two special administrative regions (SARs). It was agreed on handover that the existing political and economic systems that prevailed before these dates would be maintained for 50 years.

Regional ethnic autonomy

In 1947 China's first, and ethnically based, autonomous region, Inner Mongolia, was established at the provincial level by the Chinese Communist Party (CCP). Then, after the foundation of the People's Republic of China (PRC) in 1949, the Chinese government began to introduce a system of regional autonomy for other non-Han ethnic areas. In 1952, the Chinese government issued the Program for the Implementation of Regional Ethnic Autonomy of the PRC, which included provisions on the establishment of ethnic autonomous areas and the composition of organs of self-government, as well as the right of self-government for such organs.

The first National People's Congress (NPC), convened in 1954, included the system of regional autonomy for ethnic minorities in the Constitution of the PRC. Thereafter, four autonomous regions appeared in China: Xinjiang Uyghur autonomous region (October 1955), Guangxi Zhuang autonomous region (March 1958), Ningxia Hui autonomous region (October 1958), and Tibet autonomous region (September 1965).

On May 31, 1984, on the basis of summarizing the experience of practicing regional autonomy for non-Han ethnic minorities, the second session of the Sixth NPC adopted the "Law of the People's Republic of China on Regional Ethnic Autonomy." The Law, which was further amended in 2001, has been the basic legal document for implementing the system of regional autonomy for ethnic minorities. It defines the relationship between the central government and the ethnic autonomous areas, as well as the relationship between different ethnic groups in ethnic autonomous areas.

In most cases, the name of an ethnic autonomous area consists of the name of the place, the name of the ethnic group, and the character indicating the administrative status, in that order. Take the Ningxia Hui autonomous region as an example: "Ningxia" is the name of the place, "Hui" is the name of the ethnic group, and "region" indicates the level of administration. At present, China has five provincial-level autonomous regions as following:

- Guangxi Zhuang autonomous region
- Inner Mongolia autonomous region
- Ningxia Hui autonomous region
- Tibet autonomous region
- Xinjiang Uyghur autonomous region

China has 30 non-Han autonomous prefectures (APs) in nine provincial administrations:

- Gansu province: Gannan Tibetan AP and Linxia Hui AP
- Guizou province: Qiandongnan Miao-Dong AP, Qiannan Buyi-Miao AP, and Qianxi'nan Buyi-Miao AP
- Hubei province: Enshi Tujia-Miao AP
- Hunan province: Xiangxi Tujia-Miao AP
- Jilin province: Yanbian Korean AP
- Qinghai province: Yushu Tibetan AP, Hainan Tibetan AP, Huangnan Tibetan AP, Haibei Tibetan AP, Guoluo Tibetan AP, and Haixi Mongolian-Tibetan AP
- Sichuan province: Ganzi Tibetan AP, Liangshan Yi AP, and Aba Tibetan-Qiang AP
- Xinjiang Uyghur autonomous region: Bayingolin Mongolian AP, Bortala Mongolian AP, Kizilsu Kirgiz AP, Changji Hui AP, and Yili (Ili) Kazak AP
- Yunnan province: Xishuangbanna Dai AP, Dehong Dai-Jingpo AP, Nujiang Lisu, Dali Bai AP, Diqing Tibetan AP, Honghe Hani-Yi AP, Wenshan Zhuang-Miao AP, and Chuxiong Yi AP

In addition, China has established 119 county-level autonomous administrations in 18 provincial administrations.

Communities of one ethnic group may establish, according to their respective sizes, different autonomous administrations. If we take the Hui ethnic group as an example, this includes:

(i) a provincial-level administration, called Ningxia Hui autonomous region;
(ii) a prefectural-level administration, called the Linxia Hui autonomous prefecture of Gansu province; and
(iii) a county-level administration, called the Mengcun Hui autonomous county of Hebei province.

In places where different ethnic groups live, each autonomous administration can be established based on either one ethnic group (e.g., Tibet autonomous region, Liangshan Yi autonomous prefecture of Sichuan province, and Jingning She autonomous county of Zhejiang province); or two or more ethnic groups (e.g., Haixi Mongolian-Tibetan autonomous prefecture of Qinghai province and Jishishan Bao'nan-Dongxiang-Salar autonomous county of Gansu province). If a minority ethnic group lives in an autonomous area of a bigger ethnic group, the former may establish its own subordinate autonomous areas. For example, Yili (Ili) Kazak autonomous prefecture and Yanqi Hui autonomous county are both found in the Xinjiang Uyghur autonomous region.

Organizationally, China's non-Han ethnic administrative areas are oriented in a multiethnic manner. For example, in addition to deputies from the ethnic group or groups exercising regional autonomy in the area concerned, the people's congresses of the autonomous areas also include an appropriate number of members from other ethnic groups who live in that autonomous area. "Among the chairman or vice chairmen of the standing committee of the people's congress of an autonomous area, there shall be one or more citizens of the ethnic group or groups exercising regional autonomy in the area concerned. The head of an autonomous region, autonomous prefecture, or autonomous county alike shall be a citizen of the ethnic group exercising regional autonomy in the area concerned. Other members of the people's governments of the autonomous areas shall include an appropriate number of members of the ethnic group exercising regional autonomy alongside members of other ethnic minorities."[1] The functionaries of the working departments subsidiary to the organs of self-government should be composed in a similar fashion.

By autonomy, it generally means that the head of government would be an ethnic majority in the region. However, the head is always subordinate to the secretary of the autonomous regional committee of the CCP, who was usually a Han Chinese. As a result, the role of the non-Han ethnic groups in the high-level decision making of the autonomous region is very limited.

Hierarchy, size, and efficiency

Hierarchy of power and efficiency

At present, China has the most complicated hierarchies of administrative divisions in the world. In addition to two SARs that have applied to Hong Kong and Macau, there are at least eight levels of administrative divisions in China, as following:[2]

(i) Provincial-level administrative divisions, including autonomous region (zìzhì qū), province (shěng), and municipality directly under central government (zhíxiá shì)

(ii) Subprovincial-level (fu shengji) administrative divisions, including subprovincial-level city (fu shengji shi), subprovincial-level autonomous prefecture (fu shengji zizhi zhou) (i.e., Ili Kazakh autonomous prefecture [IKAP]), subprovincial-level new area (fu shengji shixia qu) (i.e., the Binhai New Area of Tijian and the Pudong New Area of Shanghai, and so on

(iii) Prefectural-level administrative divisions, including prefectural-level city (diji shi), autonomous prefecture (zihi zhou), prefecture (diqu), league (meng), and so on

(iv) Subprefectural-level administrative divisions, including subprefectural-level city (fu diji shi)

(v) County-level administrative divisions, including district (shixia qu), county-level city (xianji shi), county (xian), autonomous county (zizhi xian), banner (qi), autonomous banner (zizhi qi), ethnic district (minzu qu), special district (tequ), and so on

(vi) Subcounty-level administrative divisions, including subcounty district (fu xianji qu), and so on

(vii) Township-level administrative divisions, including jiedao (district), zhen (town), xiang (township), minzu xiang (ethnic township), xianxia qu (district), sumu, minzu sumu (ethnic sumu), and so on

(viii) Village-level administrative divisions, including jumin weiyuan hui (neighborhood committee), shequ (community), cun (village), and gacha

[1] See "Law of the People's Republic of China on Regional Ethnic Autonomy" (1984, amended in 2001). Available at http://www.china.org.cn/english/government/207138.htm (accessed 2015-5-13).
[2] Based on Guo (2013b, p. 13) and miscellaneous news clippings.

An organizational pattern involving more classes of administrative divisions has been generally known to have a lower level of administrative efficiency. Recently, some provinces have been granted permission by the central government to practice the reform of administrative divisions (i.e., to eliminate the second-class administrative divisions) to increase spatial economic efficiency.

However, it seems that this administrative reform has encountered difficulties in large provinces. For example, in Henan or Shandong province, there are more than 100 counties and county-level administrative divisions (Guo, 2013b, p. 13). Without the participation of the prefecture-level administrations, it would be very difficult, if not impossible, for a single provincial governor to exert any effective influence on all of these county-level magistrates concurrently. This requires the decentralization of provincial powers and other, related political reforms at the provincial level or, alternatively, the reconstruction of China's provinces (especially oversized provinces).

Administrative size and efficiency

Although the formation of most provinces had taken place well before the founding of the PRC, in recent decades, a few of the others were divided into new provinces. In 1988, Hainan island, Guangdong province, was established as a new province, and, in 1997, Chongqing city and its surrounding areas, all of which had belonged to Sichuan province, became a province-level municipality under the direct control of the central government. Over recent decades, the total number of China's provincial administrations has increased from 29 in the mid-1950s to 30 in 1988 and 31 in 1997. But economic geographers and regional scientists still believe that the introduction of more (and smaller sized) provinces may help to improve the spatial efficiency of the Chinese economy.[3]

China's large provincial administrations, although they have some comparative advantages over the small ones in some circumstances, have been known to lack spatial administrative efficiency. Generally, the sources of benefits for large administrations may be grouped into two categories:

(i) The large administrations can make relatively efficient use of their fixed cost and hence gain considerable advantages over small administrations.
(ii) Marketing in a larger economy has many benefits, but the main economies of scale from marketing include the bulk purchases and distribution potentialities.

A number of advantages can lead to larger administrations experiencing risk-bearing economies. The underlying factor is that large administrations frequently engage in a range of diverse activities, so that a fall in the return from any one unit of economy does not threaten the stability of the whole economy. Although increases in size frequently confer advantages on an administration, there is a limit to the gains from growth in many cases. In other words, there is an optimal level of

[3] For example, the optimum numbers of China's provinces have been suggested as 58 by Hong (1945a and b), 40 to 43 by Hu (1991), and 43 by Guo (1993), cited from Liu (1996, pp. 153–6).

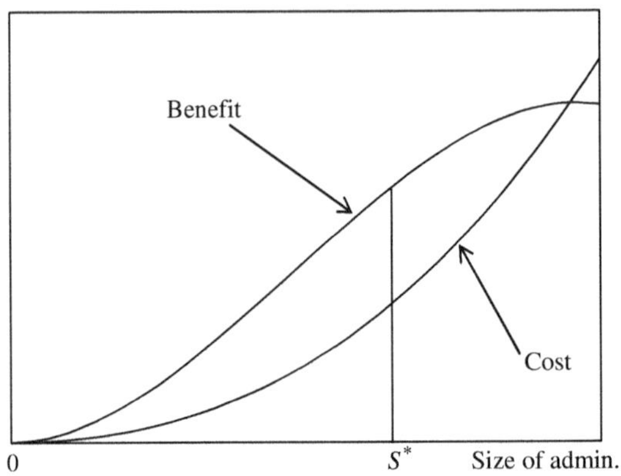

Figure 6.1 The optimal size (S^*) of an administrative (admin.) division.

capacity, and increases in size beyond this level will lead to a loss of economies of size and manifest themselves in rising average cost (Figure 6.1).[4] Without doubt, the increasing complexity of managing a large administration is the major source of administrative inefficiencies when its size grows beyond a certain level, and management of diverse socioeconomic affairs and risks become increasingly difficult.

Given China's huge size and enormous population, establishing new provincial administrations (including provinces or other provincial-level units) can serve two positive functions. The first concerns the increase of the efficiency of spatial administration over the peripheral areas, and the second relates to the realization of increased economies of scale by separating the marginal areas out of the oversized provincial administrations. In terms of spatial economics, by dividing large administrative areas into smaller ones, one may obtain significant economic benefits, especially for administrative areas that are under a centralized political system. Specifically, peripheral areas will usually benefit from the spatial division of a large administrative area into smaller ones even though previous central area may become a loser.[5]

To be clearer, let us look at Figure 6.2 in which the net benefit curves of *AB* and *BC*—two new administrative areas—are much more flat than that of Area *AC* (See Annex 6.2 at the end of this chapter for a more detailed mathematical analysis). As a result, the spatial economic disparity can be reduced automatically if Area *AC* is divided into Areas *AB* and *BC*. In addition, Area *AC*'s peripheral areas (i.e., around *A* and *C* in Figure 6.2) would have the largest increase of net benefit than any other areas even though its central area (i.e., around *B* in Figure 6.2) would have the largest reduction of net benefit than any other areas.

[4] A more detailed mathematical description of this mechanism can be found in Annex 6.1 at the end of this chapter.

[5] Note that geographical centers may not be political or economic centers. However, under such conditions as defined at the beginning of Annex 6.1, geographical and political and economic centers are usually the same.

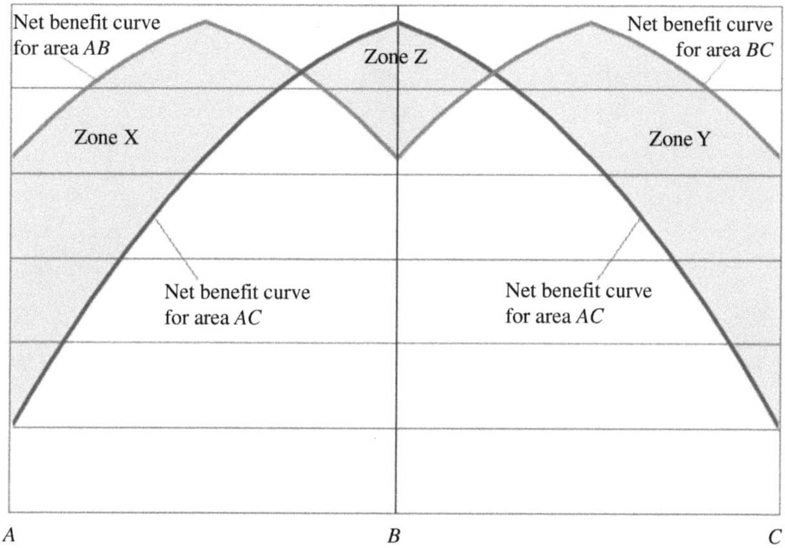

Figure 6.2 Spatial economic effects of centralized administrations. *AC* denotes a large administrative area, which can be divided into two independent administrative areas (*AB* and *BC*). Zones X and Y denote positive economic effects for Areas *AB* and *BC*, respectively, after the latter become independent. Zone Z denotes negative economic effects for the central area of AC or the cross-border area of AB and BC after the latter become independent. *Source*: Drawn by author based on Annex 6.2 in Chapter 6.

Dividing Xinjiang: A proposal

Southern Xinjiang as a new autonomy

With the most complicated hierarchy of administrative divisions in China, Xinjiang is divided into two prefecture-level cities, seven prefectures, and five autonomous prefectures for the Mongol, the , Kazakh, and Hui minorities (of which IKAP is a subprovincial-level administration). These are then divided into 11 districts, 20 county-level cities, 62 counties, and 6 autonomous counties (Guo, 2013a, p. 320). In addition, five or six subprefectural level cities (see Table 2.2 in Chapter 2), which do not belong to any prefecture, are administered by the Xinjiang Production and Construction Corps (XPCC), a de facto subprovincial (fu shengji) unit under the Chinese central government.

As a provincial-level administrative division of the PRC, Xinjiang has about one sixth of China's total land area. It also has much larger spatial ethnic diversities than any other provinces in China. Specifically, southern Xinjiang is dominated by Uyghurs, and the Han people account for a larger share of population in northern Xinjiang, with the exception of Turpan (dominated by the Uyghurs) and Altay (dominated by Kazakhs) (Figure 6.3).

Since the founding of the PRC in 1949, the Chinese central government has made various efforts to keep the peripheral, non-Han Chinese areas under its

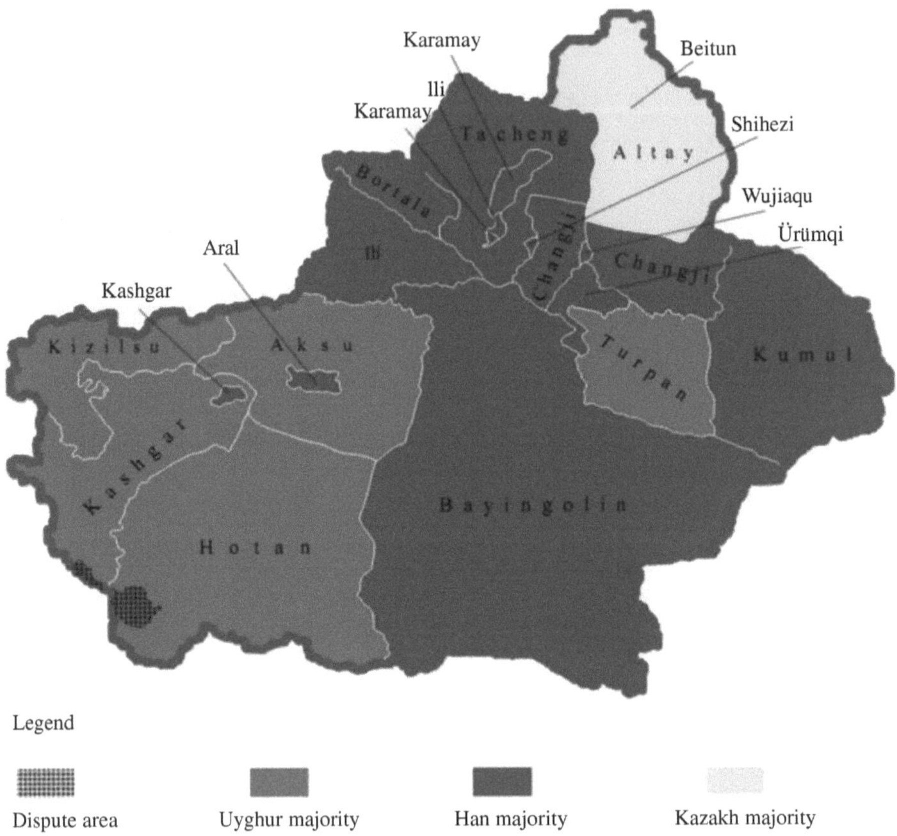

Figure 6.3 The ethnic divisions of Xinjiang.

effective control and to achieve a harmonious and prosperous society for China as a whole. In October 1955, Xinjiang Uyghur autonomous region was established. However, the costs spent have been quite high, and the outcomes achieved have rarely been encouraging. Is there any smart (or low-cost) way for China to put Xinjiang under its effective management?

Given Xinjiang's large territorial size on the one hand and its great spatial ethnic disparity on the other hand, it seems that the only way to achieve the effective management of Xinjiang is to divide it into smaller administrative areas.

Because Aksu prefecture (plus Aral Municipality), Kizilsu Kirgiz autonomous prefecture, Kashgar prefecture (plus Tumushuke Municipality), and Hotan prefecture are dominated the Uyghurs[6], a more purely Uyghurs-dominated autonomous region can be established in the southern part of Xinjiang. Specifically, the newly

[6] Specifically, as shown in Table 5.5 in Chapter 5, the Uyghurs of Aksu prefecture, Kizilsu Kirgiz autonomous prefecture, Kashgar prefecture, and Hotan prefecture account for 71.9%, 64.0%, 89.3%, and 96.4%, respectively.

established provincial administration may be named as "Nanjiang [southern Xinjiang] Uyghur autonomous region."

Compared with the previous Xinjiang Uyghur autonomous region, the Nanjiang Uyghur autonomous region is now more ethnically homogeneous. As a result, the Chinese central government's decision making can take into fuller account the ethnic features of Nanjiang. And, indeed, the new Nanjiang government, which is more representative of and on behalf of the Uyghurs in Nanjiang than before, is now more prepared to bargain with the central government for the benefits of its entire Uyghurs in Nanjiang.

The basic indicators of this new autonomous region can be found in Table 6.1. Obviously, Nanjiang Uyghur autonomous region can be treated as an ideal provincial administration. Compared with Xinjiang as a whole, in which there are two major ethnic groups (i.e., the Uyghur and the Han Chinese, with population shares of 45.2 percent and 40.6 percent, respectively), Nanjiang has now only one ethnic majority (i.e., the Uyghur, with a population share of 84.8 percent) and therefore can be called a true "Uyghur autonomous region." As for Xinjiang, the per capita

Table 6.1 After Xinjiang is divided into two smaller administrative divisions: Selected indicators, 2010

Indicator		Xinjiang as a whole	New provincial administrations	
			Nanjiang*	Beijiang†
Land area (thousand sq. km)		1,660	563	1,097
Population (million persons)		21.85	8.90	12.95
Population density (persons/sq. km)		13	16	12
Gross regional product (GRP) (million yuan)		653,315.08	89,846.22	563,468.86
Per capita GRP‡	Average level (yuan)	29,900	10,095	43,511
	Top region (yuan)	121,387	15,872	121,387
	Bottom region (yuan)	5,181	5,181	15,633
	Interregional gap (top-to-bottom ratio)	23.43	3.06	7.76
Ethnic groups	Uyghur (%)	45.2	84.8	18.0
	Han (%)	40.6	12.3	60.0
	Kazak (%)	6.7	0.0	11.3
	Others (%)	7.5	2.8	10.7
Ethnic diversity score§		0.6210	0.2650	0.5834

*Nanjiang Province includes Aksu prefecture (including Aral municipality), Hotan prefecture, Kashgar prefecture (including Tumushuke municipality), and Kizilsu Kirgiz autonomous prefecture.

†Beijiang Province includes Altay prefecture, Bayingolin Mongol autonomous prefecture, Bortala Mongol autonomous prefecture, Changji Hui autonomous prefecture (including Wujiaqu municipality), Ili Kazakh autonomous prefecture, Karamay municipality, Kuitun municipality, Kuitun municipality, Kumul prefecture, Shihezi municipality, Shihezi municipality, Tacheng prefecture, Turpan prefecture, and Urumqi municipality.

‡All monetary values are measured at current prices.

§Calculated based on Annex 5.2 in Chapter 5.

Source: Calculated by author based on Xinjiang Bureau of Statistics (2011) and Tables 5.1 and 5.5.

gross regional product (GRP) of the richest region (i.e., Karamay Municipality) was 23.43 times that of the poorest region (i.e., Hotan prefecture) in 2010; after Nanjiang Uyghur autonomous region is established, the top-to-bottom ratio of per capita GRP can be reduced to only 3.06. As discussed in Chapter 5, social unrest is usually less likely to occur in a more ethnically homogeneous and less economically divergent region.

Northern Xinjiang as a new province

After the "Nanjiang Uyghur autonomous region" is established for the southern part of Xinjiang, it can be found that most of the northern part of Xinjiang is dominated by the Han Chinese (see Figure 6.3). Naturally, the northern part of Xinjiang can be established as a new provincial administration. The newly established provincial division may be named "Beijiang [northern Xinjiang] Province."

Then how to deal with the final political status of the other non–Han-dominated areas in Beijiang province? In the current Xinjiang Uyghur autonomous region, Turpan prefecture's Uyghurs account for 70.0 percent of its total population, and Altay prefecture's Kazakhs account for 51.4 percent for its total population (see Table 5.5 in Chapter 5). As the first step, they may be established as two prefectural-level autonomies that are directly under the administrations of Beijiang province. Tentatively, they may be named Turpan Uyghur autonomous prefecture and Altay Kazakh autonomous prefecture.

After Beijiang province is established, the new provincial government should relinquish Bayingolin and Bortala, which are two Mongol autonomous prefectures in the current Xinjiang Uyghur autonomous region. As a matter of fact, as of 2010, the population shares of Mongols in Bayingolin and Bortala Mongol autonomous prefectures are only 3.70 percent and 5.64 percent, respectively.[7] As a result, according to China's existing system of regional ethnic autonomy, Bayingolin and Bortala should have been defined as Uyghur or Kazak (if not Han) autonomous prefectures in current Xinjiang Uyghur autonomous region. Nevertheless, in the new Beijiang province, these formerly autonomous prefectures may be simply changed to Bayingolin prefecture and Bortala prefecture.

The basic indicators of this new province can be found in Table 6.1. Obviously, Beijiang province can be treated as an ideal provincial administration. Compared with Xinjiang as a whole, in which there are two major ethnic groups (i.e., the Uyghur and the Han Chinese, with population shares of 45.2 percent and 40.6 percent, respectively), Beijiang has now only one ethnic majority (i.e., the Han Chinese, with a population share of 60.0 percent). As for Xinjiang, the per capita

[7] According to the Sixth National Population Census of the PRC conducted in November 2010, the population shares of Bayingolin Mongol autonomous prefecture are 56.68% (Han Chinese), 33.82% (Uyghurs), 3.70% (Mongols), and 5.80% (others), and those of Bortala Mongol autonomous prefecture are 67.19% (Han Chinese), 12.53% (Uyghurs), 9.14% (Kazaks), 5.64% (Mongols), 4.49% (Hui Chinese), and 1.01% (others).

GRP of the richest region (i.e., Karamay Municipality) was 23.43 times that of the poorest region (i.e., Ili prefecture) in 2010; after Beijiang province is established, the top-to-bottom ratio of per capita GRP can be reduced to only 7.76. As discussed in Chapter 5, social unrest is usually less likely to occur in a more ethnically homogeneous and less economically divergent region.

Rationale for the proposal

Historically and geographically, Xinjiang is divided into two parts, southern Xinjiang (or Nanjiang) and northern Xinjiang (or Beijiang). In older English-language reference works, the area of Xinjiang was often referred to as Chinese Turkestan, Sinkiang, East Turkestan, or Uyghuristan. More specifically, the term East Turkestan only referred to the Xinjiang area south of the Tian Shan mountains, North of the Tian Shan was called Zungaria (or Dzungaria).

The boundary of the division is the Tianshan mountain range. On both sides of the mountain range, different geographical and environmental features exist. Whereas the south side—traditional home to the Uyghurs—is mainly covered by Gobi deserts, with some arable land suitable to agriculture, the north side—which was dominated by the Mongols and the Kazakhs in history and is now the place where the Han Chinese is the majority—features mountains and grassland.

It is not new for China to create a province in Xinjiang. As early as the 1880s, the Xinjiang province was already established there by the Qing court. And Xinjiang's province status was not abolished until October 1, 1955, when the Xinjiang Uyghur autonomous region was founded by the PRC. In terms of geopolitics and culture, the northern–southern division of Xinjiang is quite rationale. For example, before 1831, only a few hundred Chinese merchants lived in southern Xinjiang, and only a few Uyghurs lived in northern Xinjiang (Millward, 2007, p. 104–105).

Yet the major portion of the southern Xinjiang area has many different ethnic, social, and religious elements from the rest of China. This can be witnessed in Eimer's (2014, p. 6) travelogue:

> *The longer I stayed in Kashgar, the more I began to realize that Xinjiang was a country within a country, one with far closer connections to its central Asian neighbors than to China. The Sunday market, the social event of the week, was an exhilarating mix of local tongues and minorities. Ethnic Kyrgyz and Tajiks from the surrounding countryside arrived on donkey carts piled high with watermelons, or trailing dispirited lines of sheep, to join the Uyghurs and Pakistanis in selling their wares. The different languages vied with each other to such overpowering effect that I no longer felt I was in China.*

If taking the XPCC and the IKAP into account, Xinjiang is already under, in addition to a provincial-level administration, two other subprovincial-level administrations. However, the XPCC is a quasimilitaristic organ composed of and established by the People's Liberation Army. If the XPCC was a necessary unit during the early stage of the PRC, its legitimacy has been now challenged, especially when the PRC government decides to implement the peaceful development strategy. To this end, the Chinese government may consider other, alternative measures by which to replace the XPCC.[8] On the other hand, the IKAP is the only subprovincial-level autonomous prefecture that has been created in China, reflecting its crucial geopolitical and cultural positions in Xinjiang and China as well.

There is another benefit of dividing Xinjiang into two smaller provincial administrations. As in other large provincial administrations in China, Xinjiang Uyghur autonomous region has the most complicated hierarchies of administrative divisions. As of 2013, there exist seven levels of administrative divisions in Xinjiang:

(i) Subprovincial-level (fu shengji) administrative divisions, such as the XPCC and the IKAP
(ii) Prefectural-level administrative divisions, including prefectural-level city, autonomous prefecture, prefecture, and so on
(iii) Subprefectural-level administrative divisions, such as Shihezi city and Wujiaqu city
(iv) County-level administrative divisions, including district, county-level city, county, autonomous county, banner, autonomous banner, and so on
(v) Sub-county-level administrative divisions
(vi) Township-level administrative divisions
(vii) Village-level administrative divisions

After the Nanjiang Uyghur autonomous region and the Beijiang province are established, the new provincial leaders are able to optimize the hierarchies of administrative divisions of their own. Because Nanjiang is much smaller than Beijiang and other inland Chinese provinces, it may follow the Hainan model (i.e., only retaining three levels—county, township, and village—of administrative divisions). As a result, the spatial administrative efficiency of Nanjiang province can be increased accordingly.

The northern–southern division of Xinjiang, although quite a necessary measure for the effective management of Xinjiang, still has some weakness. For example, after the political division, Turpan prefecture (or "Turpan Uyghur autonomous prefecture" in the newly established Beijiang province)—with more than two thirds of its population being Uyghurs—has not been incorporated into the Nanjiang Uyghur autonomous region. Instead, it now becomes a Uyghur autonomous prefecture of Beijiang province. In addition, the Kazakhs, who share the same religious belief as the Uyghurs, may not be happy after they find that they will be ruled under a Han-dominated provincial administration. However, if some appropriate arrangements are made, all possible negative effects could be minimized, if not removed.[9] Above

[8] Note that even within the XPCC, large disparities in economic development still exist. According to the statistical data released by the XPCC (2011), Divisions 8, 4, 6, and 7 (all located in northern Xinjiang) have much higher levels of per capita GRP than Divisions 3, 10, 9, and 14 (all located in southern Xinjiang).

[9] For example, the Chinese government may persuade the Uyghurs in Turpan of that the "Turpan Uyghur Autonomous Prefecture, Beijiang Province" itself is not different from—or may even be better than—its former name "Turpan Prefecture, Xinjiang Uyghur Autonomous Region."

all, this division can not only better reflect the principle of spatial economic efficiency (as discussed under Administrative Size and Efficiency), but it can also help the central government to design and implement differentiated, flexible policies for different parts (and, of course, different ethnic groups) of today's Xinjiang.

Indeed, the making of Xinjiang as two different subpolitical divisions can achieve "one-stone-for-two-birds" results. Specifically, the Chinese central government is able to enrich the content of "autonomy" for the non-Han provincial-level autonomy in southern Xinjiang. On the other hand, with regard to Beijiang province, where the Han Chinese are the ethnic majority, China is now free to implement more Sinolized policies as long as the remaining non-Han minorities living there are not affected. Now, the degree of ethnic heterogeneity (or diversity) is much smaller in both Nanjiang and Beijiang than Xinjiang as a whole (see Table 6.1). As a result, the chance for any interethnic unrest within each of the newly established provincial divisions can be reduced accordingly.

Since the founding of Xinjiang Uyghur autonomous region in 1955, the Xinjiang government has made various efforts in order to keep Xinjiang's peripheral, non-Han areas under its effective control. However, the costs spent have been quite high, and the outcomes achieved have rarely been encouraging, especially in southern Xinjiang (or Nanjiang).[10] It can be sure that all the above arrangements will not only conciliate the Uyghurs in Nanjiang and the Han Chinese in Beijiang, but it will also save much energy that the old Xinjiang government and the PRC government as well have had to put into the management of the peripheral, non-Han Chinese areas.

Nevertheless, the Han–Uyghur unrest cannot disappear automatically in Xinjiang. Instead, some of it may have transformed from intraregional (i.e., within current Xinjiang) to interregional (i.e., between Nangjiang and Beijiang) patterns. However, if additional political and physical measures (or barrier walls, in the worst situation) are taken, interregional ethnic conflicts can be more easily managed than intraregional ones. Above all, most, if not all, of the Uyghurs and the Han Chinese are now happier than before because both of them have become the ethnic majorities in their newly established provincial administrations.

Broader implications

China has invested much heavily in Xinjiang to progressively and fully assimilate everything in Xinjiang into the PRC. China has been the second largest economy in the world—and, definitely, if based on purchasing power parity (PPP) rates, its economy would have already surpassed that of the United States. China is now much richer than any period in its history. However, China's current policies toward Xinjiang are unsustainable. It seems that, until now, Xinjiang has been a big

[10] Obviously, we may observe from Table 3.1 in Chapter 3 that most of the past Han–Uyghur unrest occurred in southern Xinjiang.

burden to China. And what China has gained—politically and economically—is far less than what it has paid. China needs smart policies.

It should be noted that by establishing more provincial administrations, China can achieve better development opportunities for peripheral areas, especially in large areas such as Xinjiang. This is particularly so given that the Chinese economy is still operated under a highly centralized system. However, it seems unlikely that the central government will be willing to create and, of course, be able to deal with any more provincial administrations under the current political and economic systems. This requires further political reforms. Of course, this chapter only presents some preliminary ideas about the future of Xinjiang. If the PRC government is smart enough, the proposals suggested in this chapter could be further developed into more practical measures. Furthermore, they can be applied not only to Xinjiang but to other territorial issues as well.

More than three decades ago, when addressing Hong Kong's return to China's sovereignty in 1997, Deng Xiaoping proposed "one country, two systems." According to the mini-constitution "Basic Law," "[t]he Hong Kong Special Administrative Region may on its own, using the name of 'Hong Kong, China,' maintain and develop relations and conclude and implement agreements with foreign states and regions and relevant international organizations in the appropriate fields, including the economic, trade, financial and monetary, shipping, communications, tourism, cultural and sports fields."[11]

It should be noted that Hong Kong and its people are not the only winner for the post-1997 arrangement of Hong Kong, a former colony of United Kingdom. Mainland China has also benefited by granting Hong Kong as a "quasi-state" under the framework of "one country, two systems." Since the return to its motherland, Hong Kong has not only avoided becoming a "troublemaker" to mainland China's socialist system, but it also has helped to raise China's international influences. For example, the appointment of Margaret Chan as the Director-General of the World Health Organization (WHO) in 2006 with the extensive back up from the Beijing government triumphs the success of "second-tier sovereignty" system in modern state diplomacy (Shen, 2009, pp. 361–382). In the WHO, Mrs. Chan not only represents "Hong Kong, China"; she also represents China as a whole.

If the PRC's new leaders are wiser than Deng Xiaoping, they could successfully apply the Hong Kong mode (or a revision of it) to Xinjiang's Uyghur-dominated areas, given that the latter's independent-state status cannot be recognized. In this way, China's soft power could be greatly enhanced. Furthermore, if both sides of the Taiwan Straits are wiser than their predecessors, the PRC and Taiwan—both of which share a single Chinese ancestor—can form a "Greater China Community" or a "Pan-Chinese Union." Only when that day comes can China itself eventually realize its "dream of a strong nation."

[11] Cited from "The Basic Law of the Hong Kong Special Administrative Region of the People's Republic of China" (Chapter VII: External Affairs, Article 151). Available at http://www.basiclaw.gov.hk/en/basiclawtext/index.html (accessed 2015-5-13).

Annex 6.1. Spatial optimization of an administrative area

Let us first consider an administrative area which applies an authoritative system or can be simply called an authoritative state. The term "authoritative" is used here to simply denote that all economic activities are highly centralized. In addition, we make the following assumptions:

(1) There are high-level tariff and nontariff barriers between the state and the outside world.
(2) All socioeconomic factors are uniformly distributed throughout the state.
(3) There exists an isotropic communication and transport network in the state.
(4) The aim of the state is to maximize its well-being through the behavior of its economic agents.

Obviously, assumption 1 is also characteristic of isolated states, which means that most economic activities are domestically conducted. Assumptions 2 and 3 are very common in most spatial economic analyses. Finally, assumption 4 simplifies our topic to a pure economic issue in which consumers seek to maximize satisfaction and firms seek to maximize their return from productive activity.

On the basis of the above assumptions, we can further define that the cost (c) and benefit (r) resulting from the transactions between a given site (x, y) and any other site (x', y') of the state (denoted by Ω) are related to the distance (l) between the two sites. Here, l ranges between 0 and L (L is the longest distance within the given state). The total cost and benefit of the given site (x, y) within the state can be expressed by different integral calculus functions with respect to distance. As for the total cost function, i.e., $C(l)$, we have

$$C(x, y) = \oint_{\Omega} c(l)\mathrm{d}l, \text{ with } l \in (0, L) \text{ and } (x,\ y) \in \Omega. \tag{6.1}$$

For simplicity of exposition, we only analyze the one-dimension case. Consider Figure 6.4 in which A and B (with the coordinates of 0 and L, respectively) symbolize the borders of the state and O (with the coordinate of $L/2$) is the center of the area. According to assumptions 2 and 3, the transaction cost (c) and benefit (r) between any two sites in the state can be expressed respectively by the monotonously increasing and monotonously decreasing functions of the distance (l) between the two sites. In the simplest case, we use two linear functions:

$$c(l) = a + bl, \text{ with } a \geq 0 \text{ and } b \geq 0. \tag{6.2}$$

$$r(l) = e - fl, \text{ with } e \geq \text{ and } f \geq 0. \tag{6.3}$$

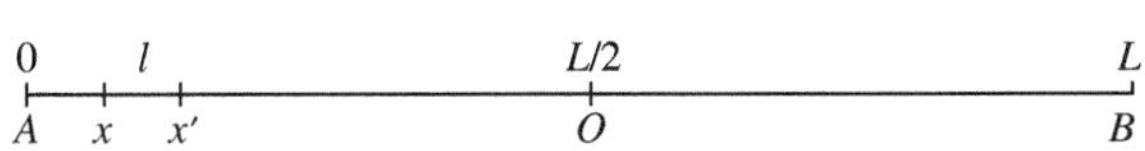

Figure 6.4 A simplified authoritative state.

In Equations 6.2 and 6.3, we define that there exist two parts for the cost and benefit, respectively: (1) fixed cost (a) and the fixed benefit (e) are constant and have nothing to do with distance (l) and (2) variable cost (bl) and variable benefit ($-fl$) are related to distance (l). Obviously, the longer the distance (l), the larger the variable cost and the smaller the variable benefit. Literally, b is defined as "marginal cost on distance," and $-f$ is defined as "marginal benefit on distance."

According to assumptions 2 and 3, the total cost of the state can be further expressed as a function of the location (i.e., x in the one-dimensional case). Inserting Equation 6.2 into Equation 6.1, we have

$$C(x) = \int_0^x (a + bl)\mathrm{d}l + \int_0^{L-x} (a + bl)\mathrm{d}l, \text{ with } x \in (0, L). \tag{6.4}$$

Finally, after solving Equation 6.4, we obtain a nonlinear function of the total cost (C) with respect to the location (x):

$$C(x) = bx^2 - bLx + aL + bL^2/2 \tag{6.5}$$

Let the differential of C with respect to x be zero, that is, $\mathrm{d}C/\mathrm{d}x = 2bx - bL = 0$, we can find that when $x = L/2$, the function of the total cost (C) goes to an extremity site. Apparently, because $C = aL + bL^2/2$ is maximized when $x = 0$ and L (i.e., the peripheries), it can be seen that $C = aL + bL^2/4$ is minimized when $x = L/2$ (i.e., the center). Finally, we have the following:

- The transaction costs of an authoritative state are usually minimized at its center and maximized at its peripheries.

The assumptions at the beginning of this Annex can help us to build up a function of the total benefit with respect to the location in the state. Let Equation 6.3 denote the benefit function with respect to the distance between x and x' (shown in Figure 6.4). The function of the total benefit now becomes:

$$R(x) = \int_0^x (e - fl)\mathrm{d}l + \int_0^{L-x} (e - fl)\mathrm{d}l = -fx^2 + fLx + eL - fL^2/2, \text{with } x \in (0, L). \tag{6.6}$$

Similar to Equation 6.5, Equation 6.6 also has three kinds of marginal properties for $R(x)$ with respect to x. Let $\mathrm{d}R/\mathrm{d}x = -2fx + fl = 0$, then $x = L/2$. Specifically, (i) when $0 \le x < L/2$, $\mathrm{d}R/\mathrm{d}x > 0$, that is, R is an increasing function of x; (ii) when $L/2 < x \le L$, $\mathrm{d}R/\mathrm{d}x < 0$, that is, R is a decreasing function of x; and (iii) when $x = L/2$, $\mathrm{d}R/\mathrm{d}x = 0$. As a result, we conclude that when $x = 0$ and $x = L$, $R(0) = R(L) = eL - fL^2/2$, and when $x = L/2$, $R(L/2) = eL - fL^2/4$. In other words, $R(x)$ is maximized at the center (i.e., $x = L/2$) and is minimized on the boundaries (i.e., $x = 0$ and $x = L$).

Obviously, the benefit expressed by Equation 6.6 yields an inverted U−shape curve, that is, the state's total benefit always decreases from the center (which is represented by O in Figure 6.4) to the peripheries (which is represented by A and B in Figure 6.4). Finally, we have the following:

- The transaction benefits of an authoritative state are usually maximized at its center and minimized at its peripheries.

Next, let us investigate if there is any optimal size for an isolated administrative area. In the simplest case, we derive the total transaction cost for the administrative area by the integral calculus of Equation 6.5, that is,

$$TC(L) = aL^2 + bL^3/3 \tag{6.7}$$

And we derive the total benefit for the administrative area by the integral calculus of Equation 6.6, that is,

$$TR(L) = eL^2 - fL^3/3 \tag{6.8}$$

Subtracting TC from TR, we obtain the net benefit for the isolated administrative division $Y = TR - TC$, where TC and TR are defined in Equations 6.7 and 6.8, respectively. By deriving the first-order differential of the net benefit (Y) with respect to size (here, it refers to L) and let it be zero, we obtain

$$\mathrm{d}Y/\mathrm{d}L = TR'(L) - TC'(L) = 2(e-a)L - (b+f)L^2 = 0 \tag{6.9}$$

Solving Equation (6.9), we have

$$L^* = 2\frac{e-a}{b+f} \tag{6.10}$$

Equation 6.10 indicates that an optimal size can be found for an isolated administrative area if $e > a$, $b \neq 0$ and $f \neq 0$. On the basis of the above results, we may conclude that (i) the net benefit (Y) increases with respect to the size of the administrative area (L) when $L < L^*$; (ii) the net benefit (Y) decreases with respect to the size of the administrative area (L) when $L > L^*$; and (iii) the net benefit (Y) is maximized when $L = L^*$ (Figure 6.5). Finally, we have the following:

- The size of an isolated administrative area can be optimized at a certain level, if e > a in Equation 6.10.

The total cost and total benefit grow at different rates when the administrative area grows in size (here, it refers to L), as demonstrated in Figure 6.5. When the size administered is small, the increased total cost will decrease with respect to the increase of size because the fixed cost remains as a constant. However, when the size exceeds a certain quantity, the socioeconomic affairs will no longer be efficiently managed. As a result of the managing difficulties of the additional quantity of size, there will eventually bear a relatively higher increased rate of administrative expenditure (cost) with respect to the increase of size. If the functions of the total cost and benefit with respect to size are known, we can derive the most efficient level of the size by maximizing the net benefit Y (i.e., benefit minus cost).

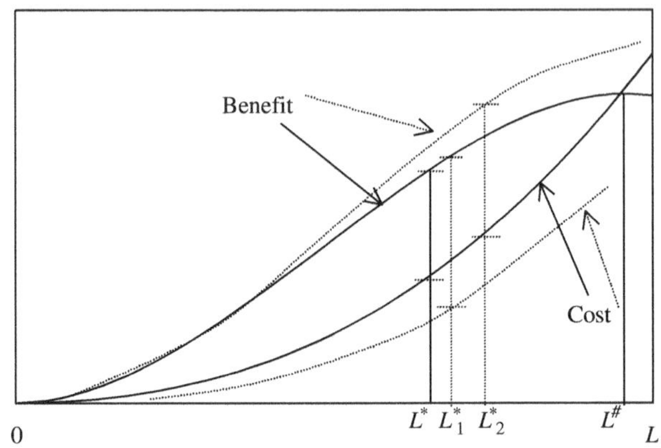

Figure 6.5 Changes of optimal sizes of an administrative area. x_1^* and x_5^* denote the places at which the largest net benefits are found for Areas *AB* and *BC*, respectively when the two areas are isolated; x_2^* and x_4^* denote the places at which the largest net benefits are found for Areas *AB* and *BC*, respectively when the barriers between Areas *AB* and *BC* are reduced; and x_3^* denotes the place at which the largest net benefits are found for Area *AC* before the latter is divided into Areas *AB* and *BC*.

Next, let us suppose that the isolated administrative area has now transformed from the backward transportation and communication network to a well-developed one. Along with the reduced transaction cost throughout the whole area, the coefficients a and b in Equation 6.2 will be reduced accordingly. Under the condition that $e > a$, the optimal the size (as illustrated by L_1^* in Figure 6.5) will be, *ceteris paribus,* larger than L^*, that is:

- The optimal size of an isolated administrative area is positively related to the stage of economic development, if $e > a$ in Equation 6.10.

Finally, let us suppose that the isolated administrative area has now transformed to an open one. The most different consequence is that the latter can benefit not only from internal but also from external trade and other economic activities. As a result, Equation 6.3 will bear the following changes: the coefficient of e will increase and that of f will decrease accordingly. At last, we may find that, if $e > a$, the optimal level of the size (as illustrated by L_2^* in Figure 6.5) will be, *ceteris paribus,* larger than L^*, that is:

- The optimal size of an open administrative area is larger than that of an isolated one, if $e > a$ in Equation 6.10.

Annex 6.2. Changes of spatial benefit curves after an administrative area is divided into smaller ones

In this section, we will discuss another issue: after an administrative area is divided to two or more smaller administrative areas, how the pattern of spatial economic disparity will be influenced.

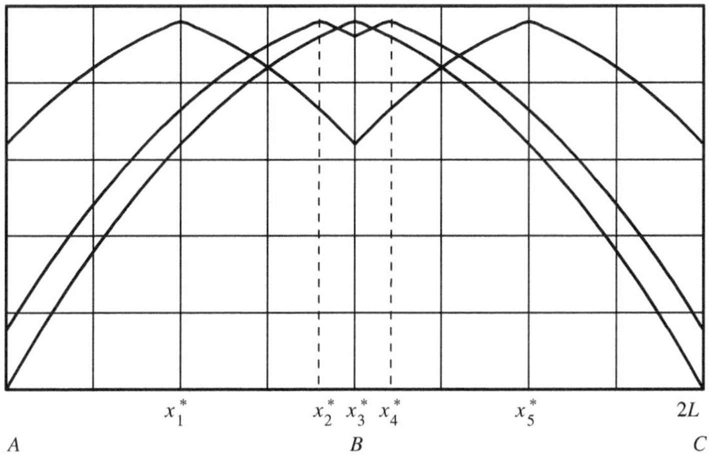

Figure 6.6 Changes of net benefit curves after Area *AC* is divided into Areas *AB* and *BC*.

To make composition easier, let us analyze two areas (*AB* and *BC*), both of which are characterized by assumptions 1 to 4 of Annex 6.1 of Chapter 6. We assume that the total cost and benefit of site x (here $0 \leq x \leq L$) within Areas *AB* and *BC* are expressed by Equations 6.4 and 6.6, respectively. When *AB* and *BC* are two isolated areas, as discussed in Annex 1.2 in Chapter 1, the largest net benefit of Areas *AB* and *BC* can be found at x_1^* and x_5^*, respectively (as demonstrated in Figure 6.6).

When *AB* and *BC* are not isolated areas, the total cost $C_{ABC}(x)$ and benefit $R_{ABC}(x)$ of the given site x within Areas *AB* and *BC* may then be expressed by

$$\begin{aligned} &C_{ABC}(x) = C_{AB}(x) + \alpha C_{BC}(x) = \\ &\int_0^x (a+bl)\mathrm{d}l + \int_0^{L-x}(a+bl)\mathrm{d}l + \alpha\int_{L-x}^{2L-x}(a+bl)\mathrm{d}l \\ &= bx^2 - (1+\alpha)bLx + (1+3\alpha)bL^2/2 + (1+\alpha)aL, \text{ with } \alpha \geq 1. \end{aligned} \tag{6.11}$$

$$\begin{aligned} &R_{ABC}(x) = R_{AB}(x) + \beta R_{BC}(x) = \\ &\int_0^x (e-fl)\mathrm{d}l + \int_x^{L-x}(e-fl)dl + \beta\int_{L-x}^{2\mathrm{L}-\mathrm{x}}(e-fl)dl \\ &= -fx^2 + (1+\beta)fLx - (1+3\beta)fL^2/2 + (1+\beta)eL, \text{ with } \beta \in (0,1). \end{aligned} \tag{6.12}$$

In Equation 6.11, when the inter-area tariff and nontariff barriers change from the maximum to the minimum level, α will decrease to 1 accordingly. In Equation 6.12, when the inter-area barriers change from the maximum level to 0, β will increase from 0 to 1 accordingly. In the extreme case, when $\alpha = \beta = 1$, there do not exist any inter-area barriers.

If the net benefit is expressed by the total benefit less total cost—that is, $Y_{ABC} = R_{ABC}(x) - C_{ABC}(x)$—then, by deriving the first order differential of the net benefit (Y_{ABC}) with respect to x (i.e., $dY_{ABC}/dx = -2fx + (1+\beta)fL - 2bx + (1+\alpha)bL = 0$), we obtain

$$x^* = \frac{(1+\alpha)b + (1+\beta)f}{2(b+f)}L = \frac{L}{2} + \frac{\alpha b + \beta f}{2(b+f)}L \tag{6.13}$$

at which the net benefit is maximized. Obviously, because $b > 0$, $f > 0$, $L \geq 0$, $\alpha \geq 1$, and $\beta \geq 0$, then we have $x^* \geq L/2$. This result implies that the optimized economic center of Area *AB* will move away from its core (*O*), as a result of the removal of inter-area barriers.

Let us look at the extreme case. When all inter-area barriers are removed (i.e., $\alpha = \beta = 1$), Equation 6.13 becomes $x^* = L/2 + L/2 = L$, indicating that the largest net benefit of Areas *AB* and *BC* can be found at the peripheral area (i.e., x_3^*), as demonstrated in Figure 6.6.

In most circumstances, the net benefit of Area *AB* is maximized at a place from x_1^* to x_3^* and that of Area *BC* is maximized at a place from x_3^* to x_5^*. And from Figure 6.5, one may observe that the spatial benefit curve will become flatter after a large administrative area (i.e., *AC* in this research) is divided into two smaller ones (i.e., *AB* and *BC* in this research).

References

Alesina, A., & Ferrara, E. A. (2005). Ethnic diversity and economic performance. *Journal of Economic Literature*, *43*(3), 762–800.

Al Jazeera (February 29, 2012). Deadly knife attack reported in China. *Al Jazeera English*. Available at: <http://wwwaljazeera.com/news/asia-pacific/2012/02/20122294486118604.html> Accessed April 19, 2013.

Anderson, J. E., & Marcouiller, D. (2002). Insecurity and the pattern of trade: Empirical investigation. *The Review of Economics and Statistics*, *84*, 342–352.

Anonymous (April 25, 2013). Xinjiang's counter-terrorist actions face new challenges. *Wen Wei Po*. Available at: <http://paperwenweipo.com/2013/04/25/WW1304250003.htm> Accessed April 25, 2013.

Arceneaux, K., & Huber, G. A. (2007). What to do (and not to do) with multicollinearity in state politics research. *State Politics and Policy Quarterly*, *7*(1), 81–101.

Associated Press. (August 25, 2010). Police arrest 4 in bombing in restive west China. Available at: <http://www.google.com/hostednews/ap/article/ALeqM5i3E80IT1fQrscs2ThcPaY-BuipzwD9HQH1880> Accessed March 18, 2013.

Avery, N. (August 4, 2008). Xinjiang border patrol attacked, 16 dead, Xinhua says. *Bloomberg*. Available at: <http://wwwbloomberg.com/apps/news?pid=20601087&sid=aWA1HpopOpWg&refer=home> Accessed March 19, 2013.

Barriaux, M. (November 9, 2009). China executes nine over Xinjiang unrest. *Agence France Press*. Available at: <http://www.google.com/hostednews/afp/article/ALeqM5i86FMEClVmUn3KnSfvPjP7JuhHQA> Accessed March 18, 2013.

BBC. (January 8, 2007). China "anti-terror" raid kills 18. BBC News. Available at: <http://news.bbc.co.uk/2/hi/asia-pacific/6241073.stm> Accessed March 19, 2013.

BBC. (July 7, 2009). Riots engulf Chinese Uyghur city. BBC News. Available at: <http://news.bbc.co.uk/2/hi/asia-pacific/8137824.stm> Accessed March 18, 2013.

BBC. (September 4, 2009). "Five die" in China ethnic unrest. BBC Online. Available at: <http://news.bbc.co.uk/2/hi/asia-pacific/8238768.stm> Accessed March 18, 2013.

BBC. (December 9, 2009). New arrests over China's Xinjiang ethnic riots. BBC News. Available at: <http://news.bbc.co.uk/2/hi/asia-pacific/8404245.stm> Accessed April 15, 2013.

BBC. (September 8, 2011). Islamic militant group "behind Xinjiang attacks." BBC News. Available at: <http://www.bbc.co.uk/news/world-asia-pacific-14834042> Accessed March 18, 2013.

Beattie, V. (July 8, 2009). Violence in Xinjiang nothing new says China analyst. Voice of America. Available at: <http://www1.voanews.com/english/news/a-13-2009-07-07-voa6-68790522.html> Accessed April 15, 2013.

Becquelin, N. (2000). Xinjiang in the nineties. *The China Journal*, *44*, 65–90.

Bellér-Hann, I. (2008). *Community matters in Xinjiang (1880–1949): Towards a historical anthropology of the Uyghur*. Boston: Brill.

Berry, W. D., & Feldman, S. (1985). *Multiple regression in practice*. London: Sage Publications.

Bingtuan Daily. (December 2011). Bulletin of XPCC's major data at the Sixth National Population Census. Available at: <http://epaper.bingtuannet.com/index.asp?id=54966> Accessed March 23, 2013.

Blanchard, B. (April 30, 2014). China says three killed in attack at Xinjiang train station. Available at: <http://www.reuters.com/article/2014/04/30/us-china-xinjiang-blast-idUSBREA3T0HX20140430> Accessed May 9, 2014.

Blanchard, B., & Buckley, C. (February 29, 2012). Twenty dead in attack in China's restive west. *Reuters.* Available at: <http://www.reuters.com/article/2012/02/29/us-china-xinjiang-idUSTRE81S0TV20120229>

Bluedorn, J. C. (2001). Can democracy help? Growth and ethnic divisions. *Economic Letters, 70*, 121–126.

Boisso, D., & Ferrantino, M. (1997). Economic distance, cultural distance and openness in international trade: Empirical puzzles. *Journal of Economic Integration, 12*, 456–484.

Bovingdon, G. (2005). *Autonomy in Xinjiang: Han nationalist imperatives and Uyghur discontent. Political Studies 11*. Washington, DC: East-West Center. Available at: <http://www.eastwestcenter.org/fileadmin/stored/pdfs/PS011.pdf> Accessed March 18, 2013.

Branigan, T., & Watts, J. (July 5, 2009). Muslim Uyghurs riot as ethnic tensions rise in China. *The Guardian.* Available at: <http://www.guardian.co.uk/world/2009/jul/05/china-Uyghur-riots-xianjing> Accessed March 23, 2013.

Bristow, M. (October 21, 2009). Many "missing" after China riots. BBC News. Available at: <http://news.bbc.co.uk/2/hi/8317644.stm> Accessed April 18, 2013.

Bristow, M. (August 19, 2010). Blast kills seven in China's Xinjiang. BBC News. Available at: <http://www.bbc.co.uk/news/world-asia-pacific-11021645> Accessed March 25, 2013.

Buckley, C. (July 10, 2009). Chinese police break up Uyghur protest after prayers. *Reuters.* Available at: <http://wwwreuters.com/article/2009/07/10/us-china-xinjiang-demonstration-sb-idUSTRE5691HI20090710> Accessed March 18, 2013.

Castets, R. (2003). The Uyghurs in Xinjiang—The malaise grows. *China Perspectives.* Available at: <http://chinaperspectives.revues.org/648>

CCTV. (March 8, 2004). Official: West-east gas pipeline to be in operation this year. CCTV News, Available at: <http://www.cctv.com/english/20040308/101582.shtml> Accessed April 16, 2013.

CCTV. (September 7, 2009). Urumqi calms after syringe attacks. Available at: <http://english.cctv.com/program/chinatoday/20090907/101680.shtml> Accessed March 31, 2013.

CPPCC Daily (August 19, 2010). *The inland senior middle schools for Xinjiang: 10 years of interethnic exchange and solidarity.* Beijing: Chinese People's Political Consultative Conference (CPPCC). Available at: <http://www.qstheory.cn/zz/shzyzzzd/201008/t20100819_43387.htm> Accessed August 31, 2014.

Chang, A. (August 20, 2010). Official: Attack in western China targeted police. *Businessweek.* Available at: <http://www.businessweek.com/ap/financialnews/D9HN6NP80.htm> Accessed April 18, 2013.

China Association of Communications and Transportation and the National Development and Reform Commission of the PRC (2001). *China Communications Yearbook 2000.* Beijing: China Communications Yearbook Press.

China Association of Communications and Transportation and the National Development and Reform Commission of the PRC (2011). *China Communications Yearbook 2010.* Beijing: China Communications Yearbook Press.

China Daily. (September 4, 2009). Nearly 200 arrest warrants issued. Available at: <http://www.chinadaily.com.cn/china/2009-09/04/content_8653710.htm> Accessed March 18, 2013.

China Daily. (September 9, 2009). Syringe attacks persist in Urumqi. Available at: <http://www.chinadaily.com.cn/china/2009-09/09/content_8669084.htm> Accessed March 23, 2013.

China Daily. (May 26, 2014). Anti-terror campaign launched. Available at: <http://www.chinadaily.com.cn/language_tips/cdaudio/2014-05/26/content_17540525.htm> Accessed May 26, 2014.

China Radio International (February 28, 2012). Xinjiang terrorist gets death sentence. Available at: <http://english.cri.cn/6909/2012/03/28/189s689660.htm> Accessed February 18, 2013.

China Radio International (October 16, 2012). China starts constructing 3rd west-to-east gas pipeline. Available at: <http://english.cri.cn/6909/2012/10/16/2361s727502.htm> Accessed April 2, 2013.

Chi-yuk, C. (July 22, 2011). Ban on Islamic dress sparked Uyghur attack. *South China Morning Post.*

Chi-yuk, C. (July 25, 2011). Hotan attack takes a toll on business. *South China Morning Post.*

Cihai (1999). *Cihai.* Shanghai: Shanghai Cishu Press.

Clem, W., & Chi-yuk, C. (July 14, 2009). Conflicting stories emerge after police shoot dead Uyghur pair. *South China Morning Post*A1.

Cnradio. (November 10, 2006). News—Qingzang railway transported 0.73M passengers, boosts Tibet economy (in Chinese). Available at: <http://www.cnradio.com.cn/2004news/internal/200611/t20061110_504324840.html> Accessed April 15, 2013.

Combes, P.-P., Lafourcade, M., & Mayer, T. (2005). The trade-creating effects of business and social networks: Evidence from France. *Journal of International Economics, 66*(1), 1–29.

Dasgupta, S. (July 20, 2011). China finally ready to admit Pak's role in Xinjiang violence. *The Times of India* Available at: <http://articles.timesofindia.indiatimes.com/2011-07-20/china/29793567_1_uyghur-east-turkistan-islamic-movement-contemporary-international-relations> Accessed April 26, 2013.

Deardorff, A. V. (1998). Determinants of bilateral trade: Does gravity work in a neoclassical world? In J. A. Frankel (Ed.), *The regionalization of the world economy* (pp. 7–22). Chicago: University of Chicago Press.

Delabroye, C., & Le Belzic, S. (August 4, 2008). At least 16 policemen reportedly killed in bomb attack. France 24. Available at: <http://www.france24.com/en/20080804-attack-xinjiang--policemen-china-killed-olympic-games&navi=MONDE> Accessed March 26, 2013.

Denyer, S. (May 22, 2014). Attack on market in China's restive Xinjiang region kills at least 31, injures 90. *Washington Post* (World News).

Denyer, S. (September 1, 2014). China's campaign for mixed marriages spreads to troubled Xinjiang. *Washington Post,* Washington, DC. Available at: <http://www.washingtonpost.com/blogs/worldviews/wp/2014/09/01/chinas-campaign-for-mixed-marriages-spreads-to-troubled-xinjiang/> Accessed September 2, 2014.

Dillon, M. (2003). Xinjiang: China's Muslim Far Northwest *(Durham East Asia Series).* London: Routledge.

Dwyer, A. (2005). *The Xinjiang conflict: Uyghur identity, language policy, and political discourse. Political Studies 15.* Washington, DC: East-West Center. Available at: <http://www.eastwestcenter.org/fileadmin/stored/pdfs/PS015.pdf> Accessed March 25, 2013.

Easterly, W., & Levine, R. (1997). Africa's growth tragedy: Policies and ethnic division. *Quarterly Journal of Economics*, *112*, 1203–1250.

Eaton, J., & Tamura, A. (1994). Bilateralism and regionalism in Japanese and U.S. trade and direct foreign investment patterns. *Journal of the Japanese and International Economics*, *8*, 478–510.

Eichengreen, B., & Irwin, D. (1995). Trade blocs, currency blocs and the reorientation of trade in the 1930s. *Journal of International Economics*, *38*(2), 89–106.

Eimer, D. (2014). *The emperor far away: Travels at the edge of China*. New York: Bloomsbury.

Epstein, G. (July 5, 2009). Uyghur unrest. Forbes. Available at: <http://www.forbes.com/2009/07/05/china-riots-xinjiang-opinions-beijing-dispatch.html> Accessed March 21, 2013.

Fan, W.-C. (September 6, 2009). *Chinese doctors say some claims of needle-stabbings are mistaken*. CNN. Available at: <http://edition.cnn.com/2009/WORLD/asiapcf/09/05/china.urumqi.unrest/index.html> Accessed April 12, 2013.

Foroutan, F., & Pritchett, L. (1993). Intra-sub-Saharan African trade: Is it too little? *Journal of African Economics*, *2*(May), 74–105.

Foster, P. (July 7, 2009). Han Chinese mob takes to the streets in Urumqi in hunt for Uyghur Muslims. *The Daily Telegraph (London)*. Available at: <http://www.telegraph.co.uk/news/worldnews/asia/china/5766327/Han-Chinese-mob-takes-to-the-streets-in-Urumqi-in-hunt-for-Uyghur-Muslims.html> Accessed February 25, 2013.

Frankel, J. A., Stein, E., & Wei, S.-J. (1997a). *Regional trading blocs in the world economic system*. Washington, DC: Institute for International Economics.

Frankel, J. A, Stein, E., & Wei, S.-J. (1997b). Trading blocs and the Americas: The natural, the unnatural, and the super-natural. *Journal of Development Economics*, *47*(1), 61–95.

Frankel, J. A., & Wei, S.-J. (1995). European integration and the regionalization of world trade and currencies: The economics and the politics. In B. Eichengreen, F. Frieden, & J. von Hagen (Eds.), *Monetary and fiscal policy in an integrated Europe* (pp. 23–51). New York: Springer.

Gladney, D. C. (2003). Islam in China. In D. L. Overmyer (Ed.), Religion in China Today *(The* China Quarterly *Special Issues No. 3)*. Cambridge: Cambridge University Press.

Gladney, D. C. (2004a). Islam in China: Accommodation or separatism? In R. Michael Feener (Ed.), *Islam in world cultures: Comparative perspectives* (pp. 161–183). New York: ABC-CLIO.

Gladney, D. C. (2004b). The Chinese program of development and control, 1978–2001. In S. Frederick Starr (Ed.), *Xinjiang: China's Muslim Borderland* (pp. 63–98). New York: M.E. Sharpe.

Global Security (2008). Uyghur developments in the 1990s. *Global Security Military News*. <http://www.globalsecurity.org/military/world/war/Uyghur-5.htm> Accessed April 29, 2013.

Greene, W. H. (2002). *Econometric analysis* (5th ed.). Upper Saddle River, NJ: Prentice-Hall.

Guiso, L., Sapienza, P., & Zingales, L. (2006). Does culture affect economic outcomes? *The Journal of Economic Perspectives*, *20*, 23–48.

Guo, R. (1993). *Economic analysis of border-regions: Theory and practice of China (zhongguo shengji bianjie diqu jingji fazhan yanjiu)*. Beijing: China Ocean Press.

Guo, R. (2004). How culture influences foreign trade: Evidence from the U.S. and China. *The Journal of Socio-Economics*, *33*, 785–812.

Guo, R. (2007a). *Territorial disputes and resource management: A global handbook*. New York: Nova Science.

Guo, R. (2007b). Linguistic and religious influences on foreign trade: Evidence from East Asia. *Asian Economic Journal*, *21*(1), 100–121.

Guo, R. (2009). *Intercultural economic analysis: Theory and method*. New York: Springer.

Guo, R. (2012). *Territorial disputes and conflict management: The art of avoiding war*. London: Routledge.

Guo, R. (2013a). *Regional China: A business and economic handbook*. London: Palgrave-Macmillan.

Guo, R. (2013b). *Understanding the Chinese economies*. Oxford: Academic Press/Elsevier.

Guo, R. (2014). *China's spatial (Dis)integration: Tibetan-Han unrest and the development strategy for Tibet*. Draft (forthcoming by Springer, Berlin).

Guo, R. (forthcoming). Spatial (dis)integration and multiethnic economies: Evidence from China's interprovincial data. Draft.

Havrylyshyn, O., & Pritchett, L. (1991). *European trade patterns after the transition*. Policy, Research and External Affairs Working Paper *No. 74*. Washington, DC: The World Bank.

Heckscher, E. F. (1919). The effect of foreign trade on the distribution of income. *Ekonomisk Tidskrift*, *21*, 497–512.

Helpman, E. (1987). Imperfect competition and international trade: Evidence from fourteen industrial countries. *Journal of the Japanese and International Economies*, *1*(Mar.), 62–81.

Hille, K. (July 21, 2011). Tense mood prevails after Xinjiang attack. *Financial Times*. Available at: <http://www.ft.com/intl/cms/s/0/6a1558cc-b39d-11e0-b56c-00144feabdc0.html#axzz1TOSCFiJu> Accessed April 2, 2013.

Hille, K. (July 25, 2011). Symbol of hope in Hotan yet to reap rewards. *Financial Times*. Available at: <http://www.ft.com/intl/cms/s/0/976f39a6-b41e-11e0-9eb8-00144feabdc0.html> Accessed March 2, 2013.

Hong, F. (1945a). On the "new provincial regions" (xin shengqu lun), *Ta Kung Pao*, October 2.

Hong, F. (1945b). Reconstructing provincial regions: A preliminary discussion (chonghua shengqu fang'an chuyi). *Oriental Journal*, *43*(6).

Hu, H. (1991). The past, present, and future administrative divisions in China (zhongguo xingzheng qu de guoqu, xianzai he weilai). In Chinese Society for Administrative Divisions (Ed.), *Studies of China's Administrative Divisions* (zhonguo xingzheng quhua yanjiu), Beijing: China Social Press, 1991, pp. 144–167.

Hu, Y., & Xiaoxun, L. (July 18, 2009). Urumqi riot handled "decisively, properly." *China Daily*. Available at: <http://www.chinadaily.com.cn/china/2009-07/18/content_8444365.htm> Accessed March 5, 2013.

Huang, C. (February 9, 2011). The successful practice of pairing-aid mechanisms (in Chinese). *China Ethnic Daily*. Available at: <http://www.mzb.com.cn/html/report/172316-1.htm> Accessed March 2, 2013.

Huntington, S. P. (1996). *The clash of civilization and the remaking of world order*. New York: Simon and Schuster.

Iredale, R. N., Bilik, F., Guo, S., Wang, & Hoy, C. (2001). *Contemporary minority migration, education and ethnicity in China*. Cheltenham, UK: Edward Elgar.

Jia, C. (December 5, 2009). Riot woman sentenced to death for killing. *China Daily*. Available at: <http://www.chinadaily.com.cn/cndy/2009-12/05/content_9122992.htm> Accessed March 25, 2013.

ia, C. (July 5, 2013). Pain lingers after Xinjiang terrorist attack. *China Daily*. Available at: <http://www.chinadaily.com.cn/2013-07/05/content_16731733.htm> Assessed July 7, 2013.

Jia, C., & Xiaodong, W. (June 27, 2013). 27 killed as rioting hits Xinjiang. *China Daily* (US edition), p. 3.

Jia, Z. (January 1, 2013). The electrified Lanzhou-Xinjiang Railway completes. *Xinjiang Economic Daily*, Urumqi. Available at: <http://news.hexun.com/2013-01-01/149693574.html> Accessed April 22, 2013.

Kim, H. (2004). *Holy war in China: The Muslim Rebellion and State in Chinese Central Asia, 1864–1877*. Stanford, CA: Stanford University Press.

Krishnan, A. (July 21, 2011). Analysts see Pakistan terror links to Xinjiang attack. *The Hindu*. Available at: <http://www.thehindu.com/news/international/article2277362.ece> Accessed April 5, 2013.

Krugman, P. R. (1995). Growing world trade: Causes and consequences. *Brookings Papers on Economic Activity*, *1*, 327–362.

La Porta, R., Lopez de Silanes, F., Shleifer, A., & Vishni, R. W. (1999). The quality of government. *Journal of Law, Economics and Organization*, *15*(1), 222–279.

Li, H., & Hu, B. (2010). An investigation into interethnic marriages in an Uyghur village of Hunan province (in Chinese). *Journal of Huaihua University*, *29*(9), 5–8.

Linder, S. B. (1961). *An essay on trade and transformation*. New York: John Wiley and Sons.

Linders, G. -J. M., Slangen, A., de Groot, H., & Beugelsdijk, S. (2005). Cultural and institutional determinants of bilateral trade flows, Tinbergen Institute Discussion Paper No. 074/3.

Linnemann, H. (1966). *An econometric study of international trade theory*. Amsterdam: North-Holland.

Liu, J. (1996). *China's administrative divisions: Theory and practice (zhongguo xingzheng quhua de lilun yu shijian)*. Shanghai: East China Normal University Press.

Liu, Q., Yongbin, Z., Zheng, W., & Yanling, D. (2009). A study of China's regional economic disequilibrium, extremity, and its evolutions (in Chinese). *Statistics and Decision*, *12*, 1–12.

Lu, F., & Jianhua, X. (2004). China's regional economic disparities: Evidence from the Gini and the Theil coefficients. The Working Papers of RCEWCC (Vol.1). East China Normal University, Shanghai.

Ma, D. (2002). *State interest override everything: Thoughts about the Xinjiang security problems* (in Chinese). Urumqi, China: Xinjiang People's Press.

Macartney, J. (July 7, 2009). Riot police battle protesters as China's Uyghur crisis escalates. *The Times* (London). Available at: <http://www.timesonline.co.uk/tol/news/world/asia/china/article6655225.ece> Accessed April 25, 2013.

Mackerras, C. P. (2005). People's Republic of China: Background paper on the situation of the Tibetan population, A Writenet Report commissioned by United Nations High Commissioner for Refugees, Protection Information Section (DIP). Available at: < http://www.unhcr.org/cgi-bin/texis/vtx/refworld/rwmain/opendocpdf.pdf?docid = 423ea9094 > Accessed 25.04.13.

Mallory, J. P., & Mair, V. H. (2000). *The Tarim Mummies: Ancient China and the Mystery of the earliest peoples from the West*. London: Thames & Hudson.

Markusen, J. (1986). Explaining the volume of trade: An eclectic approach. *American Economic Review*, *76*, 1002–1011.

Mauro, P. (1995). Corruption and growth. *Quarterly Journal of Economics*, *110*, 681–712.

McDonell, S. (April 19, 2014). Seven killed in China-Vietnam border shootout. Available at: <http://www.abc.net.au/news/2014-04-19/an-seven-killed-in-shootoutonvietnam-china-border3a-vietname/5399600> Accessed April 23, 2014.

McLaughlin, K. E. (July 17, 2009). Fear grips Shaoguan's Uyghurs. *Far East Economic Review*. Available at: <http://www.feer.com/politics/2009/july58/Fear-Grips-Shaoguans-Uyghurs> Accessed March 5, 2013.

McMillen, D. H. (1981). Xinjiang and the production and construction corps: A Han organization in a non-Han region. *The Australian Journal of Chinese Affairs*, *6*, 65–96.

Millward, J. A. (1998). *Beyond the pass: Economy, ethnicity, and empire in Qing Central Asia, 1759–1864*. Stanford, NJ: Stanford University Press.

Millward, J. A. (2007). *Eurasian crossroads: A history of Xinjiang*. New York: Columbia University Press.

Montalvo, J. G., & Reynal-Querol, M. (2005). Ethnic polarization, potential conflict and civil war. *American Economic Review*, *95*(3), 796–816.

Mullen, J. (June 27, 2013). Report: Unrest in China's Xinjiang kills 27. CNN. Available at: <http://edition.cnn.com/2013/06/27/world/asia/china-xinjiang-violence/index.html?iref=allsearch> Assessed June 29, 2013.

National Bureau of Statistics (2001). *China statistical Yearbook 2000*. Beijing: China Statistics Publishing House.

National Bureau of Statistics (2011). *China statistical Yearbook 2010*. Beijing: China Statistics Publishing House.

Noland, M. (2005). Affinity and international trade. Working Paper Series WP 05-3. Washington, DC: Institute for International Economics.

Ohlin, B. (1933). *Interregional and international trade*. Cambridge, MA: Harvard University Press.

Olsen, A. (July 19, 2011). China says 14 extremists killed in Xinjiang attack. Associated Press. Available at: <http://www.deseretnews.com/article/700164452/China-says-14-extremists-killed-in-Xinjiang-attack.html> Accessed March 21, 2013.

Olsen, A. (September 4, 2011). China sentences 4 Uyghur men to death over attacks. Associated Press. Available at: <http://www.google.com/hostednews/ap/article/ALeqM5iOpqZmsdAMEIxkU8IsMofjfnrqmA> Accessed March 25, 2013.

Olsen, K. (August 28, 2014). *Uyghur entrepreneur confronts prejudice in China*. Beijing: French Press Agency (AFP). Available at: <http://news.yahoo.com/Uyghur-entrepreneur-confronts-prejudice-china-054039215.html > Accessed September 1, 2014.

O'Neill, M. (April 13, 2008). The conqueror of China's wild west. *Asia Sentinel*. Available at: <http://www.asiasentinel.com/index.php?option=com_content&task=view&id=1148&Itemid=31 > Accessed March 13, 2013.

Ottaviano, G., & Peri, G. (2004). The economic value of cultural diversity: Evidence from US cities. NBER Working Paper No. 10904 (November), National Bureau of Economic Research, Cambridge, MA, USA.

Pomfret, J., & Tarrant, W. (June 26, 2009). *Ethnic tensions spark brawl at China factory: Report*. Beijing: Reuters. China Digital Times. Available at: <http://chinadigitaltimes.net/2009/06/ethnic-tensions-spark-brawl-at-china-factory-report/ > Accessed March 25, 2013.

Poncet, S. (2005). A fragmented China: Measure and determinants of Chinese domestic market disintegration. *Review of International Economics*, *13*(3), 409–430.

Pöyhönen, P. (1963). A tentative model for the volume of trade between countries. *Weltwirtschaftliches Archiv*, *90*(1), 93–99.

Qian, W. (2012). Comparative case studies of rent-seeking in China's state-owned enterprises: the Ministry of Railway and China Mobile. CMC Senior Theses. Paper 498. Available at: <http://scholarship.claremont.edu/cmc_theses/498> Accessed March 26, 2013.

Qian, X., Zhuo, W., Yamada, K., & Wang, Q. (2012). Pairing aid system in disaster relief and recovery management: Lessons from Wenchuan Earthquake in China. Proceedings of international conference on disaster management. Available at: <http://iiirr.ucalgary.ca/files/iiirr/A3-2_.pdf> Accessed March 2, 2013.

Radio Free Asia. (August 19, 2010). Slain patrolmen "checked" Uyghurs. Available at: <http://www.rfa.org/english/news/uyghur/Uyghur%20policemen%20killed%20in%20 attack-08192010163454.html> Accessed March 21, 2013.

Rajan, D.S., & Tiku, A. (July 29, 2011). Understanding the Hotan (Xinjiang) riot in China. *Sri Lanka Guardian* (Chennai). Available at: <http://www.srilankaguardian.org/2011/07/understanding-hotan-xinjiang-riot-in.html> Accessed March 25, 2013.

Rana, S. (June 6, 2013). Building on ties: New premier indicates plan to link Gwadar with China. *The Express Tribune*, p. 1.

Rauch, J. E. (1999). Networks versus markets in international trade. *Journal of International Economics*, *48*(1), 7–35.

Rauch, J. E. (2001). Business and social networks in international trade. *Journal of Economic Literature*, *39*(4), 1177–1203.

Rauch, J. E., & Trindade, V. (2002). Ethnic Chinese networks in international trade. *Review of Economics and Statistics*, *84*(1), 116–130.

Reuters. (March 27, 2012). China sentences Uyghur man to death over Xinjiang attacks. Available at: <http://in.reuters.com/article/2012/03/27/china-xinjiang-idINDEE82Q03A 20120327> Accessed March 22, 2013.

Reuters. (April 24, 2013). China sentences Uyghur man to death over Xinjiang attacks. Available at: <http://www.reuters.com/article/2013/04/24/us-china-xinjiang-idUSBRE 93N15C20130424> Accessed April 25, 2013.

Rodríguez, P. A. (2013). Violent resistance in Xinjiang (China): Tracking militancy, ethnic riots and_knife-wielding' terrorists (1978–2012). *Historia Actual Online*, *30*, 135–149.

Rodrik, D (2007). *Normalizing industrial policy*. Draft, Harvard University. Available at: <http://www.hks.harvard.edu/fs/drodrik/Research%2520papers/Industrial%2520Policy %2520_Growth%2520Commission_.pdf> Accessed March 25, 2013.

Rose, A. K. (2004). Macroeconomic determinants of international trade. NBER working paper. Cambridge, MA: National Bureau of Economic Research.

Rossabi, M. (2005). *Governing China's multiethnic frontiers*. Seattle, WA: University of Washington Press.

Rumbaugh, T., & Blancher, N. (2004). China: International trade and WTO accession. IMF Working Paper WP/04/36, Washington, DC: International Monetary Fund (IMF).

Saiget, R. J. (April 19, 2005). Caucasians preceded East Asians in basin. *The Washington Times* (News World Communications).

Sainsbury, M. (January 2, 2010). The violence has ended in Urumqi but shadows remain in hearts and minds. *The Australian.* Available at: <http://www.theaustralian.com.au/news/world/the-violence-has-ended-in-urumqi-but-shadows-remain-in-hearts-and-minds/story-e6frg6so-1225815346008> Accessed March 5, 2013.

Seymour, J. D. (2000). Xinjiang's production and construction corps, and the sinification of Eastern Turkestan. *Inner Asia*, *2*, 171–193.

Shanghai Daily. (July 9, 2009). Kindness found amid the violence. *Shanghai Daily*, Shanghai.

Shanhaijing. (2001). *The classic of mountains and seas*. An ancient Chinese book written in the Eastern Zhou dynasty (771–221 BC) and compiled by Liu Xin (c. 53–23 BC). Beijing: Beijing Yanshan Press.

Shao, W. (July 21, 2011). Attack on police station was 'long-planned'. *China Daily*, Beijing. Available at: <http://www.chinadaily.com.cn/china/2011-07/21/content_12947603.htm> Accessed March 12, 2013.

Shao, W. (April 3, 2012). XPCC ranks second among China's provincial economic growth rates (in Chinese). *China Daily*, Beijing. Available at: <http://www.chinadaily.com.cn/dfpd/2012-04/03/content_14974971.htm> Accessed April 16, 2013.

Shen, S. (2009). Borrowing the Hong Kong identity for Chinese diplomacy: Implications of Margaret Chan's World Health Organization election campaign. *Pacific Affairs*, *81*(3), 361–382.

Shenzhen Daily. (May 16, 2014). Islamist group claims Xinjiang station bombing. Available at: <http://www.szdaily.com/content/2014-05/16/content_9511754.htm> Accessed May 18, 2014.

Sima, Q. 104 bc (1997). *Shiji (Records of the Great Historian) (in Chinese)*. Beijing: Taihai Press.

Simon, L.J. (2004). Detecting multicollinearity using variance inflation factors, Penn State Department of Statistics, The Pennsylvania State University. Available at: <http://online.stat.psu.edu/online/development/stat501/12multicollinearity/05multico_vif.html> Accessed April 13, 2013.

Smith, W. (March 16, 2014). Kunming terrorist attack: A resident's perspective. <http://thediplomat.com/2014/03/kunming-terrorist-attack-a-residents-perspective/> Accessed April 13, 2014.

Starr, S. F. (2004). *Xinjiang: China's Muslim Borderland*. New York: M.E. Sharpe.

Starr, S.F. (July 22, 2013). Most Xinjiangers do not want separations—An interview (in Chinese), *Huanqiu Times*. Available at: <http://mil.huanqiu.com/observation/2013-07/4156361.html> Accessed July 23, 2013.

State Council. (2003). History and development of Xinjiang. State Council of the People's Republic of China, Beijing, May. Available at: <http://www.china.org.cn/e-white/20030526/9.htm> Accessed April 12, 2013.

State Ethnic Affairs Commission (2008). *National border defense work conference*. Beijing: State Ethnic Affairs Commission. Available at: <http://www.seac.gov.cn/gjmw/zt/2008-12-15/1229136023815597.htm> Accessed April 12, 2013.

State Ethnic Affairs Commission, various years, *China Ethnic Statistical Yearbook*. The State Ethnic Affairs Commission of the People's Republic of China, Beijing, China.

Statistical Bureau of the Xinjiang Production and Construction Corps. (March 28, 2013). A statistical bulletin of national economic and social development of the Xinjiang Production and Construction Crops in 2012 (in Chinese). Available at: <http://tjj.xjbt.gov.cn/xxgk/sjzx/tjgb/206213.htm> Accessed April 4, 2013.

Stewart, J. Q. (1948). Demographic gravitation: Evidence and applications. *Sociometry*, *2*, 31–58.

Tang, D., & Watt, L. (May 26, 2014). City in China bombing divided by ethnic tension. Available at: <http://news.yahoo.com/city-china-bombing-divided-ethnic-tension-160618469.html> Accessed May 26, 2014.

Tinbergen, J. (1962). An analysis of world trade flows, the Linder hypothesis, and exchange risk. In J. Tinbergen (Ed.), *Shaping the world economy*. New York: The Twentieth Century Fund.

Toops, S. (2004). Demographics and development in Xinjiang after 1949. Washington, DC: East-West Center, Working Papers (East-West Center), Available at: <http://www.east-westcenter.org/fileadmin/stored/pdfs/EWCWwp001.pdf> Accessed March 15, 2013.

United Nations. (March 1, 2014). 7 Security Council condemns the terrorist attack at Chinese train station Kunming leadmin/stored/pdfs/EWCWwp001.pdfleadmin/stored/pdfs/EWC Available at: <http://www.un.org/apps/news/story.asp?NewsID=47256&Cr=China&Cr1=> Accessed April 14, 2014.

United Nations Development Program (2010). *China Human Development Report 2009/2010*. Beijing: United Nations Development Program (UNDP) and Renmin University of China.

Wan, W. (October 30, 2013). Chinese police say Tiananmen Square crash was in University of ChinaKunming hinaKunmstron, *Washington Post* (Asia Pacific News).

Watson, B. (1993). *Records of the Grand Historian of China: Han Dynasty II.* Translated from the Shiji of Sima Qian. Columbia University Press, New York. Revised Edition.

Watts, J. (July 10, 2009). Old suspicions magnified mistrust into ethnic riots in Urumqi. *The Guardian (London)*Available at: <http://wwwguardian.co.uk/world/2009/jul/10/china-riots-Uyghurs-han-urumqi > Accessed April 11, 2013.

Wong, C. (September 3, 2014). Mixed marriages get cash gifts in Xinjiang. *Global Times.* Available at: <http://www.globaltimes.cn/content/879657.shtml> Accessed September 3, 2014.

World Trade Organization. (2011). World Trade 2010, prospects for 2011 (Trade growth to ease in 2011 but despite 2010 record surge, crisis hangover persists), World Trade Organization (WTO) Press/628, April 7. Available at: <http://www.wto.org/english/news_e/pres11_e/pr628_e.htm> Accessed April 5, 2013.

XBS (Xinjiang Bureau of Statistics) (2001). *Xinjiang Statistical Yearbook 2010.* Beijing: China Statistics Publishing House.

Xia, Y. (August 13, 2010). China and Pakistan plan to construct a rail line, still not able to form a major energy channel. *China Business Times.*

Xinhua (March 25, 2008). *Questions, answers about casualties, damages of recent riots.* Beijing: Xinhua News Agency. Available at: <http://news.xinhuanet.com/english/2008-03/25/content_7857168.htm> Accessed April 12, 2013.

Xinhua (June 27, 2009). *Han Chinese launch revenge attacks on Uyghur property.* Beijing: Xinhua News Agency. Available at: <http://www.china.org.cn/china/news/2009-06/27/content_18023576.htm> Accessed February 15, 2013.

Xinhua (July 12, 2009). *Number of injured in Urumqi riot increases to 1,680.* Beijing: Xinhua News Agency. Available at: http://news.xinhuanet.com/english/2009-07/12/content_11696865.htm. Accessed April 16, 2013.

Xinhua (August 5, 2009). *Innocent civilians make up 156 in Urumqi riot death toll.* Beijing: Xinhua News Agency. Available at: http://news.xinhuanet.com/english/2009-08/05/content_11831350.htm > Accessed March 15, 2013..

Xinhua. (September 4, 2009). Urumqi quiets down after protest about syringe attacks. Available at: <http://news.xinhuanet.com/english/2009-09/04/content_11992622.htm> Accessed April 11, 2013.

Xinhua (November 16, 2011). *New progress in development-oriented poverty reduction program for rural China.* Beijing: Xinhua News Agency. Available at: <http://news.xinhuanet.com/english2010/china/2011-11/16/c_131249948.htm> Accessed April 11, 2013.

Xinhua. (April 30, 2013). 11 more Xinjiang terrorist suspects captured. Available at: <http://usa.chinadaily.com.cn/china/2013-04/30/content_16462776.htm> Accessed April 30, 2013.

Xinhua (June 30, 2013). *Fugitive of Xinjiang attack captured.* Beijing: Xinhua News Agency. Available at: <http://news.xinhuanet.com/english/china/2013-06/30/c_132498990.htm> Accessed July 1, 2013.

Xinhuanet (March 3, 2005). *News—the Qingzang Railway will no longer let 100 yuan to be only 54 yuan.* Beijing: Xinhua News Agency. Available at: <http://www.qh.xinhuanet.com/2005-03/03/content_3810355.htm> Accessed April 15, 2013.

Xinhuanet (June 25, 2003). *To build the Qingzang Railway and to benefit multiethnic people.* Beijing: Xinhua News Agency. Available at: <http://www.qh.xinhuanet.com/qztlw/2003-06/25/content_639390.htm> Accessed April 15, 2013.

Xinjiang Bureau of Statistics (2011). *Xinjiang Statistical Yearbook 2010*. Beijing: China Statistics Publishing House.

Xinjiang Production and Construction Corps (2001). *Xinjiang production and construction crops statistical yearbook 2000*. Beijing: China Statistics Publishing House.

Xinjiang Production and Construction Corps (2011). *Xinjiang production and construction crops statistical yearbook 2010*. Beijing: China Statistics Publishing House.

Xiong, C. (July 7, 2012). *Xinjiang's key role emerges as oil and gas production rise steadily*. Beijing: Xinhuanet. Available at: <http://news.xinhuanet.com/local/2012-07/07/c_112382386.htm> Accessed April 10, 2013.

Yan, H., Geng, R., & Ye, Y. (July 18, 2009). Xinjiang riot hits regional anti-terror nerve. Xinhua. Available at: <http://news.xinhuanet.com/english/2009-07/18/content_11727782.htm> Accessed April 11, 2013.

Yu, L. (January 26, 2010). *China sentences four more to death for Urumqi riot*. Reuters. Available at: <http://uk.reuters.com/article/2010/01/26/uk-china-xinjiang-idUKTRE60P3HM20100126> Accessed April 2, 2013.

Yu, M. (July 20, 2011). Inside China. *The Washington Times* Available at: <http://www.washingtontimes.com/news/2011/jul/20/inside-china-110063105/> Accessed March 15, 2013.

Zhai, I. (September 13, 2009). Out of harm's way, but far from normality. *South China Morning Post*A6.

Zhang, L. (January 16, 2013). *Xinjiang's coal output exceeds more than 1.4 tons last year*. Beijing: China Energy Network. Available at: <http://www.china5e.com/show.php?Contentid=263424> Accessed March 15, 2013.

Zhang, Y. (April 21, 2014). Shooting sounds alarm for cross-border activities. Global Times. Available at: <http://www.globaltimes.cn/content/855733.shtml#.U1eF85VZrmQ> Accessed April 23, 2014.

Zipf, G. K. (1946). The P^1P^2/D hypothesis: On the intercity movement of persons. *American Sociological Review*, *11*(6), 677–686.

Index

Notes: AP = autonomous prefecture; P = prefecture; PM = prefectural level municipality; SPM = sub-prefectural level municipality (administered by the Xinjiang Production and Construction Corps)

FSC
www.fsc.org
MIX
Papier | Fördert
gute Waldnutzung
FSC® C083411

Kolibri 360 GmbH
Ferdinand-Jühlke-Straße 7
99095 Erfurt, Deutschland
produktsicherheit@kolibri360.de